SOCIAL CAUSATION

R. M. MacIVER

SOCIAL CAUSATION

GLOUCESTER, MASS.

PETER SMITH

1973

THE QUOTATIONS in Chapter Two from works by Dr. Kurt Rietzler and by Professor W. P. Montague are reproduced with the kind permission of the respective publishers, Yale University Press and Prentice-Hall, Inc., and of the authors.

Reprinted, 1973, by Permission of
XEROX COLLEGE PUBLISHING

ISBN: 0-8446-2504-3

SOCIAL CAUSATION
Copyright, 1942, by Ginn and Company.
Introduction to the Torchbook edition and Select
Bibliography *(Revised, 1964)* copyright © 1964
by R. M. MacIver.
Printed in the United States of America.
This book was originally published in 1942 by
Ginn and Company, and is here reprinted by arrangement.
First HARPER TORCHBOOK edition published 1964 by
Harper & Row, Publishers, Incorporated
49 East 33rd Street, New York, N.Y. 10016.

CONTENTS

v

INTRODUCTION TO THE TORCHBOOK EDITION

A PHILOSOPHER friend of mine, the late W. P. Montague, who read the original typescript of *Social Causation*, wrote me: "You will probably get some hot and angry comments which will be all to the good." While I would not say the comments were angry, they were certainly warm enough. The barrage came from the champions of positivism and behaviorism and was directed almost entirely at the first two chapters. In the original Preface, I had suggested that since the introductory part, and particularly Chapter Two, was concerned with the philosophical background of causal investigation, it could be skipped over without prejudice to an understanding of the main subject of the book. Perhaps it would have been better to have omitted the introductory chapters altogether, since then the main analysis might have received all the attention. Though I remain unconvinced by the attacks on these chapters, I shall not here endeavor to rebut them. I would merely like to point out that this book is a study of a much neglected subject, *social* causation, and that I believe the advancement of the social sciences (and, not least, that of sociology) depends to a great degree on a more thorough grappling with the exceedingly complex problem of the causation of social phenomena.

Allow me to illustrate from an area with which I have been particularly concerned in recent years: juvenile delinquency. In the text I had commented on the inadequacy of Clifford R. Shaw's explanation of the volume of delinquency in certain urban areas as primarily due to "the invasion of residential communities by business and industry," with the consequent "disintegration of the community as a unit of social control." The conclusion, it was remarked, was "apposite and suggestive," but still remained a one-sided, and therefore misleading, interpretation of the evidence. Since the original text failed to provide any full-scale illustrative case, I take the opportunity to deal with this one at some length.

Shaw was of course well aware that many conditions and happenings conspire to produce any social phenomenon. A delinquent youth is one who has developed certain attitudes and habits over a period of time — there has been a process of conditioning of which habitual delinquency is the outcome. It is hopeless to search for any single complex of conditions that will be applicable to all cases; the variations of heredity, temperament, upbringing, associations, environmental impacts, and casual events are endless. What concerns us here, as in a great number of social inquiries, is a group phenomenon, the greater and the lesser frequency of delinquency for different groups under different conditions or within different environments. What Shaw is offering is a causal explanation of the higher level of delinquency of youth within a particular type of urban area.

Obviously there are many differences between the environments of the higher-delinquency and lower-delinquency areas and also between the people who inhabit them and the kind of lives they lead. Our problem then is to distinguish those factors that provoke or encourage or sustain the delinquent tendency from those that are irrelevant or incidental to it. We may look for a particular "syndrome" or complex or cluster of conditions that together are more closely linked with the phenomenon, as shown by their frequent association with the cases of delinquency occurring in the area, or by their being frequently associated with delinquency elsewhere. Such conjunctures may be of various kinds. One, for example, might consist of school retardation, truancy, staying out late in the streets. Or we might think of a variety of concomitant factors that form a "vicious circle," each of them stimulating another concomitant factor; and in a situation so conceived we might find evidence that one link in the chain frequently exhibits itself prior to the others, triggering as it were the whole vicious circle. We might, for example, find such a triggering factor in parental neglect or brutality or failure to exercise discipline. Or we might look for some basic condition, some development of a broad kind that comes first in time and seriously changes a total situation in such a way that within the changed situation there is a higher incidence of delinquency.

Each of these three leads, the statistically significant cluster of conditions, the presumptive trigger of the vicious circle, the critical change introduced into a situation that thereafter exhibits a higher rate of delinquency, offer only hypotheses, promising hypotheses that must be tested and followed up if we are to arrive at any causal interpretation. Shaw's conclusion in the passages cited is an hypothesis belonging to the third category. It is no more than a first approach to a conclusion. The invasion into a previously residential area of plants, factories, warehouses, and so forth, is not directly a cause of the social disorganization of a community, however we may interpret social disorganization. In the first place, when industry or commerce invades a neighborhood it is accompanied and followed by a change of residents also, since residential desirability falls and a lower economic group takes over. In the second place, while in Chicago at the time of Shaw's study the high-delinquency areas were largely those in which business and industry had invaded residential districts, in other cities, such as New York, many of the high-delinquency areas are not to any considerable extent permeated by industrial concerns. Zoning regulations or other agreements protect the more prosperous residential areas from invasion, so that manufacturers, wholesalers, and dealers of various kinds must locate in the poorer areas, which not infrequently were previously higher grade neighborhoods. These considerations, however, are secondary. The primary consideration is that in all cities the deteriorating areas with their populational congestion are almost always also the areas of high delinquency. In short, Shaw's emphasis on the priority of business invasion is misleading. Business invasion may drive people out of areas that thereafter become high-delinquency areas, but what drives people into areas where high delinquency develops is poverty and economic helplessness.

We have taken this illustration as one of the numerous examples of imputation on the basis of correlation or concomitant variation. The causal explanation of the disparate incidence of a social phenomenon, of the changing more or less within the greater flux of change, is beset with many difficulties. It is so in the case we have cited. Let us consider why.

We take as our datum the higher rate of delinquency, let us say, in a particular city, in certain areas as compared with certain other areas. We shall assume that the statistic disparity is at least roughly indicative of a genuine difference in the actual amount of delinquency in the contrasted areas. We have, let us say, discovered that the high-delinquency areas are characterized by the poverty of the inhabitants, by the deterioration of the housing, by populational congestion, and by the high percentage of recent immigrants they contain. We note also that the immigrants differ ethnically or racially from the majority of the city's residents.

Further research reveals that the high-delinquency areas are characterized also by a considerably higher than average incidence of a number of various socio-pathological phenomena, as shown by admissions to mental hospitals, psychiatric clinic cases, home relief cases, public assistance cases, rates of infant mortality, and cases of tuberculosis. Incidentally, these concomitant phenomena should be reflected on by those who think that juvenile delinquency is due to the "low morality" of the people of these areas. On their own terms, what then makes the morality low?

How far are we toward an explanation of the higher rate of delinquency in these areas when we have found that high delinquency is highly correlated with inferior health conditions, more mental troubles, more dependency and so forth, as well as with squalor, congestion, inadequate housing, and lack of most social amenities? At least we can conclude that such areas, exhibiting such conditions, are breeding grounds of delinquency. This may seem a very obvious conclusion. Perhaps so, but what about the rather obvious corollary, that considerable delinquency will persist in these areas so long as they remain the kind of slums we have indicated?

With apologies for the digression let us note that to speak of breeding grounds still leaves open the question: is it the soil or the seed, the area or the people in it, that is primarily responsible? There are some who claim that the higher delinquency rates of these areas are to be mainly attributed to "lower class morality" or "lower class culture." The *prima facie* basis of the claim is that the high delinquency areas are areas inhabited by the very poor, the lower class. Some of these writers regard the resort to delinquency as congenial to the cultural outlook of

this class. Others find the clue in the contention that the youth
of this lower class are schooled to accept the values and aspirations of the middle class and, since they meet with frustrations
in seeking to attain them due to their poverty, lack of connections, poorer education, and so forth, they turn to illegitimate
means to compensate in some way. We would question such
claims on several grounds. We might as well claim that the
greater susceptibility to certain diseases within these areas is due
to lower-class morality. Moreover, high delinquency does not
characterize all lower-class groups but chiefly those living under
certain conditions characteristic of congested and deteriorating
urban areas. Within these areas we can observe, as has been done
and recorded by workers in them, the manner in which the
handicaps, the mean pressures, and the lack of opportunities
vitiate the life of the family, the relations of parents and children, and frustrate the natural aspirations of the young, so that
the more susceptible are liable to resort to delinquent ways. It
is not merely their failure to achieve "middle-class" aspirations,
it is their inability to attain the satisfactions, within the family,
in the school, and in other relationships, that youths everywhere,
in every class, normally seek to attain.

We accept then the conclusion that the physical environment
is itself one of the determinants of the higher delinquency within
it, through both its direct and indirect impact on the life of the
young. But again, since we find, though infrequently, a crowded
low-income urban area that is not characterized by high delinquency — the Chinese area of New York City used to be an instance — and since the volume of delinquency varies somewhat
in equally depressed urban areas, we must also take under consideration the people, usually some ethnic group or a mixture
of ethnic and racial groups, who live under such conditions.
Differences in backgrounds, mores, religious convictions, and
culture will mean different responses to problems, different degrees of resistance to adverse conditions. The cohesiveness of the
group, its capacity to organize its resources, and other tendencies
within it, will have some significance for the training of the
young and the attitudes they develop. Again, since there are always differences in the extent to which various families follow
any particular way of life, some of the young will be more, some
less, protected against the handicaps of the neighborhood conditions.

Almost all income groups exhibit a high delinquency rate in the type of physical environment already specified. Quite exceptionally, there is a highly insulated group, such as the Chinese have been, or a group tightly bound by a strict religious orthodoxy, particularly some Jewish group which shows a marked divergence from the common pattern. Such groups are also less affected by another factor that is often enough an additional impediment to the prospects of the youth who live in depressed areas — the attitude of discrimination and prejudice exhibited toward them by the surrounding community.

We conclude, thus far, that the conditions of life within over-congested poverty-stricken urban areas are conducive to above-average delinquency in the young of these areas, a consequence that regularly occurs except in the rare cases where the group within the area exhibits a high separatist group cohesion, usually on the basis of a religious orthodoxy that insulates them from the rest of the community.

But even in the most deplorable areas and even among the least coherent groups a large proportion of the young do not exhibit any marked tendency to delinquency. And when we ask why some succumb or others do not, a whole new range of investigation is called for. Part of the answer we find in the differentials of the social milieu, differences in family life, in new associations, in personal experiences of various kinds, and so forth. But an important part of the answer is to be found in the mental and psycho-physical differences between the youth themselves. Here we have to depend on evidence provided mainly by psychologists, social psychologists, and psychiatrists. It is too complex a story to deal with in our space. It must suffice to say that there is broad agreement, amply verified by evidence, that children who are rejected at home, badly neglected, or given no proper discipline, are more liable to become delinquents; that retardation at school, accompanied by chronic truancy, rather frequently leads to delinquency; that there is a psycho-pathic type, whether it be attributable to congenital make-up or to social pressure, which is marked by over-aggressiveness, hatred of all authority, and repudiation of friendly approaches and finds delinquency the line of least resistance. These, however, are only a few of the leads that have been discovered. In general, we know enough to be assured that certain types of mentalities and certain forms of mental disturbance, sometimes accompanied by physical handicaps, are significantly associated with delinquency. We know also that some of these disturbing factors are developed or accentuated by the conditions of life in our high-delinquency areas.

To sum up, if we are asked the broad question, why is there more delinquency in certain areas than in others, we have no simple answer. What we have is a considerable amount of information, resulting from a great variety of researches, that gives us very important clues toward an explanation. We know that there is more delinquency in these areas because of an accumulation of adverse conditions, resulting in the reduction of the life-chances of the young and not infrequently in serious frustrations, rebelliousness, and a detestation of authority. We know that young persons of certain temperaments, mentalities, physical abnormalities, including the neurotic and those suffering from certain bodily defects, are more subject to disturbance and disorientation under the pressures of their living conditions. There are still many unsettled or controversial issues, but our knowledge of causation is already reasonably sufficient as a guide to the strategy necessary for the control and reduction of delinquency, whether in low-delinquency or high-delinquency areas.

A very large percentage of our inquiries in the social sciences involve questions of the less and the more, between the then and the now, the here and the there, this group and the other group. Alike they call for analysis of evidences of disparate kinds, pertaining to the physical environment, the various circles of the social environment, and the patterning of the mental and somatic characteristics of individuals and groups, thus revealing conjunctures of conditions that are somehow registered in what we have ventured to name the dynamic assessment. Our discovery of causation is consequently always incomplete and at best progressive, always leaving room for future investigation.

R. M. MacIver

July 1964

PREFACE

IT CAN scarcely be doubted that if we could learn better how to investigate and how to interpret the phenomena of social change the social sciences would advance to a higher level. This work is devoted to that cause. It is addressed to students of the social sciences, and more especially of sociology. Part One is broader in its range, since it undertakes to refute sceptical attacks on the principle of causality. Since philosophical doubt percolates into sociological writings the author has found it desirable to include this preliminary part. Students who are not troubled by such doubt or who lack training in philosophical analysis may be advised to omit Chapter Two. This can be done without prejudice to the understanding of the succeeding argument.

Of the work here presented a small portion, consisting of the second section of Chapter One and the second section of Chapter Seven, has already appeared in the form of articles. I am indebted to the *Journal of Social Philosophy* and to the *American Journal of Sociology* for permission to reprint these sections. I desire also to record my indebtedness to the Columbia Council for Research in the Social Sciences, for a grant enabling me to survey the relevant periodical literature of a number of European countries. My thanks are due also to various research assistants, and particularly to Mrs. Thea Field and to Mr. Joseph Gidynski.

R. M. MacIver

COLUMBIA UNIVERSITY

PART ONE

SCIENCE AND CAUSALITY

CHAPTER ONE

CAUSALITY

I

PRIMACY OF THE CONCEPT

BACK of all our conscious activity, whether we think things or do things, lies some concept of causation. Some philosophers, like David Hume, have denied that we have any valid ground for the attribution of cause and effect; but there has been no one who did not at every turn act and think, live and breathe, as though that ground existed. It was all very well, and no doubt very salutary, for David Hume to challenge us to discover anything more in nature or in experience than *one object following another*, [1] but in putting that challenge on paper did he not expect that it would have some *effect*, at least on the thoughts of others? When we speak of cause and effect we certainly do not *mean* " one object followed by another." The light of mid-day is followed by the darkness of night; it is a sequence perhaps more invariable than any other, but we do not think of the light as the cause of the darkness. The noise of a train is heard before the train appears in sight, but we do not think of the noise as the cause of the appearance of the train. The fall of a stone in water is followed by a splash, and we do think of the stone as the cause of the splash. The concept of sequence,

---

[1] *An Essay on the Human Understanding*, Section VII.

even invariable sequence, is one thing; that of cause is
definitely another. We are not here concerned with the
validity, but only with the universality, of the application of the concept. Whenever we set about any task we
assume causation. Whenever we use an active verb we
postulate a cause, and whenever we use a passive one we
postulate an effect. Whenever we attribute continuity or
process, we imply causation. In all doing and suffering
we experience, or at least believe we experience, cause
and effect. Hume took the stand that we do not *perceive*
causation, that we have no sense " impression " of it, and
therefore no right to impute it. The obvious answer is
that, if we employ the term as he did, we have no sense
" impression " of anything that is a relationship. We have
no sense " impression " even of succession, but only a succession of sense " impressions." [2] Hume's one object following another becomes instead one sensation, or one mental
image, habitually associated with another. We are trans-
ported into a shadow-land of impotent " impressions,"
and there is no way out any more into the objective realm.
The " phenomena " are in our " minds," not in nature.
And our minds, too, become a succession of moments of
awareness, save that even the succession becomes a figment of the mind figment that thinks it. Dissolve all relationships into Hume's sense " impressions," and we dissolve
our world. Deny the concept of cause, and every other
concept — succession, change, continuity, time itself —
vanishes into thin air. Let us consider, for example, the
concept of time. Time has meaning for us as the pre-
condition not merely of change, but of change as caused.
We cannot conceive of change except as caused change.
Otherwise it would be the idle flux of meaningless appear-
ances, at most the moving picture on a screen, which can

---

[2] See, for example, G. H. Mead, *The Philosophy of the Act* (Chicago,
1938), pp. 646–651.

be run backward as well as forward, which can be slowed or accelerated, which can be repeated again and again — provided that, though there is no causation in change itself, there is beyond it some cause that idly plays with the idle sequence. Change obviously implies three things, that which changes, that which is constant relative to that which changes, and the span of time in which the change takes place. But if change were uncaused, then it would have no necessary direction in time, and time itself would become directionless and be no more, since the one-way signposts of change are all effaced.

The world we experience is a world of continuity and change. We perceive change and therefore continuity. We perceive continuity and therefore change. It is a world in which the concept of causation reigns over our experience. Our life is a process signalized by events. Succession is transition, a one-way road from the past to the future. The road has no breaks in it. The discontinuous signposts, the events of experience, merely reveal the continuity of passage. Things happen *to* us and *in* us continually. We react to the happenings, and the totality of happenings and reactions — our strivings, emotional tensions, controls, comprehensions, anticipations — is our experience. Our experience has the finality that belongs not to mere change, but to irrevocable change. As an ancient Greek poet said, even God cannot make undone the things that have been done. Hence our experience must always assume the character of a causal nexus. There is no escape from the web of cause and effect.

Whether we could derive any conception of causation from the mere observation of external change, may be doubtful. Possibly from that alone we could get no further than the concept of succession, that of " one object followed by another," to which Hume reduced our knowledge of cause and effect. But speculation on this head is vain, since the capacity to observe external change already implies the causative activity of the observer. To live, as we shall bring out at a later stage, is itself a special causal activity, and to be aware of anything is also to be aware of this causal activity of ourselves. In being aware there is at least implicit the concept of causation. But the causal nexus we attribute to the changes of the external world differs in one important respect from the causal nexus we discover when we are ourselves the authors or sources of change. In the latter case we often foresee, in some part, the changes we bring about; we undertake the activity in order to bring about the foreseen change. Such activity introduces a factor of causation that physical nature nowhere reveals to us. Besides other differences, there is here a different relation of time and change. In the physical universe each instant, so far as our science goes, determines that which succeeds it. Given the moment, there is present all that the next moment requires for its coming to birth. But for teleological activity, wherever or in whatever degree we find it, the moment is not enough. Here the causal process has another quality, that of *duration*. The image of what is yet to be informs the process of its becoming. We do not merely observe in the present the signs of the direction of approaching change. The teleological impulse, previsioning the change, is itself dynamic. It exists prior to the change and persists through the process of its accomplishment. It may lie low and work in the twilight of consciousness or it may emerge into conscious purpose. In the latter form it constitutes the distinctive quality of causation within the socio-psychological realm. In the teleological process the effect, not yet as actuality but as prevision and end of action, operates to bring itself about. The effect, dimly adumbrated or clearly conceived, exists as projection in advance of the physical process from which, as actuality, it emerges. This reversed relationship is the essential factor in the control that the living thing, or the social group, exercises within its environment, when it is no longer content merely to adapt itself to that environment but has undertaken the greater adventure of adapting also that environment to itself. When it reaches this stage, the living being exists not only in the ever-enduring present; it exists, as it were, *in the time dimension*, embracing at each moment the future and the past with the present. So the concept of time and the concept of causation are essentially interdependent.

There are those who, acknowledging the paramount role of the concept of causation in human experience, nevertheless conclude that it has no scientific warrant when applied to the outer world of physical nature. " Technical and mathematical language . . . is surely, if slowly, replacing expressions of causal relations with mathematical functions or equations, which are neutral to all anthropomorphic hypotheses." [3] This position we shall critically examine at a later stage. For the present we are not concerned with the valid reference of the concept to the phenomenal world, but only with its universality for human experience.

We experience change everywhere, and wherever we experience change we summon the concept of causation. For human life change is a one-way sequence. It is here, in the irreversible character of change, that we find the essence of causality, something that no " mathematical functions or equations " can ever represent, or even suggest. Moreover, the concept of causation embraces not only that which changes but also that in terms of which it changes. Change is always relative to something else that does not similarly change. The earth moves in relation to the sun,

---

[3] M. R. Cohen, *Reason and Nature* (New York, 1931), pp. 224–225.

the train moves in relation to the earth, the passenger moves in relation to the train, and his hand moves in relation to his organism. Nothing changes, nothing passes away, except as against that which by contrast endures. A change, then, is a difference occurring within a relatively determinate system. Change and the unchanging are correlative, and as we cannot think of the one without the other we cannot think of either except in the light of the principle of causation.

Everything is in process of change, except conceivably the infinitesimal units of " matter " or " energy " of which all things consist. Everything that is now is different from what it was: its form, place, properties, relations, functions, undergo change incessantly. The elements alone — or rather most of them — seem indifferent to the processes they endure, for though changed by changing temperature, pressure, and exposure to the action of other elements, they alone can return the road they travelled, back to their former state again. But for all constructed things, for all things that assume character and function in space and time, for all the works of nature and the little works of man, for all things that expend energy, for all that live, there is no return to a former state. For them all the process of change is irreversible.

This primary datum gives determination, law, meaning, finality, within the universe. Were the process reversible, like a mere mathematical function, there would be no significant history. Life would lose its order, its quality, its sting — and so would death. Change would be an irrelevant incident, an episode in chaos, affecting the whole as little as the waves affect the surface of the sea.

II
MODES OF THE QUESTION WHY

All living creatures are meshed in the universal process of irrevocable change, subjected to it from within and from without. So the first question of the enquiring mind, the first question on the lips of a child, is *Why? Why does it grow dark? Why does it rain? Why does the engine go? Why does it hurt? Why must I go to bed? Why is it wrong to use that word?* These many whys, like those of its elders, are all requests to have something explained. Feeling the insistent impact of change it asks the explanation of this happening, this difference, this prohibition, this command. The answer always begins: *Because.* But sometimes it is concerned with a reason that is not a cause. *Because it's not good for you. Because mother wants you to. Because nice people don't use that word. Because God will be angry.* What is common to all the whys is the request: *Show me the connection* — between this and that, between before and after, between what I do and suffer and the world it happens in. The connection shown may not be a causal nexus. Usually it is not causal when the why is posed in terms of values or standards of behavior. *You should do this because it is customary, proper, right, established, commanded.* The causal why asks for a nexus of dependence or interdependence between a phenomenon and a scheme of things already in some measure known. The more limited the knowledge and vision of the enquirer, the less meaningful is his why, the less significant for him is the answer of those whose knowledge is more advanced. For that reason most of the child's whys are essentially unanswerable. And for the same reason most of the adult's whys are at best answerable only in degree. The scientist too has his persistent whys that stretch far beyond his attained science, though he actually occupies himself only with those whys that lie on the frontiers of what he already knows.

1. The man in the street points to the gathered clouds. The farmer says it rains on account of this or that, say the

Why Does It Rain?

steady east wind of the past two days. But it does not always rain when the clouds gather; and sometimes the east wind does not bring rain and sometimes the west wind does. The scientist tells us that it rains because clouds form and water vapor condenses under certain meteorological conditions, such as the meeting of cold and warm currents in the air. If then we ask him why water vapor condenses under these conditions he may tell us about the phenomena of contraction and expansion. But at some point he stops. Always he stops when he arrives at an invariant sequence or concomitance of phenomena. Where he stops he says in effect: " This is the nature of things." The whys of the physical scientist are addressed to the discovery of the order that all things exhibit, the order that is itself the nature of these things. In the last resort he tells us *how* things belong together and *how* they are bound together in specific processes of change. His why resolves itself always into a how. If he reaches his fundamental how — the invariant sequence and concomitance of unit properties — he does not proceed to ask: " *Why* is it invariant? " For him that question conveys no implication. If it is invariant, it is the nature of things — it is necessity. But the necessity is merely a construction of the " invariance." So the why of physical science is the Why of Invariant Order.

This fundamental nexus has no confines. It permeates the organic world as well as the inorganic. The invariant order is revealed in the beating of the heart and in the process of glandular secretion no less than in the weathering of the rocks and in the motions of the stars. It holds in the relation between the animal's synapses and its modes of behavior. It holds in the relation between the inconceivably complex structure of the human brain and the dreams, inventions, beliefs, philosophies, of men.[4]

Nonetheless and without any contradiction of what has just been said, there are other kinds of causal nexus besides that which the physicist pursues. There are whys that seek an answer the physicist never gives, that do not have recourse to the principle of invariant order, and that are equally legitimate, equally scientific, and no less answerable on their own terms. We shall leave aside for the present the non-causal whys, all the whys that are concerned with a normative " ought " or an imperative " must," or with the logical " therefore." Several other types have to be considered.

2. Consider, for example, these questions. *Why do plants assimilate carbon? Why does the liver secrete bile? Why do the leaves of Venus's fly-trap have sensitive upright bristles?* Here our why is directed to something else than the linkages within physico-chemical processes. The production of carbon plays a part in the economy of the plant. The secretion of bile has a role in the digestion of food. The bristles of Venus's fly-trap enable it to capture the insect food that it absorbs through the leaves. An organism is a biological unity; it functions as a living whole through the specific interdependent functioning of its parts. What our questions are addressed to is the functional significance of organs, processes, or activities in their relation to the organism as a whole. We cannot answer these questions in the terms of the physicist. We are concerned no longer

---

[4] This statement does not involve a philosophy of "materialism," which is a metaphysical and perhaps ultimately meaningless doctrine, like its counterpart "idealism." The scientist assumes that there is invariant order everywhere, even if he arrives at a principle of "uncertainty" ; and the whole advance of science is a partial confirmation of his assumption.

merely with interaction, concomitance, and sequence. We now view these relations in the light of function. Observe the difference between the questions we have selected and such questions as these: *Why does bile emulsify fats? Why does the leaf of Venus's fly-trap close when the bristles are touched?* Now the causal nexus we are seeking is directly in the physico-chemical realm. We are enquiring into organic processes without reference to organic function. The difference in the character of the two types of question is revealed by the fact that often we can answer the one when we are unable to answer the other. There are organs of the body that are, or are believed to be, functionless, like the pineal gland; there are other organs the functions of which are still obscure. Again, there are organs whose functions are definitely known, though the manner in which they perform them, the physico-chemical nexus, remains unknown. We know the functions of the bile that the liver secretes but we know practically nothing of the process of secretion. In short, there is a distinctive type of why that is properly relevant to the biological level. We shall call it the Why of Organic Function.

3. We pass to another level that presents its own distinctive why. Now we are interested in the nexus between overt or externalized activity and certain operations or conditions that we must name " psychical " or " mental." To discover this nexus is the aim of the commonest questions we ask concerning one another. *Why did he do this? Why did he say this? Why did he vote that way? Why did he pursue that policy?* A complete answer to any such question would involve an almost inconceivable knowledge of the make-up of the personality concerned, including physiological as well as psychological aspects. But the question has usually a much more limited range. It seeks to relate

the overt act to a mode of determination that is peculiar to beings endowed with consciousness, beings who are in some degree aware of what they are doing and who are in some sense purposive in doing it. We shall therefore speak of this relationship as the teleological nexus. We are not thereby assuming that the conscious purpose is other than the flickering light of some urge or drive whose depths remain shadowed and unplumbed. It may well be that, as was said long before modern explorations into the unconscious, our consciousness at any moment is " but the phosphorescent ripple of an unsounded sea." Nevertheless, this fact of awareness not only makes all whys possible but constitutes the distinctive quality, the differentia, of one great area of causation, the area within which social causation belongs.

a. Let us begin with examples that at first view seem to lie within the realm of physics. *Why are airplane engines air-cooled? Why are electric light filaments made of tungsten?* Here we seem to be asking for the nexus between a physical phenomenon and a particular physical structure. But the nexus in which we are interested is not given to us by nature; it is contrived by man. There would be no electric light bulbs, or tungsten filaments in them, were it not for human contrivance. The relation is a means-ends relation. If we answer the why by saying that tungsten filaments give a better light, we imply that better light is an objective that explains the phenomenon. We imply further that this better light is obtained under conditions of convenience and relative economy. The " better " is defined by utility. We have left the realm of nature in the sense of the physicist and entered the teleological realm. So the causal nexus we are seeking is of the same character as if we had asked: *Why do we plan so and so?* or *Why do we follow this road?* or *What is the goal we are trying to reach?* It is the Why of Objective, if we understand by objective the foreseen and intended end-result of any act or series of acts.

Observe particularly that the new causal factor introduced by the why of objective is not of the same order as those that fall within the system of physical causation. Given the appropriate conditions of the atmosphere, the meeting of cold and warm currents will condense the moisture in the air and result in precipitation, whether we desire it or not. If man could effect these conditions with the intention of producing rain, they would still achieve this result as before. The meteorological conditions combine to produce rain, but meteorological conditions and human intentions do not *combine* to produce rain. Nor do tungsten filaments, a vacuum bulb, an electric current, *and* the desire for better illumination *together* produce electric light. The intention that makes the result also an objective is outside the specific physical nexus, adds nothing to it, has no meaning for it. The intention initiates a set of operations that collocate and organize a certain physical pattern that *as such* produces or constitutes the intended phenomenon. At this point we approach an ultimate problem. We saw that the why of invariant order always resolves itself into a how; the why of objective never does so. It exists independently of the how. The crucial juncture of the two remains an enigma. We know *why* we move our arm; we do not know *how* we move it — we do not fathom the primary nexus between intention and the organic motion that itself belongs to the physical order and initiates the physical processes involved in the realization of the objective.

b. The objective is, however, only one aspect of the teleological nexus. We can always go further and ask: *Why then do you seek this objective? Why did you build this house? Why did you go that journey? Why did you sell that stock?* The answer may be in terms of a more inclusive objective — or it may be in terms of *motive. I did it out of pity. I did it because I was afraid of something. I did it for the fun of doing it.* This we shall speak of as the Why of Motivation, referring motivation to the subjective conditions, emotions, dispositions, attitudes, that move man to act in a particular manner, to pursue this or that objective.

Objective and motive merge subtly in one another and therefore the distinction between them must be stated more explicitly. Money and power, when men seek them, are objectives; ambition, greed, envy, jealousy, are clearly not objectives, but motives. Objective externalizes itself in action, is the completion or culmination of a series of activities; motive is at best only inferred, is not externalized. Therefore the same objective may be attributable to any one or any combination of a considerable variety of motives. Motive is an aspect of the personality of the agent, not something that he does or achieves. When we attribute motives to any person we make the often dubious assumption that we know his hidden feelings and desires. When we ask a person what his motives are we assume that he knows himself well enough to answer, but even if he is willing to reveal himself we cannot test the accuracy or the extent of his self-knowledge. At a later stage we shall be much concerned with the fact that the agent's revelation of his motives is precarious and subject to bias, while the outsider's imputation of them is highly inferential.

The why of motivation lies, often obscurely, behind the why of objective. Whether we ignore it or not depends on the nature of our interest, on what it is we are seeking to understand. If we want to know why electric light filaments are made of tungsten, we need not concern ourselves with the motives of the inventor or of the manufacturer.

In the realm of technology, and broadly of utility, we can usually afford to neglect motives. But if our interest centers not in the contrivance but in the contriver, if what we are trying to understand is the personality, the human nature, of the agent, then we must face the difficult and frequently baffling task of getting at his motives. In passing we may note that the difficulty is less when we are investigating the motives of a group, especially a large group acting in concert, than when we endeavor to explore the motives of a single personality.

c. There remains for consideration a third aspect of the teleological nexus. Here we come to another type of question. *Why did you build this style of house? Why did you paint this kind of picture? Why do people get married in church? Why do people wear clothes of a certain cut at dinner parties?* The last two questions may seem to belong to a different order from that represented by the first two, but for our classification they are only another variety of a single type. In the thirteenth century people built houses after a different pattern from that followed today. The modern artist paints a different kind of picture from that characteristic of the renaissance artist. They have different marriage ceremonies in England and in Japan. The style of clothes worn on formal occasions was quite different in the eighteenth century. In all these and a myriad other activities men follow a pre-defined design, a pattern socially imposed or culturally acceptable. In a sense each activity realizes an example of an established style, " imitates " it, " reproduces " it. The nexus is between the copy and the prior pattern, the example and the exemplar, the particular embodiment and the prevailing style. It is clearly a kind of causal nexus, for the pattern or style is prior and determinant. We may call this nexus the Why of Design, meaning by design not the objective but the general pattern, exemplified in a cultural product, a utilitarian device, or a mode of behavior.

It may clarify our meaning if we compare the why of design with Aristotle's "formal cause," one of the famous list of "four causes" advanced in the *Physics*. Aristotle points out that before the builder erects a house he has a prior "idea" of the house, a type or model or standard or definition that he then proceeds to realize in the materials he employs. Similarly the physician has a positive definition of health before he practises his healing art. Aristotle thus conceives of a form or pattern existing in the mind of the agent before it is imposed on the material with which or on which he works. Our why of design has a more limited range. It is more determinate and more determining. The Aristotelian "form" sometimes tends, as in Aristotle's example of health, to coalesce with the objective, the Aristotelian end or final cause. Furthermore, the builder of a house is usually aware of many different ways of building a house, may have a number of patterns or "ideas" among which to choose. Only one of these enters the causal nexus; the others remain idle or unavailing. Why one pattern is selected is the question to which we are addressing ourselves. The answer is not in universal terms, to the effect that the pattern pre-existed in the imagination of the builder, but in socio-psychological terms. The pattern is invested with value, utilitarian, aesthetic, or social, and thus, in a sense, with power. It has a dynamic quality for the individual, for the group, for the age. As such it enters specifically into the causal nexus. The process of realizing the design is not necessarily one of copying, imitating, or in a narrow sense reproducing an original. It may be so, as when a group strictly conforms to a ritual. But all intellectual and aesthetic activity abjures mere imitation. The form or pattern may be susceptible of a vast variety of concrete expressions. The genuine painter does not imitate his contemporaries when he paints in the style of his age. The constructive architect adapts the selected style to the special needs and opportunities of the situation. The novelist has sufficient freedom within the framework of the accepted form to endow it with all that his personality can give. When a style seems no longer capable of sustaining free creative activity it is already dated and a new one has already begun to emerge.

4. Still within the world of human experience, we find another type of causal nexus. We pass now from the teleological, or socio-psychological, nexus to one that is explicitly social. *Why does bad money drive out good? Why are ground values high in the centers of cities? Why is a declining death-rate normally associated with a declining birth-rate? Why is greater division of labor a concomitant of advancing technology?* We cannot answer directly in terms of objective, motive, and design. Nobody intends that bad money should drive out good. No social legislation prescribes that a declining death-rate shall be accompanied by a declining birth-rate. Obviously our previous categories no longer fit. The phenomena we are referring to are the social resultants of a great many individual or group actions directed to quite other ends but together conspiring to bring them about. It is thus that the social structure is for the most part created. We include here not only the trends and cycles and configurations of social phenomena that are discoverable by statistical and other methods of investigation but also the standards, customs, and cultural patterns that men everywhere follow. They do not foresee and then design these larger patterns of collective behavior. It is only after they are formed that our why of design becomes operative. Nor do they create them by concerted action directed to one objective, as men co-operate to construct a machine.

These patterns emerge instead from the conjuncture of diverse activities directed to less comprehensive and more immediate ends. They are for the most part as unintended as the hexagons constructed by the honeybee. Here and there a portion of the existing social scheme is deliberately torn up and reconstructed, a set of usages is codified, a politico-economic system is planned. But such set designs, great as their practical importance may be, still leave endless play for the conjuncture of individual and group activities that weave the continuous texture of social life.

This nexus between social phenomena and a mass of individualized activities will occupy us at a later stage. Here we merely point out its distinctive place in the whole system of causation. Unlike the physical nexus it does not exist apart from the objectives and motives of social beings; unlike the teleological nexus it is not itself a means-ends relationship. This why is not answered by direct reference to the ends men seek but only in the light of their interaction and conjuncture. We shall therefore distinguish it as the Why of Social Conjuncture.

5. Our list is now complete unless we include the whys that ask for a reason that is not a cause. These we may divide into two groups. One of them is concerned with the logical, as distinct from the causal nexus. *Why are the three angles of a triangle equal to two right angles?* The answer is a logical demonstration. We deduce the conclusion. We show that it follows, once we understand the nature of a triangle. Something that was there all the time comes to light for us. Here there is no preceding cause and succeeding effect. Here there is instead a timeless connection that is revealed to us through a process of inference. We are not looking for a cause that makes the three angles equal to two right angles, we are looking instead for a reason that

shows them to be so. Here no change is involved except a change in our knowledge, no dynamic except the dynamic of understanding. We have taken a mathematical example, since mathematics is the supreme realm of logical connections. But wherever we infer anything from anything else, whether in scientific investigation or in everyday affairs, we are pursuing the same logical nexus. We are discovering the implications of evidences already given to us, so as to learn from them something we did not know before. The indications we possess lead us to new facts or to new principles, but they do not create the facts or the principles. Sometimes they yield certainty, sometimes at most probability. A reason does not affect the reality it predicates, does not operate in that reality. Hence it is utterly different from a cause, as we are using that term. We must therefore set up as a distinct category what we may call the Why of Inference.

▼

6. Finally there is the Why of Obligation. *Why must I do this? Why should I obey the law?* Now we are not looking for the explanation of any factual situation, present or past, but for the reasons which, if accepted as valid, may lead to a future act that still remains hypothetical. We are not asking why things are so, we are asking how potential alternatives of behavior are related to some standard of value. The relation is always invincibly contingent. *I ought to do this.* There is no implication here that I will do it. *You ought to do this.* Here a double contingency has to be surmounted before the " ought " becomes dynamic and determinant of behavior. First, the asserted validity must be accepted; next, it must overcome all motivations that prompt an alternative course of action. Should the double contingency be surmounted, then, for the explanation of the consequent behavior, we return to the teleological nexus. The dynamic " ought " has been translated into

objective and motive. Only in this transformation does it enter into the realm of causality. For in the causal scheme we are concerned with actual objectives, not potential ones; with operative and not merely contingent motives; with designs actualized in the external world, not with designs that merely appeal for actualization. The answer to the why of obligation offers a value-judgment, not a nexus already established in the relevant facts.[5] Although these value-judgments exercise the most powerful influence over human conduct, we cannot admit them as such into the causal nexus, but only after their translation into our teleological determinants.

In conspectus our classification appears on page 24.

III

AXIOMS OF CAUSATION

Our first axiom is easily misunderstood. We do not mean that when a thing changes some particular force or agency has done something to it. We do not think of cause as a detachable entity or power that *intervenes* to make things happen. What is meant is that every happening is the manifestation of a specific causal nexus, that the event or the change is a consequent stage of a specific process, that it would not have happened had there not been present, within the totality that contained it, a specific conjuncture of conditions such that, wherever this conjuncture occurs, the event or the change also occurs. The axiom bids us seek the prior conjuncture. This is what the scientist does

AXIOM 1

*Whatever Happens
Has a Cause*

---

[5] We use the term "obligation" in a comprehensive sense, to include all the normative, authoritarian, and imperative "reasons" which are directed to contemplated or future acts but which remain only potential grounds of behavior unless and until they are converted into the operative processes of the teleological nexus.

TABLE I[6]

Modes of the Question Why

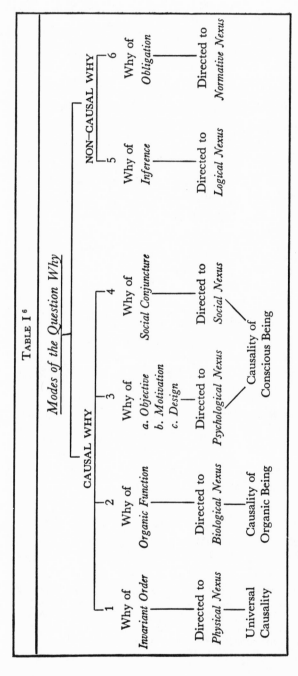

	CAUSAL WHY			NON-CAUSAL WHY	
1	2	3	4	5	6
Why of *Invariant Order*	Why of *Organic Function*	Why of a. Objective b. Motivation c. Design	Why of *Social Conjuncture*	Why of *Inference*	Why of *Obligation*
Directed to *Physical Nexus*	Directed to *Biological Nexus*	Directed to *Psychological Nexus*	Directed to *Social Nexus*	Directed to *Logical Nexus*	Directed to *Normative Nexus*
Universal Causality	Causality of Organic Being	Causality of Conscious Being			

[6] Our schema has been constructed with particular reference to the type of causation that will occupy us hereafter, viz., social causation. It should be observed that we have in this area two types of nexus, the psychological or socio-psychological and also another derivative type which, since it is found only in society, we distinguish as being peculiarly the social nexus. Our main concern will be the causality of conscious being as it is exhibited in social phenomena. But it already appears that these types of causation postulate the other types as well and that they cannot be comprehended except in the light of the entire system.

when he seeks, for example, the cause of a disease. It is what, in one way or another, the scientist is forever doing.

We know that if we apply a certain amount of heat to wax, the wax will melt; and that if we apply a certain amount of heat to water, the water will turn to steam. We know that if we combine oxygen and hydrogen in a certain proportion under certain conditions water will result. Given the conjuncture of the antecedents we predict the consequence. We know from observation that heat has melted wax before, that winds have raised waves, that water has quenched fire; and we know also from observation that the conditions under which these things happen are relatively independent of a great many other conditions within the universe. We know by experiment the proportion in which oxygen and hydrogen have combined to produce water, and we can state precisely from our experiments the pattern of conditions under which this has happened and will continue to happen in the future. It is a quite limited kind of knowledge, but adequate for the purpose of prediction — provided our axiom holds. For our prediction is more than a guess that what happened once will happen again. It assumes that certain things change together or follow one another by a law of their being, in other words by a kind of necessity. It is not chance, it is the way of things. Often things are so numerously or so complexly bound together that we cannot predict what will happen from a particular combination of them, that we cannot infer, when something happens, the conditions under which it will happen again. Or it may be that the immanent potentialities of things, particularly of living things, have only in part unfolded themselves, and we cannot know them except as they have been already revealed. This is not a contradiction of our axiom but merely an application of it. Even with relatively few variables, such as those on which the weather of the next few days depends, the conjunctures are so complex that prediction is still very inexact. This uncertainty applies to a great many of the specific happenings of nature. The biologist cannot tell which of the qualities of the parents will be inherited by any one of their offspring. The seismologist cannot tell what earthquakes will occur a year hence. The expert on epidemic diseases cannot tell when or where the next outbreak of a particular epidemic will take place. Similarly, when it comes to the conjuncture of human affairs, so many variant factors are involved that our predictions of what is going to happen are at best precarious and our explanations of what has happened seem more secure only because they are made after the event and cannot be refuted by it. To explain anything is to discover the order within which it falls. Sometimes the order is simple and relatively isolable, sometimes it is bafflingly complex. But always we seek the order to which the event belongs. And the first axiom of the order of events is that whatever happens has a cause.

▼

AXIOM 2

Where There Is Difference in the Effect There Is Difference in the Cause

It is said that one man's meat is another man's poison. If so, there must be a relevant difference in the digestive organs of the two. Somehow the difference in the consequent depends on a difference in the antecedent. In this sense the route of cause-effect is invariant. The effects of the same drug, under the same conditions, on two identical organisms would be identical. There are certain mushrooms that some authorities mark as poisonous and others as harmless.[7] But no scientist takes the position that this conflict of opinion means that the

---

[7] For example, *gyromitra esculenta*.

identically same mushroom can have opposite effects on identical organisms. In so far as the effects are different we assume, in accordance with our axiom, that there was variation in the conditions or in the organisms or in both. It is readily seen that this axiom is implicated in the search for causes and that unless it holds the search would be blind and unavailing. The order we find in the universe would be lost if the same train of conditions now led in this direction and now in that. Our experiments would prove nothing, and the contradictory nature of their results would not be a challenge to further experiments but a denial of their worthwhileness.

How deep this order reaches we do not know. We may here observe that although the route of cause-effect must be taken as invariant there may nevertheless be several routes to the same effect. Poisoning is one of many roads to death. Different drugs may serve the same remedial function. Possibly the answer is that what we call the effect is itself a complex conjuncture and that, being interested only in some aspects of it, we regard it as the same only by selective or imperfect definition. It would still be possible to maintain that the same effect — if by effect we mean the whole sequent stage of any causal complex — is associated only, as well as always, with the same cause. But this consideration raises problems that lie beyond our range. For the everyday purposes of science it may suffice that a difference in the consequents proclaims a difference in the antecedents.

Here we insist on a point that will gain greater significance as we proceed, to wit that the search for causes is directed to the differences between things. If we ask why something happens we imply that but for certain conditions this particular something would not have happened. If we ask why a thing is so we imply that but for certain conditions it would have been otherwise. Difference is always the spur of curiosity, difference between the then and the now, difference between the there and the here, difference between the way this thing behaves and the way that similar thing behaves, difference between the fact and the expectation. Underneath all our questioning lies the implicit acceptance of the axiom that no difference exists without a cause. The axiom is the ground of our questioning, the why of our asking why.

Cause is dynamic. Its sense is not given in the neutral statement that one thing follows another — whether sometimes, usually, or always. When we search for causes we want to know how one thing is *bound* to another. At least we want to know what things are bound in what sequences to what things. To impute causation is to claim that one thing is bound to another, does not merely follow upon it — bound to it by a necessity that is the nature of them both. Conversely, whenever we attribute activity to anything we are introducing the concept of causation. The difficulties of dynamic imputation we shall have to face presently. At this point it is enough to say that if we reject dynamism we reject causation. The notion of cause is not merely weakened when its dynamic quality is abstracted — it is entirely destroyed. Everything, except the inconceivable whole of things, both acts and is acted upon. There is no cause apart from effect, and no effect apart from cause. Often what we designate as cause is more strictly a *factor* of a total cause-effect relationship, whereas what we designate as effect is a sequent *stage* of the total cause-effect relationship. We speak, for example, of the spark as the cause and the explosion as the effect, but the cause and effect so designated are not properly correlative. The explosion is the sequent stage of the conjuncture of spark, gunpowder, and so forth. It is often convenient to designate as cause a specific factor or element of a causal conjuncture, but we must not on that account be misled as to the nature of causal imputation. Cause is a conjuncture of factors; effect is a conjuncture of factors continuous with and sequent upon the former.

Cause is the conjuncture viewed as active; effect, the conjuncture viewed as being acted upon. Activity and passivity are, however, relative. We say that the arrow flies and that the bird flies. The logic of causation might seem to require another use of language — the bird flies and the arrow is flown. But the distinction is still relative and must not be pressed too far. We might perhaps say that the cause of the difference between the arrow at rest and the arrow in motion lies wholly outside the arrow, while we cannot make a like statement concerning the bird at rest and the bird in motion, or concerning the aeroplane at rest and the aeroplane in motion. In being shot from the bow the arrow is acted upon, motion is imparted to it. But now in motion it is also active, a flying arrow that does things the resting arrow could not do. It is both acted upon and acting at the same time. So is everything in its degree and relation. That is what it means to be a thing, to have any kind of existence whatever. The concept of causation and the concept of thinghood are inseparable. In acting, a thing presents the aspect of cause; in being acted upon it presents the aspect of effect. The two aspects are eternally bound together. Together they constitute the stream of change. The phenomena of change, the immediate stimulants of the causal quest, are the differences that occur in things in the endless reciprocity of their acting and being acted upon.

We have just seen that the concept of cause is at
the same time a concept of the reality of things, of their
thinghood, that is, of their particular
and limited actuality. A thing is itself and not something else. It is —
or has — a more or less enduring configuration of attributes, defined in
space and time. Its existence means
that it acts and is acted upon, no matter how relative,
partial, dependent, transient, incomplete, and aspectual
that existence may be. For this attribution it matters not
whether the thing be a cloud, a wisp of smoke, a shadow,
or a mass of iron, a star, a galaxy. It matters not whether
it be a " material " thing or a thought, a dream, a halluci-
nation. Because things, in their fleeting or more lasting existence, act and are acted upon, the world of time is a world
of processes and events, in other words, of change, of continuous difference. When we seek for causes we seek to derive the differences of things as existent at a given moment
or period of time from the state of things at a prior moment
or period. The prior and posterior are always relative,
are predicable of all things always, and thus there is no
limit to the regress of causes. Causation is continuous,
though events are discontinuous. Causation is continuous,
though the systems in which it is manifested are discontinuous or relatively self-contained. Causation is not a
series of steps or stages called causes and effects. It is revealed in persistence as well as in change. It is revealed
alike in equilibrium and in disequilibrium, alike in regularity of sequence and in the breakdown of regularity.[8]
We seize on a moment of change in the endless process —
for practical purposes, for convenience of investigation,
because we are interested in it, because it is significant or

AXIOM 3
*Every Cause Is the Effect
of a Prior Cause
and Every Effect
Is the Cause
of a Posterior Effect*

---

[8] The inability to appreciate this point vitiates certain philosophies
that identify causality with uniformity or regularity of sequence.

novel or salient. But causation is no less present in the calm than in the storm, in the routine than in the cataclysm.

Causation is thus, axiomatically, universal. Were there any gap in it, any failure of it, its existence anywhere would be impugned. Where it failed, things would cease to be things. A thing would at the same time in the same relation be itself and something different from itself. The primary postulate of all our reasoning, all our science, all our practice, would be challenged.

There are indeed certain doctrines that deny, or seem to deny, this axiom. One is the doctrine of " free will," but we shall show later that this doctrine, where it denies causality, is founded on a misconception.[9] A more specious denial is suggested by certain doctrines of " vitalism," including Bergson's doctrine of the *élan vital*. Such doctrines are sometimes stated in a loose or vague manner that is not in conformity with the universal reign of causality. But their essential claim is of a quite different character. It is that there is in living things a life principle or energy that has its own potency, its own quality or mode of being, its own causal efficacy, such that it cannot be reduced to what we know as physico-chemical properties. With the validity of these doctrines we are not here concerned. What alone we need point out is that their proper challenge is not directed against the principle of causality but against the assumption that *all* causation, in the total realm of nature, falls within the physico-chemical order, as that order is commonly understood and limited. Thus the Bergsonian doctrine is in essence a protestation against the universality of scientific mechanism, as applicable equally to the organic and the inorganic, to the living present no less than to the dead past. It claims that though the event,

---

[9]Chapter Eight, § 2.

once determined, is sealed forever, the other and more significant aspect of causality, throughout organic nature, is the creative process of the unborn event, an activity as dynamic and untiring to-day as in the dawn of life or of history. In short it claims that the dynamism of organic nature is indeed dynamic, not merely confined to the established lines of its own past creation, but constantly overthrowing them, remaking them, so that no present ever repeats its past.[10]

Finally, there are those who hail certain revolutionary discoveries and doctrines of modern physics as overthrowing the principle of causality in the very sphere where its supremacy seemed most fully established. This conclusion has been drawn by some philosophers, and even by some scientists, from the remarkable application made by Heisenberg along the lines of the new quantum mechanics of Planck. Heisenberg pointed out that the means we use to determine the position of the electron is light energy of certain wave lengths. These wave lengths impart, in terms of the quantum theory, a change of velocity and of direction, itself of unpredictable amount, to the electron thus brought under observation. The inability to measure at the same time both the precise position and the precise velocity of the electron is not due to some uncertainty inherent in the nature of things but to the causal relation between our measuring instruments and the objects to be measured. It means that we must at present be content, within certain limits, with probability instead of quite exact knowledge. This conclusion is in no sense a denial of causality in its proper sense. Heisenberg's principle of indeterminacy is not really a principle of indeterminism. Every revolutionary discovery, including that of Planck, compels us to recast our conceptions of causality, and

---

[10] H. Bergson, *L'Évolution créatrice*, Chap. I.

whenever this happens there are those who proclaim that the principle of causality has itself been overthrown.[11] It is not within our province to expound the significance in this respect of the great advances made by Planck and Heisenberg. It will be enough to appeal to the testimony of Planck himself. He tells us that " physical science, together with astronomy and chemistry and mineralogy, are all based on the strict and universal validity of the principle of causality." [12] And he sums up the argument in these words: " Scientific thought is identical with causal thought, so much so that the last goal of every science is the full and complete application of the causal principle to the object of research."[13]

Our axioms, it will be seen, are not independent statements of the nature of causation. Each is an implication of the other. If any one of them holds, all of them hold. They are not, strictly, inductions from experience. They reach deeper than that, for they are the preconditions of our experiencing. They are not, on the other hand, deductions from more universal propositions. There is no prior principle from which they can be derived. The principle of causality, of which these axioms are merely variant expressions, is rather, as Mill put it, " the ultimate major premiss of all inductions." [14] Every advance of science may be said to provide additional evidence of its validity, but we accepted it before we could obtain the evidence, and we must continue to accept it so long as we continue to investigate nature or reality. Wherever we find order or law

---

[11] A good example of this tendency is the article by L. K. Frank, " Causation: an Episode in the History of Thought," *Journal of Philosophy* (August, 1934), Vol. 31, pp. 421–428. Some popularizers of modern science, such as Sir James Jeans (*The Mysterious Universe*, London, 1932, pp. 17 ff.), are guilty of the same looseness.

[12] Max Planck, *Where Is Science Going?* (New York, 1932), p. 147.

[13] Ibid. p. 158.

[14] J. S. Mill, *A System of Logic*, Book III, Chap. III.

in nature we have vindicated our trust in the axioms. Wherever we seek to extend the realm of science we are renewing our faith in them. Nevertheless it remains a faith, the faith on which all science rests. But this faith is implicit in our practical life before it becomes explicit in our reflection. When we till the soil and sow seed, when we build engines, when we navigate the seas, when we use water to quench fire, when we use any means in pursuit of any end, we are witnessing to this faith. As John Dewey put it, " The first thinker who proclaimed that every event is effect of something and cause of something else, that every particular existence is both conditioned and condition, merely put into words the procedure of the workman, converting a mode of practice into a formula." [15]

But reflection is like time in that it is apt to devour its own children. In recent philosophy the Humian assault on the concept of causation has been resumed with new vigor and with new weapons. Lest our faith in the axioms prove too naive, it may be well, before we turn to our main theme, to test our faith against this fresh assault.

---

[15] *Experience and Nature* (Chicago, 1926), p. 84.

CHAPTER TWO

VINDICATION OF THE PRINCIPLE

I

DIFFICULTIES AND RETREATS

EVERY EFFECT, we say, has a cause. Do we mean that the cause does something, produces something, called the effect? The cause, we say, determines the effect. Do we mean that the cause exerts force, compels the effect to happen? Outside the volition of conscious beings what does it mean to say that one thing compels another to happen? What evidence have we of any such occurrence in nature? Does the water *compel* the fire to go out? Does, then, the match compel the fire to kindle? Some fires go out when water is poured on them, but there are substances that burn in water. Sometimes the applied match is followed by a blaze — and sometimes not. In one state of the universe one thing is followed by a certain other thing; in another state it is not so followed. What, then, is the compulsion, or the necessity? Does the first thing, say the lighted match, exert force that sometimes produces an effect and sometimes does not? But the exertion of force is a notion we derive from our own conscious strivings, our efforts to achieve our purposes. We cannot attribute it to non-conscious nature. Nature never reveals it to us.

In the light of these and other considerations some modern philosophers have followed Hume, though for perhaps different reasons, in dismissing the notion of cause as a human imagination that has no relevance to the real world. Some, it is true, merely reject the transference to natural phenomena of the dynamic we find in human relations. It is anthropomorphic to speak of a physical cause as *producing* an effect. " A cause indeed, in the sense of a something which forces another something called an effect to occur, is so obvious a phantom that it has been rejected even by metaphysicians." [1] But others attack the notion root and branch. " The word ' cause,' " says Bertrand Russell, " is so inextricably bound up with misleading associations as to make its complete extrusion from the philosophical vocabulary desirable. . . . In advanced sciences such as gravitational astronomy, the word ' cause ' never occurs. . . . The law of causality, I believe, like much that passes muster among philosophers, is a relic of a bygone age." [2]

Morris Cohen takes the same position. " We may grant at the outset that the positivists are right in regarding the popular use of the word *cause* as embodying remnants of primitive animism. When we popularly speak of a thing's causing something else, we undoubtedly tend to attribute to the thing something analogous to human compulsion, something of muscular tension or the feelings of activity and passivity when we wilfully push or are pulled contrary to our will. Such animism is out of place in modern scientific physics. The Humian analysis of causation and its replacing of the ideas of production, of power and force (as synonyms of compulsion) by the idea of regular sequence, was the *coup de grâce* which modern thought administered to the scho-

---

[1] C. K. Ogden and I. A. Richards, *The Meaning of Meaning* (New York, 1930), Chap. III.

[2] " On the Notion of Cause," *Proceedings*, Aristotelian Society (1913), Vol. 13, pp. 1–26; reprinted in *Mysticism and Logic, and Other Essays* (London, 1919), Chap. IX.

lastic physics of occult qualities and powers. Technical and mathematical language, however, is surely, if slowly, replacing expressions of causal relations with mathematical functions or equations which are neutral to all anthropomorphic hypotheses." [3]

The reader will more fully apprehend the nature of these attacks on the notion of cause if he recalls that primitive man has an inevitable tendency to endow inanimate objects with souls or spirits. There are spirits that ride the thunder-cloud and the storm, spirits that strike men with pestilence, spirits that guide the sun and the moon, spirits that inhabit the woods and the waters, the mountains and the valleys. This primitive animism is apt to persist in our notion of force, as implying strain or effort or compulsion, in our attribution to things of "occult qualities and powers," in the teleological conception of the universe, in the "pathetic fallacy" that regards external nature as the friend or enemy of man, as kindly or angry, as mourning with us or as deluding us. How persistent these attributions are the whole history of science reveals. A good example of how animistic elements have clung to the notion of force is found in the work of Kepler. "The great German astronomer, for example, in his *Mysterium cosmographium* and his *Astronomia nova*, ascribed a vital faculty to the sun and the planets. In the 1621 edition of the former work, however, he said that one can substitute the word force for soul." [4] The modern followers of Hume, finding that all such concepts as force, efficacy, production, determination, necessity, when referred to causal relations, are tainted with animism or at least anthropomorphism, reject

---

[3] M. R. Cohen, *Reason and Nature*, p. 224.
[4] Quoted from Carl B. Boyer, *The Concepts of the Calculus* (New York, 1939), p. 177n. The references are to J. Kepler, *Opera Omnia* (Frankfort on the Main, 1858–1870), Vol. I, p. 174; Vol. II, p. 270; Vol. III, pp. 176, 178–179, 313.

them all, would banish them altogether from the realm of science, and would substitute for them the neutral and directionless formulas of mathematical equations.

We can better appreciate the retreat from causality if we look somewhat more closely at certain of the logical embarrassments inhering in the popular notion of cause-effect. We say that A is the cause of X, the spark of the explosion. But the powder, its dry condition, the small space in which it is confined, the state of the atmosphere, and so on, are also " causes " of the explosion, and back of these are many other " causes," so that in the end we may have to include as the cause of the explosion the whole antecedent state of the universe. The cause of X becomes not one phenomenon A but an infinitely vast array of phenomena, and not as separable factors but as a total conjuncture. Moreover, this total conjuncture must then be viewed as the cause not only of A but of all the other events that emerge within or from the previous state of the universe. And if this is true of mere events it is obviously more true of processes; if it is true of particulars it is also true of the uniformities of sequence in which science is interested. So we are told that the simple statement, "A is the cause of B," is scientifically useless, if not entirely invalid.

The same difficulty presents itself when we investigate the causation of social phenomena. We begin by attributing, say, a war to an emperor, a dictator, a cabal of statesmen, but as we go on thinking about it we discover that thousands and thousands of other factors were present and active without which the war would not have happened. As Tolstoi says of Napoleon's campaign against Russia, " In order that the will of Napoleon and Alexander (on whom the whole decision appeared to rest) should be effective, a combination of innumerable circumstances was essential, without any one of which the effect would not

have followed." [5] We begin by ascribing the frequency of
crime in the United States to this or that factor or narrow
conjuncture of factors, but as we proceed we discover that
the " factors " we select are inextricably interwoven in the
total situation from which we select them. And we may
conclude with the author of a recent study: " The amount
of crime in the United States responds to all of the factors
and forces in American life. . . . The relationship between
the criminal and the community is a total relationship and
not a partial one. He is the product of the sum of our
institutions." [6] In a similar way a careful student of the
causes of suicide concludes that to understand them we
must comprehend the total situation, " neglecting neither
the great collective currents nor the particular circumstances but envisaging them together as a complex and
indecomposable totality." [7]

Nor can we evade this conclusion by singling out certain factors as dominant or weighty and dismissing the rest
as subsidiary or insignificant. Such valuations lie outside
the problem. If any circumstance whatever is causally
linked with the phenomenon we are seeking to explain, it
is a circumstance without which the phenomenon would
not as such occur. If all the factors are necessary, all are
alike necessary — necessity cannot be reckoned by degrees.
From the standpoint of human responsibility, within a
scheme of social valuations, we may attach greater significance to one factor than to another. But as we shall see
later, the concept of responsibility is by no means to be
identified with the concept of causation. For the purpose
of causal analysis we cannot assign different weights to the

---

[5] *War and Peace*, Part IX, Chap. I. See the further discussion of this
point, pp. 181–184.

[6] Frank Tannenbaum, *Crime and the Community* (Boston, 1938),
p. 25.

[7] Maurice Halbwachs, *Les Causes du suicide* (Paris, 1930), p. 514.

factors from the combination of which the phenomenon results. A small change in a chemical formula may mean the difference between a remedy and a poison, between a dye and an explosive. The man who runs an elevator in a factory is as necessary to the operation of the plant as is the general manager. The fact that elevator men are easier to find and cost less does not make their service any less *necessary*. If the elevator man is paid twenty dollars a week and the general manager one hundred thousand dollars a year we must not construe this economic fact as though it meant that the causal efficacy of the general manager is a hundred times as great as that of the elevator man. Such arithmetic has no meaning for causal analysis.

Meeting an impasse along this road we try another. We draw a distinction between " cause " and " condition." It is a distinction readily suggested when we reflect on our own causality as conscious agents. We are presented with a situation; we intervene in order to attain some purpose. We think of the situation as the set of conditions under which we act. Conditions, so to speak, are the consentient or conspiring circumstances in which a specific causal operation occurs. There is an active " cause " and there is a set of conditions that are conceived of as relatively passive, though necessary for the operation of the cause. A bolt of lightning splits a tree. A myriad circumstances are involved if we are to explain why in the complex tensions of an electric storm the course of the lightning was along the line of the tree. But we concern ourselves only with the immediate salient event, and with any unusual or spectacular factor present in it, calling this factor the cause and all the rest the conditions. Now we shall later find reasons for drawing distinctions within the causal complex, for the better analysis of that complex. But such distinctions are never properly between causes and conditions: they are always between different elements, aspects, or stages of the causal system. There can be no conditions that are not also causes.

This point was made by John Stuart Mill. " It is very common to single out any one of the antecedents under the denomination of Cause, calling the others merely Conditions. Thus, if a person eats a particular dish, and dies in consequence, that is, would not have died if he had not eaten of it, people would be apt to say that eating of that dish was the cause of his death. . . . But though we may think proper to give the name of cause to that one condition, the fulfilment of which completes the tale, and brings about the effect without further delay; this condition has really no closer relation to the effect than any of the other conditions has. All the conditions were equally indispensable to the production of the consequent; and this statement of the cause is incomplete, unless in some shape or other we introduce them all." [8]

Again we retreat and try another road. We realize that the establishment of cause-effect relationships becomes unmanageable if we must attribute every phenomenon, every event, to the whole situation from which it emerges. It amounts to saying that the whole is the cause of the whole, a statement as unhelpful as its correlative that the whole is the effect of the whole. Our concern is to establish a specific nexus between one phenomenon and one or more other phenomena. There is, for example, a relation between the eating of a poisoned dish and the death of the eater which is certainly significant and which we wish to examine without dragging in the whole universe. It is true that a poison is poisonous only under appropriate conditions, but can we not, for the purpose of a particular

---

[8] *A System of Logic*, Book III, Chap. V, § 3.

enquiry, take these conditions for granted? There are a vast number of situations in which, if you eat a poisoned dish, you die. Death is the normal, the common sequel. Other things being equal, you die. Here, then, is our formula — " other things being equal." It is a formula of which much use has been made in economic analysis. It is a formula that admits of application only on the assumption of an invariant or static order, and thus in economics it is associated with the concept of a permanent equilibrium subject to incidental and relatively isolated disturbances. But where we are dealing with a phenomenon of change in a changing system — the typical problem of *social* causation — this device will no longer avail us.

As we shall have occasion to investigate this whole subject at a later stage we shall here content ourselves with a single illustration.[9] In a skilful piece of economic analysis R. Heberle deals with the causes of urban migration.[10] The main argument is that a change in agricultural technology, *without simultaneous change in the distribution of property*, increases the pressure towards emigration from the country to the city. Since the change in agricultural technology here referred to is of the kind that substitutes labor-saving capital for human energy, it means that fewer agricultural workers are needed to supply a given demand for agricultural products. If we postulate a relative inelasticity of demand for agricultural as compared with industrial products, then, other things being equal, there will be displaced agricultural workers; then again, other things being equal, there will be cityward migration. It is with the second of these statements that our author is chiefly concerned, and for his broad theoretical survey he

---

[9] See below, pp. 164–169.
[10] " The Cause of Urban Migration — A Survey of German Theories," *American Journal of Sociology* (May, 1938), Vol. 43, pp. 932–950.

simplifies the qualifying conditions to the one proviso —
" without simultaneous change in the distribution of
property." But in effect this proviso is extremely complex
and inclusive. A change in agricultural technology is one
aspect of a larger system of technological change. That
larger system is certainly associated with changes in the
distribution of property, and that again with numerous
aspects of economic and political and cultural change. On
all of these — on such factors, for example, as governmental
policy towards agriculture, the conditions of social and
occupational mobility, the level of business activity, the
technological and cultural conditions making for or against
the increase of non-agricultural rural occupations — will
depend the answer to the question whether there is an
effective " pull " to the city and an effective " push " from
the country. Starting as we do from the fact that there has
been over a certain period a cityward migration we com-
fortably select a particular " thing," knowing that the conjuncture of the " other things " *has been* on balance favorable. The other things are never " equal," if they enter
into the situation at all. Once more we have failed in our
efforts to evade the impasse of the " complex and indecomposable totality."

Other logical embarrassments crowd upon us. There
is, for example, the highly disconcerting business of the
time lag. The effect succeeds the cause. The concept of
causation, whatever else it includes, always expresses a
relation of antecedent and consequent. The residual relation, of one thing followed by another, was retained even
by Hume. But since he dissolved causation into mere
succession he avoided the essential difficulty. As soon as
we conceive of one thing as " determining " another we
are in the thick of it. Where one thing follows another
there is a time interval, no matter how brief. Cause and

effect are, by definition, not simultaneous, since even successive instants are still successive. If the cause is conceived not as operating at one instant of time but as enduring through a process from which the effect emerges,
nevertheless each stage of the process itself, no less than
the culminating stage in which the effect comes into being,
postulates a prior cause and a subsequent effect. In sum,
whenever we assert that one thing, or one state of things,
determines another, we assert a time interval between the
two. Or we may put the problem in the form of a dilemma.
If *A* and *B*, whether they be specific events or successive
states of the whole universe, are cause and effect, then
either there is a time interval between them or there is not.
If there is no time interval the cause and the effect are
indistinguishable and the postulated relationship becomes
meaningless. To save it we accept therefore the other
horn of the dilemma. But now we fare no better. For if
there is a time interval, there is no nexus of cause and effect.
The cause ceases to operate before the effect begins. The
bridge between cause and effect has been destroyed.

This difficulty is put in various ways by the critics of the
principle of causation. Russell, for example, states it as
follows:

" Philosophers, no doubt, think of cause and effect as
contiguous in time, but this, for reasons already given, is
impossible. Hence, since there are no infinitesimal time-
intervals, there must be some finite lapse of time τ between
cause and effect. This, however, at once raises insuperable
difficulties. However short we make the interval τ, something may happen during this interval which prevents the
expected result. I put my penny in the slot, but before I
can draw out my ticket there is an earthquake which up-
sets the machine and my calculations. In order to be sure
of the expected effect, we must know that there is nothing

in the environment to interfere with it. But this means that the supposed cause is not by itself adequate to insure the effect. And as soon as we include the environment, the probability of repetition is diminished, until at last when the whole environment is included, the probability of repetition becomes *nil*." [11]

We may note in passing that the difficulty of the time lag is closely bound up with the conception of cause to which we appear to have been driven, cause as the totality of the antecedents of the effect; and that, as Russell suggests, the difficulty becomes insuperable as soon as we accept this position. Obviously the total prior situation does not *wait* through an interval and then explode instantaneously into a series of consequents or " effects."

We may perhaps feel that the time lag problem is a logical paradox, like Zeno's problem of Achilles and the tortoise, hard to refute so long as we accept the formula in which it is stated, but yet carrying no conviction. But once we have retreated to the position that " the " cause of any phenomenon, if we continue to speak at all of cause, is the totality of its antecedents the enemy has so many grounds of attack that our situation becomes quite untenable. The relation of any two events becomes contingent, not necessary. We can no longer say: if A then X; or even if $ABC \ldots N$, then X. For our items never exhaust the totality and therefore are not adequate as a statement of the cause of X. We may say that the relation is probable; that given $ABC \ldots N$ we can with high probability predict X; but nothing short of *necessary* connection will save us and that we can no longer maintain. Moreover, what we predict is sequence, not necessity. We can with enormously high probability predict that night will be followed

---

[11] *Mysticism and Logic*, p. 187.

by day, but if we do not in this instance claim that the sequence is causal how can we make the claim for any other sequence? If there is no necessity in the relation of any two events, then there is no necessity anywhere. We observe certain uniformities of sequence, we observe also that they sometimes fail; but even if there is no hitherto recorded instance of failure we have no guarantee that one may not occur tomorrow. " In this sense we shall have to give up the hope of finding causal laws such as Mill contemplated; any causal sequence which we have observed may at any moment be falsified without a falsification of any laws of any kind that the more advanced sciences aim at establishing." [12]

In this chastened mood we turn to Mill's canons of induction, based as they are on what he calls " the law of universal causation," that " every consequent has an invariable antecedent." And we find that the simplicity and the conclusiveness they claim are illusory. All that the methods can provide for us are useful clues to probable sequences, but the assurance of a permanent nexus is another matter altogether. Mill himself admits that "unfortunately it is hardly ever possible to ascertain all the antecedents, unless the phenomenon is one which we can produce artificially." [13] But if so, the methods, taken strictly, are for the most part counsels of impossible perfection. Even the artificial production of the phenomenon under investigation will often fail to provide us with two instances that differ with respect to a single circumstance alone. And as for the " method of agreement," it would seem to be nothing short of a miracle if two instances of a phenomenon should be found that have " only one circumstance " in common. But there is a further difficulty

---

[12] Bertrand Russell, op. cit. p. 194.
[13] J. S. Mill, op. cit. Book III, Chap. VIII.

involved in the whole procedure. The formulation of the Millian methods presumes the disjunctive operation of the " circumstances " that are present or absent in the various instances of the phenomenon. But in any combination of elements, whether mechanical, chemical, or social, we have to reckon not with the mere presence or absence of a particular circumstance but with the complex interrelationship of the combining elements, parts, properties, or activities. The only difference between a car that moves and one that refuses to move may be that the latter has a disconnected wire. But it would be idle to assert that the cause of the motion of the car is the connection of a particular wire to its terminal. A small difference between two chemical formulas may mean that the one represents a food and the other a deadly poison, but it would be absurd to say that the difference is itself the poisonous agent. We cannot accept Mill's statement that " if the effect of *ABC* is *abc*, and the effect of *BC* is *bc*, it is evident that the effect of *A* is *a*." [14] The world is not a congeries of unit factors functioning as detached units, whether the units we are considering be atoms or men or stars. Frequently the examples offered us of the application of the methods contain this false assumption. Here is an instance taken from a textbook of philosophy: " If there is no barking in a house, and then, with no other change in the household conditions except the introduction of a dog, there occurs barking, we are justified in believing that barking is correlated with dog. The form of this method is:

First Instance   CDE
Second Instance   ABCDE

C, *D*, *E* represent the household conditions in the two instances. *A* represents the introduction of dog, and *B* the

---

[14] Loc. cit.

occurrence of barking." [15] The form is factitious and misleading. Dog and barking are not two distinct items A and B, any more than dog and tailwagging, and we do not proceed to eliminate CDE in order to discover that the barking is an activity of the dog.

Once again we are forced to retreat. Our first assurance in the principle of causation has been subjected to formidable assaults. We may now be ready to accept the alternative that the critics of the principle offer us. We descend to the mathematical limbo.

II

MATHEMATICAL LIMBO

That there is order, sequence, uniformity, law, in the universe is a datum of all experience, and a condition of all science. To deny it would be the most impossible feat of contradiction, since it would be to deny our very existence. This order appeared to our naive common sense to depend, more than on anything else, on the principle of causation. But we are now enjoined from the notion of cause-effect. We are told that it is outdated, a mere episode in the history of ideas.[16] We are told that it is inconsistent with the scientific attitude and has been abandoned by the more advanced sciences.[17] We are told that it is anthropomorphic and theological.[18] What, then, is the alternative, since the natural order is undeniable? It is, we are told, to substitute mathematical functions for the older expressions of causal sequence and concomitance.[19] Mathemati-

---

[15] University of California Associates in Philosophy, *Knowledge and Society* (New York, 1938), Chap. III.

[16] Cf. L. K. Frank, "Causation: an Episode in the History of Thought," *Journal of Philosophy* (August, 1934), Vol. 31, pp. 421–428.

[17] Bertrand Russell, op. cit. p. 180.

[18] G. A. Lundberg, *Foundations of Sociology* (New York, 1939), p. 260.

[19] M. R. Cohen, *Reason and Nature*, p. 224; Bertrand Russell, op. cit. p. 199.

cal formulas are the proper and most perfect instruments for the statement of all relationships.[20] Mathematical and logical relations are themselves " the intelligible substance of things." [21] " A causal sequence, which is a two-term sequence so loosely constructed that it can work only from the past to the future and besides cannot give precise quantitative results, is to a functional equation as a canoe to an ocean liner." [22] Therefore, instead of speaking of cause and effect we must now use differential equations, " which hold at every instant for every particle of the system." Instead of speaking of causal interaction we must speak of correlation, of the concomitant variation of the variables of a system with respect to the relative constants of the system. Instead of speaking of causal sequences we must speak of functional configurations, so constructed that, given the formula for the state of the system at any instant, we can calculate, in terms of a set of co-ordinates, its state at any other instant. We can no longer ask whether a particular correlation is meaningful or otherwise. The correlation itself is the whole meaning. We can no longer impute necessity to the order of succession or interdependence to the order of concomitance. The only necessity we can postulate is the necessity inherent in *logical* relations, " the necessity which connects ground and consequent." [23] And should we be baffled by the question how *logical* necessity can hold for an order that lacks any inherent or existential necessity, then we must resort to the position of Karl Pearson, who tells us, in true Humian fashion, that the necessity is merely that of the order of our sense impressions, and that the word " cause " is properly

---

[20] G. A. Lundberg, op. cit. pp. 79–80 and *passim*.

[21] M. R. Cohen, loc. cit.

[22] University of California Associates in Philosophy, *Knowledge and Society*, p. 65.

[23] M. R. Cohen, op. cit. p. 225.

used to mark " a stage in a routine of experience." ²⁴ So
used he regards it as a " clear and valuable concept."

But it is surely far from clear. For what is Pearson saying
here? That the imputation of cause is a habit of thought
due to the sequence of our " sense impressions." There is
an order of our " sense impressions," and we transfer this
order to the world without. But are we not at this point in
peril of hopeless confusion? We have seen that the concept
of causation, whether it possesses or lacks valid application,
is universally entertained — and we shall see presently
that it is entertained by the philosophers who formally
reject it. We have seen that this concept is not the same as
the concept of sequence. If so, we have still to explain why
the sequence of sense impressions should beget in us a
different concept altogether. Even if we admitted that we
perceived sequence — an admission that on Humian
grounds we have no right to make — we have hardly
advanced any nearer to the associationist derivation of the
concept of causation. The associationists must go one step
further, and say, as in effect they do, that there is a necessity of connection between our sense impressions. They
must say at the very least that the sequence of sense impressions *causes* us to entertain the concept of causality. In
short, they must admit the validity of the causal explanation as applied to mental phenomena, while denying that
it has any application to natural phenomena.²⁵ And this
is only the beginning of their troubles. They must then
admit that the sequence of sense impressions *causes* in us

---

²⁴ *The Grammar of Science* (London, 1911), pp. 128 ff. Observe what
would happen to Pearson's argument if we claimed that the " routine
of experience " involved the experience of routine.

²⁵ The resort to associationism merely transfers the role of causation
to another area, from the physical to the psychological. (See,
for example, S. P. Lamprecht, " Causality," in *Essays in Honor of John
Dewey*, New York, 1929. Cf. also H. Speier, " The Social Determination of Ideas," *Social Research* (1938), Vol. 5, pp. 182–205.) It should

the belief in the sequence of external phenomena. That means, the sequence, order, or uniformity they substitute for the concept of causality proves to be itself dependent on a particular causal nexus. These points are so obvious that they relieve us from the larger task of showing the more profound difficulties involved in the subjectivist separation of sense impressions from external phenomena. We will adduce only one further consideration. We challenge the assumption that our notions of causality are first applied to what Pearson calls " the sphere of sense impressions." Rather, they are from the first implicit in our awareness of ourselves as living beings, with needs or wants the satisfaction of which depends on a constant readjustment between ourselves and our environment. To live is a dynamic function — not a mathematical one — and in that dynamism, as we become reflective, the concept of causality emerges. Its roots are vastly deeper than mere psychological association. No doubt our reflection is exceedingly crude and inadequate, needs, and is capable of, vast clarification. But our experience as dynamic beings progressively confirms the reality of causation, and the task of reflective analysis is to reveal the scientific basis of that experience — not, because of the inadequacies and confusions of our first naive reflections upon it, to discard it altogether. We do or we leave undone, and our particular near world is changed accordingly. We struggle, suffer, and resist, achieve some temporary controls over our conditions. This realm of experience cannot be construed as

---

be observed that psychical causation is not an alternative to physical causation but only another operation of the causal principle. " For example, the fire is burning and we see a red coal. This is explained in science by radiant energy from the coal entering our eyes. But in seeking for such an explanation we are not asking what are the sort of occurrences which are fitted to cause a mind to see red. The chain of causation is entirely different. The real question is, When red is found in nature, what else is found there also? " (A. N. Whitehead, *The Concept of Nature*, Cambridge, 1926, p. 41.)

a sequence of " sense impressions," nor can it be represented through the undynamic formulas of mathematical functions.

A functional equation is an admirable device to symbolize certain highly general or universal relationships under hypothetical conditions, where, for example, a number of determinate factors or forces are assumed to constitute the structure of a closed system in a state of equilibrium. It has no relevance to a system that cannot be understood in terms of isolable factors or components. It has no application to a system the changes of which depend in any degree on the impact of factors lying outside it. It is incapable of expressing or even of indicating the nature of the changes that occur in any changeful order — which is practically the whole world of our experience. The relations it symbolizes are the concomitant variation of factors in a timeless order. For time is a one-way direction. The present moves into the past, not into the future. Of this primal necessity the functional equation is regardless. In no sense does the mathematical function symbolize our experience of time, the irreversible order that moves from present to past, *from cause to effect*. It is not constructed in terms of that experience. It has nothing to do with cause and effect. It is a fine instrument for expressing the calculable elemental attributes of physical mechanics, but it is futile to seek to apply it to the processes, trends, and happenings of the complex time-bound constructs within which we have our being. If science refuses to deal with the latter on the ground that it cannot represent them by functional equations, on the ground that they are not amenable to precise quantitative calculation, it is refusing to meet the challenge of experience. If it claims that " the intelligible substance of things " consists of those attributes that an ingenious but purely symbolic device can cope with, it is without warrant identifying the abstractions of the calculus with the realities of the universe. But the practice of the scientific investigator does not conform to these dogmas. Only the metaphysicians of science take this stand.

" Mathematical and logical relations form the intelligible substance of things." By what magic do the numerical and quantitative ratios between things become the intelligible substance of the things themselves? Why should the most abstract relations, devoid of all content, of all quality, of all potency, be the substance of things? Why should that aspect of things which is most remote from our senses, our organs of perception, be their most *intelligible* aspect? Why, for example, should correlation be more intelligible than causation, when correlation asserts nothing but the possibility of an undefined connection, whereas causation is itself a kind of connection and one the idea of which is highly congenial to our experience? If we make logical relations the substance of things we turn the world into a realm of insubstantial phantasms. In the first place logical relations are timeless relations.[26] Nothing ever happens in them or to them. In the second place they are, with respect to the world of experience, hypothetical relations. They take the form: given A, then B. If the proposition A is true, then the proposition B is also true. They are not relations between facts but relations between judgments. They are equally valid, or invalid, whether we are talking of chimaeras, ghosts, scholastic essences, idle signs, or of realities. They are not relations between things but relations between concepts or meanings, or between the symbols that stand for them. A world of meanings, apart from a world of realities, apart from a world of causal relations, would be a dream world. Logical relations, apart from

---

[26] See, for example, T. Parsons, *Structure of Social Action* (New York, 1937), pp. 482 ff.

causal relations, would be a "ghostly ballet of bloodless categories," dancing in the void of disembodied impotent mind.

Logical relations are relations between propositions or judgments, not between things. The necessity they claim is normative. They do not express the laws of nature, not even the laws of thought, but only the laws of correct inference. The whole matter is well stated in the following passage from a book in which Aristotle is imagined to be addressing a congress of modern scientists:

"If I am not mistaken there is some confusion about causality. Many of you, it seems to me, mix up the *principium rationis* with the law of causality. Each ought to be kept distinct. The *principium rationis* binds reason and consequence. When you draw your conclusions in the realm of your mathematics you are inclined to call reason the thesis to start from — say, a given triangle having a right angle. From this you proceed to the Pythagorean proportion of the squares, speaking of consequence. In doing so you refer merely to the process of your thinking. You may also start from the squares and conclude that the angle is a right angle. Then reason and consequence change places. This, your habit, is misleading. In the realm of mathematics neither the proportion of the squares nor the right angle is either reason or consequence. The reason is the axiomatic system of Euclidian geometry; the consequence is the Pythagorean theorem . . .

"Reason and consequence are not interchangeable . . . Obviously, in drawing conclusions from the right angle to the squares and vice-versa you refer between each two steps to the axioms of space. Thus you do not proceed straight from one position to the next. You set a position. You go back to the axioms, to add a second position to the first, according to the axioms.

" Now as to your causality. Your causality deals with successive states and events in time. Causality pretends that in a closed system a state at a given point of time is entirely determined by the preceding state and determines the succeeding. This is an assumption concerning the order of the Many in time — to be accepted or denied.

" Let us look at the relation between this kind of causality and the *principium rationis*. This causality presupposes an axiomatic order that underlies the successions in time and is built in a very particular way. From this reason follows the causal relation between events or states. Thus the law of causality presupposes a specific axiomatic system. You may deny this specific order and yet maintain the *principium rationis*. If there are other axiomatic systems able to cover the order of physical happenings the law of causality would have to give way to another kind of determination. The *principium rationis* would not be shattered." [27]

Mathematical and logical formulas are the empty play of mind unless we discover a reality to which to apply them, unless we apply them to a real world in order to learn more about reality, never advancing a step without a fresh appeal to our data. Mathematics and logic are not natural sciences but only the tools of these sciences. They have no content of their own. Unless there are other relations that mathematical relations can represent, unless there are other relations that logical relations can guide us to, all our thinking can do is to render luminous the void. This is the limbo, the land of the thin spirits of departed things, to which those who deny the principle of causality invite us.

But these philosophical Charons do not themselves re-

---

[27] Kurt Rietzler, *Physics and Reality* (New Haven, 1940), pp. 42–43. The whole book is a brilliant exposé of the inadequacy of the mathematico-logical conception of reality.

main on the other side. They still, openly or under disguise, return to the land of the living. They still use the
language that signifies doing and suffering. They still
speak of events as " producing effects," of " determinate
results," of " physical forces," of " real connections." [28]
They still speak of " energy," " activity," " potentiality,"
" interdependence," " chance," and so forth, using concepts that are steeped in the more pervasive concept of
causality. They must still admit that " it is essential to
perception as a source of knowledge that there should be
in the world causal series which are, within limits, independent of the rest of the world." [29] They cannot, or at
least do not, get rid of the notion of cause. The concept
survives their arguments, persistently returns. Possibly the
arguments were less conclusive than they seemed. Let us
examine them afresh.

III

RETURN TO CAUSALITY

The attack on causality has rendered valuable service,
not in demolishing the principle but in challenging our
habits of thought, in confounding our more naive conceptions, in compelling us to re-examine, re-define, and re-
vindicate the principle itself. The notion of cause is so
deeply imbedded in our most vital experience that it
seemed secure from the assaults of scepticism. At the same
time this very quality beguiled us into assuming that the
kind of dynamism associated with conscious being pervaded all nature. In an entirely intelligible sense we cause
things to happen. We manipulate certain things, we control certain things. We desire things to be otherwise, and
we strive to change them. We command and we receive

---

[28] M. R. Cohen, *Reason and Nature*, pp. 103, 236, 247, 323, 360, and
passim.
[29] Bertrand Russell, *The Analysis of Matter* (London, 1927), p. 314.

obedience. We are commanded and obey. We organize force and employ modes of compulsion. We resist the compulsion of others. And so, when we observe change in external nature we easily think that in nature too there is enforcement, exertion, tension. We easily think that there too a will commands and is obeyed. We think that somehow one thing compels another thing to happen. We think of power as magic or virtue inherent in things. But when we are challenged for evidence we can offer none. We have been transferring to nature without sanction the properties, attributes, modes of existence we find in ourselves. Seizing their advantage at this point the critics of causality attack along the whole front. As we have seen, they advance a series of crucial arguments which, unless we can meet them, must render the principle of causality entirely void and untenable. These arguments may be grouped under three main heads.

1. One of the main arguments against the notion of cause is that it is animistic or at least anthropomorphic.

The Crux of Anthropomorphism When we get rid of the last " remnants of primitive animism " we are left simply with the " idea of regular sequence," uniformity of succession.[30] But why is there no other alternative? When, for example, scientists speak of a radio-active body, of the impact of photons on electrons, of the ejection of electrons from a metal surface on which light falls, and so forth, they are not speaking of mere sequences, regular or otherwise. They do not mean merely that electrons happen to jump out when light strikes a metal surface, as though there were no connection between the two phenomena. They mean what they say, that the *ejection* of electrons is the conse-

---

[30] For example, M. R. Cohen, op. cit. p. 224; G. A. Lundberg, *Foundations of Sociology*, pp. 56–58.

quence of the *impact* of light. They do not mean that by a curious coincidence electrons detach themselves at the instant light rays reach the metal. They do not mean that by a curious coincidence the tree happens to fall when the lightning strikes it. They mean that the one event determines the other. There is nothing "animistic" or "anthropomorphic" in this conception. Russell claims that the word "determine" has no clear meaning.[31] But the meaning is scarcely in doubt, whatever may be the problem of application. A child knows what is meant when we say something makes something else happen. Even if the furthest reach of science can still not tell us how one thing makes another happen, the meaning of the words is clear and the reference to the phenomenon they denote is as common in scientific statement as in everyday observation. Everyone knows what causality *means*, even the philosophers who want to reduce the meaning to something else. But since the word expresses a primary relationship, we cannot get nearer to its meaning by substituting other words that denote other kinds of relationship.

We are apt, of course, to interpret what we know less, or more remotely, in terms of what we know more, or more immediately, and this tendency is a main source alike of error and of new knowledge. We are apt to think of physical compression as though it were a kind of restraint, of the operation of physical forces as though it were a kind of exertion similar to our own strivings. We readily apply to the realm of physical phenomena the words that convey our *feelings* of tension, strain, effort, compulsion, achievement. For this we have no warrant. But when we detach from the concept of cause the associations familiar to the causal experience of animate being we do not thereby reduce it to the concept of sequence. The lightning still

---

[31] Bertrand Russell, op. cit. p. 190.

strikes the tree. We still mean that the lightning *causes* the tree to fall. It is a different kind of causing from that which involves the fulfilment of a purpose. The generic notion of cause covers both types. It is the simple, ineluctable notion of making something happen.

In the business of living we are always making something happen. Among other things, we cause people to " change their minds." If Hume convinced me that he was right about the lack of evidence on which to base the concept of causation, he would have proved himself wrong, since it was his reasoning that caused me to change my mind. My change of mind and his reasoning would no longer be merely " one thing followed by another." If Hume means only that the notion of cause has no valid application outside of animate being, then he is denying that we have any ground to speak of causation except where it is associated with feelings, purposes, and subjective states in general. He is dividing the universe into two utterly disconnected parts, in one of which a fundamental principle of ordered knowledge is present while it is lacking in the other. Can we justify this strange dichotomy? In the world outside animate nature we discover endless sequences of events. Many of these *seem* to be more than sequences. If one phenomenon is very frequently accompanied or followed by another we suspect there is a reason — we suspect a causal relationship. We suspect that phenomenon A makes, or is contributory to making, phenomenon B happen; or more broadly, we suspect that the system in which A and B occur is so constituted as to make B accompany or follow A. The only alternative to these suspicions is the acceptance of the sequence of A and B as coincidence or chance. But chance too is a subject of scientific inference, and its probability is the inverse of the probability of non-chance. If a coin is tossed a hundred times and falls heads ninety times, we should reasonably suspect that something other than chance is operative. If it falls heads ninety thousand times out of a hundred thousand, the probability that the sequence is not chance is vastly increased, becoming a practical certainty. Chance too is subject to law.[32] No one would deny that when a loaded die falls more frequently on one side than on any of the others this is not chance, this is not one thing followed by another but one thing dependent on another. Why the universe is such that a loaded die falls more frequently on a particular side may be a very profound or a very idle question. But in either case it does not alter the fact that the sequence of faces shown by a loaded die is different on that account from the sequence of faces shown by an unloaded die. A difference in the antecedent makes a difference in the consequent. That is all we mean by causation, and that meaning is surely free from any charge of " anthropomorphism."

" No," the critics may still reply. " You have said: ' One thing *makes* another happen.' That is the anthropomorphic crux. This ' making ' belongs only to human experience. In nature we see no sign of it. We observe only occurrence, never *enforcement*. A difference in the antecedent is followed by a difference in the consequent. That is all we have a right to say. It happened so yesterday, it happened so today; tomorrow — some tomorrow — it may not happen." We might here raise the query whether the anthropomorphic risk does not lie in the identification of " making to happen " with " enforcing." We might suggest that the difficulty is created by a false distinction between the " force " of a thing and the thing itself, that the " force " of a thing is simply the presence of the thing,

---

[32] " The law of chance might be claimed to be the most fundamental and indispensable of all physical laws " (Sir Arthur Eddington, *The Philosophy of Physical Science*, New York, 1939, p. 61).

just as the " force " of will is simply the presence of will. But another line of argument may suffice. It is put as follows by W. P. Montague:

" Once grant me my first claim that real causality is a possibility, then my second claim that it is an overwhelming probability follows easily. There will now be two possible worlds — one causal, the other non-causal — with which we are confronted and between which we must choose. In external appearance the two worlds would be exactly the same. In each world there will be conjunctions of phenomena repeated with enormously greater frequencies than would be indicated by the product of their separate frequencies. . . .

" Let us take Hume's famous example of the billiard balls as a typical case of a concurrence of events that is repeated with a frequency that would be out of all proportion to the probabilities in a world lacking causal powers. Billiard ball *a* rolls with a certain velocity up to billiard ball *b*. And at the moment of contact *b* starts off with a velocity which in direction and intensity is the same as that of *a*. That this should happen once is no reason for wonder from any standpoint because it is no more peculiar or specific than any other event that would have filled the ensuing moment. But the chance that in the absence of any internal causal determination the concurrence of *b*'s motion with *a*'s contact will happen not only twice, thrice, but a million times in succession is almost zero. While if, on the other hand, there *is* internal causal determination, the continued occurrence is just what would be expected. The repeated occurrences must be either causal or casual. If the chance that they would occur in a universe in which all occurrence is casual is measured by a fraction that is almost zero, the chance that they are occurring in a universe in which there is causality is measured by one minus that fraction, which is itself a fraction almost equal to unity . . .

" The crux of my case is the assumption that there is at least the possibility of causal power in nature. If there is even that bare possibility, be it as antecedently improbable as you like, then the fact of nature's routines transforms it into an overwhelming probability. For the chance that these routines are causal is one minus the chance that they are casual. The only alternative to the hypothesis that causal power exists is the hypothesis that nature's laws are stupendous runs of luck." [33]

We do not, in short, get rid of hypothesis by taking the sceptical attitude. Instead, we shall be choosing, as between two disjunctive alternatives, the one that, since we must choose between the two, " would entail a world of perpetual miracle." To prefer the other alternative, the hypothesis of causality, is not then to be guilty of " anthropomorphism "; it is not " the shameless impudence of animal faith and hope masquerading in the garb of a logical postulate." It is to prefer the vastly credible to the vastly incredible.

▼

2. Now that we have withstood the main assault the others prove less formidable. The second argument amounts to this, that even if causality exists, investigation *The Crux* into it is idle. For the cause of any specific phe*of Totality* nomenon must be regarded as not merely some specific phenomenon or conjuncture of phenomena but the total antecedent situation. This claim discounts any attempt to establish a specific cause-effect nexus. But it misconceives the genuine problem of causal investigation. As will appear more fully at a later stage,

---

[33] *The Ways of Things* (New York, 1940), pp. 184–188. The two brief quotations that immediately follow are taken from the same passage.

when we intelligently raise the question why, what excites our interest and calls for explanation is always the *difference* between two comparable situations. Why is there a shift towards the red in the lines of the spectrum of distant stars? Why is the number of photo-electrons ejected from a metal surface proportionate to the intensity of the light, whereas their velocity is independent of the intensity of the light? Why does a billiard ball start off with the initial velocity of the ball that hit it, instead of with a different velocity? Why is there more unemployment under certain conditions than under others? Why did the general lose the battle — instead of winning it? Always there is an implicit or explicit alternative; it is always " why this instead of that." Since then it is the differential consequence we are seeking to explain we can concentrate attention on the differential conditions of otherwise similar situations. We find, for example, that a regularity of sequence is on some occasion interrupted. What is the cause of the interruption? We look for a differential factor in the antecedent of that particular occasion. If the car stalls, we do not need to invoke the whole universe to find the cause of stalling; we are seeking the difference that explains the stalling as contrasted with the regular functioning of the car. Perhaps nothing evokes our interest in causation so much as the interruption of an orderly routine. We search for some factor that has been injected into the situation — what at a later stage we shall speak of as the " precipitant " of the change.[34]

In passing, we remark that the philosophers who, like Pearson and Russell and Cohen, reduce causation to uniformity or regularity of sequence seem curiously oblivious of the fact that it is precisely the interruption of uniformity that stimulates our search for causes. If the ways of all

[34] Chapter Six.

things were eternally unchanging we could not even entertain the notion of cause. The interruption of routine and not the routine itself first prompts us to ask why — and surely the first question is no more illogical than the second. If all the conditions of two antecedent situations were identical, then, in accordance with the axiom of causality, the two consequent situations would also be identical. If a new factor is introduced into one of the two antecedent situations, then, in accordance with the same axiom, the two consequent situations would be different. In other words, the lack of uniformity of sequence expresses, no less than does uniformity of sequence, the uniform operation of the principle of causality. But even if we reject this axiom, even if we doubt whether causal determination is everywhere and always operative, we should have no more reason than before to identify causality with regularity of sequence. If causality exists anywhere it will still be causality. And since the universe is in continuous change, that causality will still be revealed by the breakdown of regular sequence as readily as by its occurrence. The position we are opposing seems to confuse uniformity of sequence with uniformity of causation.

The consideration that the universe is a changeful scheme of events and processes contains the answer to the crux of totality. Take the aspect of event. Many events are occurring simultaneously. Each event is unique, a separate manifestation of a particular conjuncture of circumstances. It is separate not from the whole, but in the whole. It is different from all the other events that are occurring at the same time in other places. It arises from a different conjuncture. We appeal to the conjuncture, to the difference, not to the totality. Here the rain falls and there the sun shines. Here a man prospers and there one goes bankrupt. Here the battle is lost and there it is won.

The conjuncture relative to the event is limited and specific — it is certainly not the whole antecedent state of the universe. Take again the aspect of process. We are concerned with change within a totality, with the change of a to a_1, of a_1^- to a_2, and so forth. A process is the passage of a continuity through a succession of changes. Each stage of the process is a different state of the continuity. The difference of the continuity at each moment of the process determines its difference at the next moment.[35] We do not enquire into the cause of existence — that is perhaps meaningless; we enquire into the change of existence. Again, the causal explanation does not need to embrace the whole wide world. If the principle of causality holds at all, then difference depends on difference. To discover how difference in the consequent depends on difference in the antecedent is the primary problem of causal investigation.

We have thus two grounds for disputing the crux of totality. In the first place the search for causes is typically the search for the differential factor of two or more comparable consequents.[36] In the second place, the situations within which we search for differential factors are themselves, for the specific investigation of causes, relatively

---

[35] On the causality of process see G. H. Mead, *The Philosophy of the Act* (Chicago, 1938), pp. 646 ff.

[36] This mode of statement avoids the over-simple and mechanical formulation of the Method of Difference given by Mill. The Method of Difference, properly formulated, remains the key method of the search for causes. To revert to our former examples, the connected wire is not the cause of the motion of the car, but the disconnected wire is the cause why one car does not run in contrast with others that do. Carbon dioxide in limited quantities performs a function in the maintenance of the organic balance, whereas carbon monoxide is a deadly poison. We cannot say that the additional atom of oxygen is the agent that carries the peculiar properties of CO_2. But we can say that the additional atom of oxygen changes a deadly poison into a normal constituent of the organism. That is only one step in the discovery of causes — behind every cause lies another — but it is definitely a step.

isolable. Possibly, if we were to include sufficiently remote links in the temporal sequence, there is no phenomenon or event that does not depend on the whole history of the universe. But the infinite regress of causes is no reason why we should not seek the connection between an immediate phenomenon and its immediate antecedents. It is a curious logic that would allow us nothing because we cannot have everything. In the present, situations are relatively isolable because they are relatively independent — not of the rest of the universe, but of the rest of the universe *in the present*. A myriad systems function at the same time in relative independence of one another. Every mechanism, every organism, every social organization, is a provisionally equilibrated system. It has its own internal structure, its own history, its own operation. We can investigate the causal relations of its specific structure and of its specific activity. Even the most momentary substructure has its own moment of equilibrium, constituted by the interdependence of its own factors. Causal sequences occur within it, in relative independence of the causal sequences that bind it to larger and larger systems. All experience testifies to this fact. Without it there could be no experience. Again we see how nihilistic and self-defeating is the denial of the principle of causality.

▾

3. We can now briefly dismiss the last of the objections to the principle of causality. It is one that comes naturally to those who regard mathematical and logical relations as the intelligible substance of things. We have seen that time, the category of irreversible, irrevocable process, cannot be comprehended or represented by means of mathematical equations. Mathematics can express the order of succession of instantaneous, or rather timeless, states, symbolized by $t_1, t_2, t_3, \ldots t_n$. These

The Crux of the Time Interval

states are not *times* as we experience them. They have no duration and no direction. They have no *passage*. They have the quality that is most alien to the time of experience — they are static, frozen. Now if we apply to cause-effect relations the concepts appropriate to mathematical equations we manufacture the crux of the time interval. It is the story of Zeno over again. We know that Achilles will catch up on the tortoise. We know that the arrow shot from the bow is not at rest until it strikes some object. Yet if we assume that time and space alike consist of an infinite series of juxtaposed and indivisible points we can maintain that Achilles will always lag behind the tortoise and we can prove that the arrow is always at rest. On these assumptions there is no differentiation between space and time, and the experiential reality of both disappears. Space becomes an infinite number of spaceless points and time an infinite number of timeless instants. These points and instants are counters, not spaces and times. " If points and instants are only subjective constructs of ours with no objective existence, Zeno's moving arrow can never get stuck in them, and we shall never have to ask whether it moves from one point to the next." [37]

In the same manner, if we refuse to accept the assumption that time is an infinite series of discontinuous instants, we are already saved from the crux of the time interval. The same reason that vindicates motion vindicates causality. The same postulate that rejects causality rejects not only motion but the whole world of experienced change. Here

---

[37] W. P. Montague, *The Ways of Things*, p. 222. This author offers a number of alternative solutions of Zeno's paradoxes. I quote only the one I find most convincing. For the mathematical treatment of the paradoxes see Carl B. Boyer, *The Concepts of the Calculus* (New York, 1939), pp. 23 ff. Bertrand Russell, in his *Principles of Mathematics* (Cambridge, 1903), gives a " solution" of the arrow paradox that is characteristically as much a denial of the reality of motion as is Zeno's own argument.

the basic denial is the denial of continuity. The denial of continuity is the denial of all intrinsic relations of things. The relations must lie somewhere " between " things, and there is no bridge between. There is no passage, no transition, because there is no continuum. From this assumption we simply return to the world of experience, for experience itself is a continuum, one aspect of the vast continuity of nature that it itself reveals. " If there is something that continues, that which is there at the present time is responsible for what is going to be there in the future." [38] There is not first an end of cause and thereupon a beginning of effect. When we speak of a causal nexus we do not mean a nexus *between* cause and effect. The causal relation is itself the nexus of things as they move from present to future. When the continuity changes gradually we call it process. When it changes with seeming abruptness, either through the acceleration of process or through the introduction of a new factor from without, we call it event. But we need not proceed further into the realm of philosophy. It suffices that if anything exists, there is continuity, and if anything continues there is causality.

By way of conclusion we draw a simple moral. The doctrines we have been criticizing have all attempted either to reduce causation to something else or to define it as something else. We have sought to show that the concept of causation is derived from experience, the primary experience of living in an environment. It is the concept of a primary relationship, so that, even if we regard it as illusory, we cannot analyze the concept itself into any simpler one. We can hardly make more clear what it *means* by stating it in other terms. The other terms are synonyms, circumlocutions, phrases in which the meaning is implicit or disguised; or else they are such as miss the meaning alto-

---

[38] G. H. Mead, *The Philosophy of the Act* (Chicago, 1938), p. 647.

gether. We have already examined instances of the latter. As an instance of the former we take Mead's definition: " The relation of any event to the conditions under which it occurs is what we term causation." [39] It is of course implied that the event is dependent on the conditions, that without the conditions the event would not occur. The relation we are referring to is not any relation but a causal relation. Such statements as that we have quoted merely *indicate* that the relation we have in mind is a causal relation. They do not, they cannot, strictly define it.

---

[39] G. H. Mead, *The Philosophy of the Present* (Chicago, 1932), p. 33.

PART TWO

CAUSATION AND THE SOCIAL SCIENCES

CHAPTER THREE

PLIGHT OF THE SOCIAL SCIENCES

I

FACILE IMPUTATION

NUMEROUS books and articles offer causal explanations of social phenomena. Some deal with social movements — the rise of fascism, the ebb and flow of democracy, the growth of some new cult, economic or religious. Some deal with social trends — urbanization, the tempo of technological exploitation, the changing phases of the " economic cycle," the decline of the birth-rate. Some deal with sociopathological problems, explaining the relative frequency of crime, delinquency, pauperism, divorce, political corruption, and so forth. The incessant impact of social change in its myriad aspects is the perpetual challenge to which these responses are made. Not only our scientific interest but also the imperative demands of public policy here give weight and urgency to the investigation of causes.

The writer made a survey of the articles dealing with these subjects as published over a period of years in journals of sociology, psychology, economics, political science, and education. In the great majority of instances either no grounds or quite inadequate ones were given in support of the causal imputations they presented. Sometimes there was displayed a meticulous care in the refinement of statistical indices or in the calculation of correlation coefficients, followed by a sweeping, unguarded, or wholly unwarranted conclusion regarding the causal nexus. Sometimes a selective description of conditions attendant on the phenomenon was the only basis for quite definite imputation. Sometimes cases or examples were offered showing the presence of the alleged cause, as though that were sufficient to establish its causal relation to the social phenomenon. Not infrequently an order of priority or importance was assigned to a number of " causes," with little or no attempt to justify or even to elucidate this rating. Occasionally an investigator ventured so far as to give numerical weights or percentages of " influence " to the various " factors." When several authors dealt with the same social phenomenon they differed considerably regarding its causation. In one instance the discrepancy went so far that an author offered as an explanation of the *declining* divorce rate in Japan an array of concomitant social changes of the same kind as those that other authors put forward to explain the *increasing* divorce rate of Western countries.[1] The almost complete lack of any well-considered methodology was very noteworthy.

For reasons that will appear more fully in the sequel, the methodological investigation of the causes of social phenomena is beset by peculiar difficulties.[2] Any social change we seek to explain is meshed in a tangled web of its inclusive history. It is dependent on conditions arising within every order of reality — physical, biological, psychological, and social. The factors we invoke embarrassingly combine the universal elements of physical causation and the human elements of teleological causation. The phenomena themselves are often hard to demarcate. What shall we include

---

[1] See the *American Journal of Sociology*, Vol. 36: November, 1930, pp. 435–446, and January, 1930, pp. 568–583.

[2] See Chapter Nine, § 2.

in a social movement? What is socialism or fascism or democracy? What is common to the different instances to which we may agree to apply the name? Each of the movements or systems we study presents a different aspect to different observers, according to their focus of interest, their experience, and their temperament. These systems, however impressed on the face of things, are not themselves " things " in the sense of being detachable or demarcated items of the objective world. As operative social systems they are the partial objectification of human conceptions, of interests and beliefs, of purposes and dreams. They have no clear boundaries marking where one ends and another begins. They have ever-changing configurations. All the time each conjuncture is undergoing subtle modifications. There is unbalance and mobility, the constant emergence or injection of new elements. What we call the movement or the trend is an aspect of an endlessly variant flux. We cannot isolate it for experimental study. We cannot find two identical instances of it, or even two instances with no relevant difference between them. Nor can we find two instances that differ only by the presence or absence of a single clearly designated factor.

In the face of these perplexities it is not surprising that much investigation into the causes of social phenomena is of a haphazard hit-or-miss character, or that various devices are employed to skirt round the difficulties of a direct attack on the problem. For example, it is not unusual to proceed on certain assumptions that simplify the task of imputation but render the conclusions thereby attained dubiously applicable to the actual world. To this order belongs the economist's conception of an equilibrium that is being forever disturbed and forever reasserting itself. To the same order belongs the recourse to the formula, " other things being equal," even where all our experience tells us that they are not so. Another device is to limit the search for causes to factors falling within the same category as the phenomenon to be explained, as when we try to account for unemployment or a decline in the volume of business solely with reference to the internal functioning of the economic mechanism, regarding political, cultural, and social changes as merely incidental disturbances, " random factors," and so forth. Such departmentalism has been widely prevalent in the social sciences. The search for causes cannot be so confined. We can describe and classify social phenomena according to the categories of tradition or of academic division. Our interest may very properly be focussed within the range of any of these categories. In fact without these categories we could scarcely make any advance towards articulate knowledge. But when we tackle the central issue of causation we must ignore all frontiers. For the quest leads us to the common substratum of social phenomena.

There is another and antithetical way of evading this requirement that is characteristic of certain schools of sociology, economics, and psychology. By way of illustration we may cite the sociological school of Durkheim, with its tendency to explain all kinds of human manifestation, cultural expressions, individual deviations, statistical facts concerning crime, suicide, and so forth, in essentially social terms. This tendency, present but somewhat controlled in Durkheim's own contributions, has been exaggerated by some of his followers. What we can charge against Durkheim himself is that his methodology, his embracing concept of organic solidarity, his ready resort to the notion of " collective representation " — illuminating as they are for certain aspects of human affairs — leave no proper place for the role of biological and individual psychological factors.[3] This is only one instance of the common tendency to make the field of one's special interest the inclusive ground within which the causes of all relevant phenomena are to be sought. Not only is this procedure congenial to us as sociologists, economists, psychologists, psychoanalysts, and so forth — but also it offers an escape from the harder problems of a more inclusive methodology. So these various academic imperialisms are encouraged to engross the larger realm of knowledge.

We could take in turn each of the social sciences, or branches of social science, and show that the degree of their inability to grapple with the issue of causation is the main obstacle to their advance. For unless we can discern the causal nexus of things we do not know the way they belong together or the way they are set apart, we do not know the nearer and the more inclusive systems they constitute, we do not know their behavior or their properties or the routes they follow in their changing relationships. We are limited to description and to insecure classification. The state of anthropology affords perhaps the best illustration, although political science might also be aptly selected. The subject of anthropology is peculiarly inclusive, being equally concerned with all the aspects, processes, and products of human living, at least within the simpler societies. The scientific organization of its data accordingly presents peculiar difficulties. Even if we limit its

---

[3] See on the subject of "sociologism" P. Sorokin, *Contemporary Sociological Theories* (New York, 1928), Chaps. VIII–X; H. Blumer, "Social Psychology," in *Man and Society* (New York, 1937), edited by E. P. Schmidt; H. Alpert, "Durkheim and Sociological Psychology," *American Journal of Sociology* (July, 1939), Vol. 45, pp. 64–70; and the wide-ranging article by A. Salomon, "Sociology and Sociologism," *Journal of Social Philosophy* (April, 1938), Vol. 3, pp. 210–222.

range to what is called "cultural anthropology" it still
includes a highly diverse group of interests. The tendency
has accordingly been towards monographic accounts of
particular peoples, particular "culture areas," and particular "culture patterns," constituting an array of valuable research materials but lacking the co-ordination and
the systematic quality of a developed science. The study
of causation has not proceeded far beyond the controversy
between "diffusionists," who seek to trace "culture
borrowing" back to various foci or even to a single focus,
and those who deny their claims. The classification of
"cultural types," resting mainly on considerations of con-
tiguities and similarities, lacks a clearly defined basis. The
earlier anthropologists found, no doubt too easily, a causal
principle in evolutionism. Present-day anthropologists
have found it advisable, on the whole, to reject this principle. Our point is, however, that unless specific causal
relationships can be established, whether between differentiated groups or types of phenomena within the same "culture" or between the various types of "culture" themselves, anthropology cannot become an articulated and
well-ordered system of knowledge.

The challenge of causation is no less urgent for the
immediately practical aspects of social science, for criminology, penology, the study of public opinion and propaganda, public finance, the arts of social work, the study
of the conditions of economic welfare, and so forth. Here
we are concerned with diagnosis, therapy, promotion, and
prevention, and unless we can discover the various causal
series from which spring or with which are bound the conditions we desire to check or to further we can never reach
our practical goal. The difficulties that beset us in this
endeavor we shall presently illustrate by a survey of the
investigations devoted to a particular "social problem."

For our last general example we turn to the field of legal studies, in which embarrassments of a quite different kind arise. The legal code determines what behavior is amenable to judicial decision and to penal sanction. The determination is normative, not the expression of causal processes inherent in the situations to which it applies. The law-makers and the courts decide what actions shall be punishable, under what conditions, and to what extent. Some legal theorists claim that the measure of responsibility, of amenity to legal sanction, is the degree of " guilt," the magnitude of the offence, or the amount of harm or loss occasioned by the punishable act. To maintain this mechanical equation of responsibility and causation it is necessary to ignore or misconstrue the sanctions attached to acts intended or attempted but unfulfilled, to acts alike in intention and in accomplishment but differing with respect to the train of consequences, to acts of " negligence," and so forth. In short, the normative system of law, like any other normative system, must find its rationale otherwise than through the exact correspondence between its various rules and the specific consequences of the acts envisaged by them. Another source of confusion is the view that the causal explanation of crime can itself be the basis of legal and judicial determinations. The causal derivation of crime may be of great value in stimulating such social reconstruction as may remove conditions evoking certain types of criminal behavior. But no system of law could be built on considerations of the causal derivation of criminal behavior, and no court could adjudicate at all, if its basic postulate, the responsibility of the offender, were made dependent on either his heredity or his environment.[4]

---

[4] On this subject see Chapter Eight, § 3.

II

BY WAY OF ILLUSTRATION: THE CAUSES OF CRIME

To bring out more fully the confusion and lack of direction that prevail in the social sciences concerning the whole issue of causation we shall survey the present state of the investigation into the causes of crime. A survey of this kind will reveal also the peculiar difficulties that must be faced in so far as the social sciences advance beyond description and classification and " measurement " to the coherence and articulation that distinguish every developed science and that in the last resort depend on the degree in which it makes effective application of the causal concept.

Let us first ask what general conclusions have been attained by the numerous and many-angled studies of the causes of crime. The answer is not easy. Let us listen to some of the conflicting voices.

" Crime is the act of a criminal. Criminals are born so. They have physical stigmata. Crime runs in families."

" If crime runs in families, it is because of economic conditions. Crime is a function of economic exploitation."

" There is no convincing correlation between economic level and the amount of crime. Even crimes against property are not always most frequent among the very poor, and the richest country in the world has the highest crime record. The cause is social disorganization — above all, the clash of cultures."

" Look at the Jukes and the Kallikaks. They weren't troubled by the clash of cultures. The difference is in the heredity. The primary cause of crime is biological inferiority."

" The Jukes had an environment as well as a heredity."

" Crimes increase with the growth of urban civilization."

" Urban crime receives more attention, but there's a

good deal of crime also in rural areas, and some types of crime, arson and certain sex offences, are more frequent there."

" Crime is mainly due to the decline of religion, and of authority in general."

" The chief source of crime is the failure to solve the emotional crises of childhood."

" Crime is a form of disease."

" The criminal is the really ' normal ' person, who does not let his instincts be suppressed by society."

" Criminality is a form of moral impairment."

" Crime results from physical impairment. Its main causes are alcohol and syphilis."

" It is due to excessive egocentricity."

" There is no use looking for particular causes. It's everything together, heredity *and* environment, the totality of group and situation. Crime in the United States is due to the United States, to all of it, its good and its evil."

" That may be true, but it is not very helpful. We are back where we started."

Let us look in more detail at this bewildering variety of attributions. First, there are those who select a single factor, biological, psychological, economic, or social, as the main determinant. To Max G. Schlapp and Edward H. Smith it is the disturbance of the endocrine glands in the criminal or in the criminal's mother.[5] To Havelock Ellis and the spokesmen of certain mental hygiene organizations it is congenital weakmindedness or some form at least of mental defect.[6] To W. A. Bonger it is the economic structure of society, in effect the capitalistic system of production for profit.[7] E. H. Sutherland lays stress on the conflict of

---

[5] *The New Criminology*, New York, 1928.

[6] *The Criminal* (London, 1907), p. 29.

[7] *Criminality and Economic Conditions*, Boston, 1916.

cultures to which immigrants and more generally those who live in a mobile society are subjected.[8] Franz Alexander and William Healy, following the lead of a number of psychoanalysts, lay stress on the emotional conflicts that arise for children in the child-parent relationship.[9]

Next, there are those who offer as the dominant cause some broadly inclusive condition or trend, scarcely to be called a single factor, since it is lacking in specific character and often is ill-defined. To E. J. Cooley crime is " in the final analysis ' an expression of faulty character.' " [10] To Franz Alexander and Hugo Staub it is the failure of youth, at the critical period of character formation, to suppress or transform its " criminal instinctual drives." [11] To Harry Best, in so far as there has been an increase of crime it is due to " restlessness and impatience with restraint " and to " individualism." [12] To Boris Brasol the underlying cause is social friction resulting from the egocentric or antisocial propensity.[13]

A third category consists of those who are content to show that some one condition, process, experience, or vicissitude is " a " cause of crime — a conclusion that has little significance unless the denominated cause is related to the causal complex. The causes thus adduced are of the most diverse nature, including " fear," " misgrading in school," " bad companions," " alcohol," " sex," " immigration," " urbanization," " bad housing," " self-indulgence," " the decline of religion," " corrupt politics," and so on through a seemingly endless array.

[8] *Principles of Criminology*, Chicago, 1939.
[9] *The Roots of Crime*, New York, 1935.
[10] *Probation and Delinquency* (New York, 1927), p. 353.
[11] *The Criminal, the Judge and the Public* (New York, 1931), p. 34.
[12] *Crime and the Criminal Law in the United States*, New York, 1930.
[13] *The Elements of Crime*, New York, 1927.

Again, there are those who put forward as the explanation of crime an assortment of heterogeneous factors. Cesare Lombroso compiled the following: meteorological and climatic influences, mountain formation, race, civilization or barbarism, density of population, the ease of obtaining subsistence, alcoholism, education, wealth, religion, early training, heredity not only of certain characteristics but of criminality, age, sex, civil status, profession, unemployment, prison, sense impression, imitation, suggestion.[14] Enrico Ferri contributed to the list a few items his compatriot may have overlooked, such as tattooing, peculiarities of the literature and jargon of criminals, and the succession of day and night! [15] Somewhat more modest lists are not infrequently offered by educationalists, psychiatrists, and sociologists. One example may be sufficient. A writer in *School and Society* explains the young criminal as the product of the following conditions: loss of loyalty to the home, thirst for public limelight, appeal of easy wealth, attractive excitement of the gangster's life, and over-emphasis of sex by the movies and popular literature.[16]

From the list-compilers we turn to our last category, those who explicitly or in effect give up the quest for causes. We can place in this category two different groups. One of these is content with the conclusion that crime is due to the interaction of heredity and environment, to the combination of individual and social factors, or to the " total situation." [17] This conclusion is indeed the only logical

---

[14] *Crime, Its Causes and Remedies* (Boston, 1911), translated by Horton.
[15] *Criminal Sociology* (Boston, 1912), translated by Kelly and Lisle.
[16] L. A. Averill, *School and Society* (1934), Vol. 39, pp. 736–741.
[17] Among those who more or less come in this category are Clarence Darrow, *Crime: Its Causes and Treatment*, New York, 1922; Frank Tannenbaum, *Crime and the Community*, Boston, 1938; G. Aschaffenburg, *Crime and Its Repression*, Boston, 1913; C. W. Reckless and Mapheus Smith, *Juvenile Delinquency*, New York, 1932.

one if we are asking the rather idle question: What are the causes of crime in general? But, as we shall see later, any pertinent investigation into the causes of crime must formulate more specific questions. It must be concerned with the relative amount of crime here or there, then or now, under these conditions or under those; with the differential crime rates of occupational classes, social classes, and other comparable groups; with the relative frequency of different types of crime under given conditions; with the relation between changes in the amount of crime and changes in the penal system, the legal system, the economic system; with the relation between crime trends and culture trends; with the relation between crime and personality type. When we make our question reasonably specific, it no longer avails us to fall back on the formula that crime is the product of the total situation.[18]

The second group arrives at a wholly negative conclusion. "It is impossible," says one of them, "in the existing state of criminological knowledge to say just what are the causes of crime. Any one who attempts to do so is far transcending the boundaries of definite knowledge."[19] The ground of this conclusion is that no general agreement has been attained concerning "the importance or the weight of any given causation factor." The positivist assumption is made that "causative factors should have an obvious, detectable, and demonstrable bearing on behavior."[20] In our later analysis we shall deal at length with the whole issue here involved. At present we merely point out that those who adopt this position, who demand objective measurement of the causal efficacy of any factor, seek a way out by resorting to the language of probability

---

[18] See Chapter Five, § 3.
[19] W. C. Reckless, *Criminal Behavior* (New York, 1940), p. 163.
[20] Ibid. p. 177.

in place of the language of causation. Criminology, they think, may have to content itself with the investigation of "factors which, while not explaining why individuals become criminal, will indicate the risk or liability for becoming criminal." [21] We shall thus obtain indices of correlation between the amount of crime and the presence of certain measurable factors. We shall learn more of the differential "risks" of criminal behavior associated with age, race, sex, class, religion, mental traits, and so forth, "just as life insurance actuaries compute the differential risk of dying at a certain age." [22] While this in itself is a commendable task we may have reason to see later that it in no sense implies the abandonment of the causal quest.

In fact it is only by seeking for the differential frequency of crimes under different but comparable conditions that we can advance our knowledge of the causation of crime. Along these lines much useful exploratory work has already been done, showing, for example, the relative frequency of certain categories of crime for particular groups of a population, for particular age-periods, for particular stages of the "business cycle," for particular psychological types, such as "schizophrenes," "catatonics," the mentally deficient, and so forth. But it is too often assumed that when we have discovered these relationships we have already solved the problem of causation. We may find that some crimes are more prevalent in the summer and others in the winter, but we should be quite unjustified in concluding that the weather is the cause of the variation. We may find over a certain period a correlation between a rise in the price of bread and the frequency of theft, but correlation as such proves nothing, and when we turn to the statistics of another period we observe that if any corre-

---

[21] Ibid. p. 181.
[22] Ibid. p. 255.

lation holds at all it is one of a reverse character. We may find that certain glandular conditions or certain physiological deficiencies are characteristic of certain groups of criminal offenders, but we do not know the incidence of these deficiencies for the population as a whole and even if we did we should still be far from our goal, since we have not explained why some only of those who exhibit them have been convicted of crimes.

Examining the literature from which our examples have been taken we discover very few attempts to face the problem of causation. Very few seriously undertake to demonstrate, by any process of scientific inference, the asserted priority of one or other factor, or the basis of selection where a list of alleged factors is presented, or the assignment of any causal efficacy to some condition they claim to be " a " cause of crime. Even where data are available and the question of causation is made reasonably specific the conclusions arrived at are often dubious, vague, conflicting, or at least unwarranted. Here are two instances, taken almost at random from a vast array. Cesare Lombroso claims that the increase of crime in civilized countries is accompanied by, and explained by, an equal increase in the consumption of alcoholic drinks.[23] Other studies show, however, that the correlation between the frequency of crimes and the consumption of spirits is very variant for different periods.[24] A German writer, making use of a variety of statistics, concludes that the explanation of the greater frequency of crime among laborers as compared with officials and business men is the poorer education of the former and the greater interest the latter have in maintaining their good names. He reaches this con-

[23] *Crime, Its Causes and Remedies* (Boston, 1911), p. 90. But see also page 99.
[24] See, for example, Dorothy G. Thomas, *Social Aspects of the Business Cycle* (New York, 1925), pp. 43–44.

clusion, although he admits that economic conditions are influential and although he does not and cannot segregate from the socio-economic complex the two dependent aspects to which he assigns priority.[25]

Our brief survey leaves us with many question marks. They would have been no less apparent had we taken any other of the great variety of social phenomena the causes of which have aroused interest and provoked investigation. The plight of the social sciences is sufficiently clear. In the exploration of causes there is much fumbling and uncertainty on the one hand, and on the other much undue and unconsidered assurance. In this essential regard the physical sciences are definitely more advanced. There are those who maintain that the trouble lies in our failure to apply to social phenomena, regardless of the difference of subject matter, the methods of the physical sciences. There are others who maintain that until we discover fundamental universal laws of a mathematico-physical character we cannot build the social sciences at all.[26] These controversies can be settled, if at all, only by exploration, analysis, and consequent construction within the field of the social sciences. The present work is offered as a contribution to this task.

III

SOME CAVEATS

Our survey of the literature devoted to the causes of crime conveys certain useful preliminary warnings against premature or ill-founded attributions of causality. It is worth while to pause over these warnings, to make clear

---

[25] F. Prinzing, " Sozialen Faktoren der Kriminalität," *Zeitschrift für Strafrechtswissenschaft* (1902), Vol. 22, pp. 557–558.
[26] Cf. Jerome Michael and M. J. Adler, *Crime, Law, and Social Science.*

their significance, to use the examples before us as illustrative of prevalent tendencies throughout the social sciences, tendencies to ignore, simplify, or short-cut the difficulties that beset any genuine investigation into the causes of social phenomena. We shall therefore set down a number of explicit cautions.

▼

1. It is vain to seek the causes of crime as such, of crime anywhere and everywhere. Crime is a legal category. The only thing that is alike in all crimes is that they are alike violations of law. In that sense the only cause of crime as such is the law itself. What is a crime in one country is no crime in another; what is a crime at one time is no crime at another. The law is forever changing, adding new crimes to the catalogue and cancelling former ones. It may even, as not infrequently happens in times of crisis or revolution, designate as the most heinous of crimes certain forms of behavior that were previously counted highly honorable. Since, then, crime varies with the law, the conditions that evoke it are equally variant. Moreover, the social conditions that increase the frequency of some categories of crime may diminish the frequency of others. Crime, then, is essentially relative. It has no inherent quality or property attaching to it as such, attaching to crime of all categories under all conditions. If indeed we do raise the question: Why crime? we are asking merely why people are so constituted that they violate laws under any conditions whatever. The question has no more specific significance than the question: Why human nature?

When a Social Phenomenon Is Defined by Law, Convention, or Any Institutional Procedure, We Should Not Assume that It Can Be Referred to Any One Set of Causes Lying Outside of the Institutional System Itself

Since crime, as a category of social action, has no inherent universal property, we cannot expect to find, in the variety of persons who are convicted of crimes, any one psychological or physiological type, any character trait whatever that differentiates them all from other persons. The crime committer may be a maniac or a genius, a scoundrel or a patriot, a man without scruple or a man who puts his scruples above the law, a reckless exploiter or a man in desperate need. All attempts to find a physiognomy of crime have failed.[27] The vaguer attempts to find a particular mentality associated with law-breaking are without warrant. The endless vicissitudes of circumstance, opportunity, and personal history preclude the expectation of any simple inclusive formula. There are, of course, criminal groups, gangs, habitual offenders who make a profession of crime under similar conditions, and these may well develop, like any other social or professional groups, their own distinctive traits.

These considerations reinforce the position we have already stated and which we shall develop more fully later on, that the only effective quest for causes is that which enquires into a specific difference between two or more comparable situations. The more determinate the difference and the more clearly comparable the situations, the more promising is the quest. If, for example, certain crimes are more in evidence during depressions than in better times, under the same social system, and if these crimes have a relative economic aspect, the problem is specific and easily attacked. But if there is a greater frequency of crime or of certain crimes among laborers than

---

[27] The most recent and most elaborate attempt is that of E. A. Hooton, *The American Criminal*, Cambridge, Massachusetts, 1939. See the searching criticism by Robert Merton and M. F. Ashley-Montagu, " Crime and the Anthropologist," *American Anthropologist* (July-September, 1940), Vol. 42, pp. 384–408.

among business people, the problem is not yet demarcated, since many other conditions besides the mode of occupation distinguish the social groups to which laborers predominantly belong from the social groups to which business people predominantly belong. Or again, if there is a greater frequency of crime among bachelors than among married men, we cannot at once proceed to the question: Why does the marital condition act as a deterrent of crime? For there may very well be other factors than the married state distinguishing the unmarried, as a broad social category, from the married. First we must analyze our difference-revealing groups and situations to discover the grounds of their comparability, relative to the phenomenon under investigation. It is only when we have discovered in this way specific relations between crime and situation that we can hope to throw much light on any larger issues regarding the incidence of crime. ▾

2. It is not unusual for writers on the subject of crime to be preoccupied with some types of crime and to explain crime in general by considerations drawn from the study of these types. We find this tendency in some authors who have made a particular study of gangs, and who consequently are apt to identify the gangster with the criminal. We should

We Should Beware of Identifying, for Purposes of Causal Derivation, the Phenomena We Are Seeking to Explain with Any Category Narrower or Broader than That Constituted by the Phenomena Themselves

observe also that the expression " the criminal " has certain connotations that limit its application. A great number of those who commit crimes are not " criminals," as that term is usually understood. Hence even if we could explain why men become criminals, or habitual offenders within a certain range of crime, we would not have thereby explained why men commit crimes.

The opposite error, but one invoking a more flagrant confusion, is attributable to those who, in dealing with the causes of crime, are mainly concerned with moral explanations. Often they write as though crime itself were almost equivalent to wrong-doing or " immorality." We find this tendency in a number of writers who are content to refer crime to " bad homes," " vicious neighborhoods," " the weakening of the moral sense," " bad heredity," " lack of social control," " individualism," " egocentricity," " the decay of religious life," " the decline of social standards," and so forth. Such explanations are in the first instance vague and inconclusive. They introduce indeterminate principles as though they were determinate causes. If these principles explain anything — though they themselves require more definition and explanation than the phenomena to which they are applied — they explain a host of other things as much, and therefore as badly. But our objection at this point is that they fail to recognize the distinction between a moral category and a legal category. No one would deny that moral attitudes are involved in violations of the legal code. But we cannot assume that there is one characteristic type of moral attitude, describable as individualism, egocentricity, and so forth, that is peculiarly associated with the commission of crime. A crime is an infraction of a legal code that is not identical with any of the diverse moral codes of groups or individuals. The numerous conjunctures of occasion, opportunity, personal experience, and socio-economic situation, to which acts of crime are responsive, make the appeal to any universal moral principle at best an inadequate and unilluminating explanation.

3. A simple correlation predicates no nexus between the correlated variables. It merely directs our enquiry in a particular direction. Where there is causation there is

also correlation, but where there is correlation there may be no corresponding causation. Many things are happening and many things are changing at the same time. Some are causally independent, some are interdependent, some are alike dependent on the same larger causal scheme but not on one another. A correlation is a clue or a question mark. Its significance is what we can infer from it or what we may learn by following the lead it provides. Sometimes we can draw no inference, sometimes the lead peters out. Correlation techniques are extremely useful in many areas of investigation, both in the physical and in the social sciences, but their heuristic value is small where the correlated variables do not fall within or cannot be brought within a single coherent order. An illustration or two may suffice.

In Our Search for Causes We Should Never Rest Content with the Establishment of a Positive Correlation, No Matter How High or How Continuous, between the Social Phenomenon to Be Explained and Any Other Phenomenon

" If bales of heavy dark wood and equally heavy bales of light colored aspen wood are compared (as to the relationship between weight and volume), then an influence of coloring on the weight might be disclosed which actually does not exist. The statistics of Russian compulsory fire insurance discloses a striking relationship between the average number of buildings destroyed in one conflagration in the country and the use or non-use of fire engines for its extinction: fires extinguished by a fire brigade furnished with a fire engine are, on the average, more destructive than others. To conclude from this that the destruction of fire engines constitutes the best means of reducing damage from fire would be . . . absurd." [28]

---

[28] A. A. Tschuprow, *Principles of the Mathematical Theory of Correlation* (London, 1939), p. 21.

Why is this conclusion absurd? Not because it is inconsistent with other correlations. Established correlations cannot contradict one another, because they assert nothing regarding the relationship of the correlated variables. The conclusion is absurd because it is inconsistent with all the causal knowledge we already possess regarding the relationship of fire engines and fires. This illustration brings out the principle that the discovery of a correlation can serve only as the starting point for further investigation and analysis. This principle has a particular significance for the social sciences. We discover, for example, various correlations of social phenomena and physical phenomena. We discover, say, that the frequency of homicide is positively correlated with the summer rise of temperature. We cannot stop there. We certainly cannot conclude forthwith that summer heat is a cause of homicide. Nor again can we conclude that wintry weather is a cause of crimes against property. The nexus between summer heat and homicide, if one exists, is not immediate. We must seek for a more direct relation between homicide and certain ways of living, certain modes of behaving, that are associated, under certain conditions of civilization, with the season of hot weather. We may thus find a nexus that is not only more direct but also more understandable, more coherent with what knowledge we already possess regarding the responses of human beings to the conditions under which they live.[29]

▼

4. The fallacy of this assumption is so simple that it ought to be immediately obvious, but it is committed rather frequently in studies of social causation. When a number of diverse factors are interactive and when a particular phenomenon is the result of their interactivity, we

---

[29] On this subject see the writer's book, *Society: A Textbook of Sociology* (New York, 1937), Chap. V.

cannot treat them as though they were independent, homogeneous units each of which produces a measurable portion of their joint product. This crudely mechanistic assumption vitiates those investigations that seek to assess, often in precise quantitative terms, the role of the various components of a causal complex. It is present when writers list in order of priority or of importance the *diverse* causes they postulate for crime, unemployment, divorce, and other phenomena, the prevalence of which is subject to statistical measurement.

We Should Not Assume that When a Number of Conditions Are Together Operative in the Production or Emergence of Any Phenomenon Each of These Conditions Can Be Assigned a Specific Weight or Influence, a Percentage of Contribution towards the Resultant Phenomenon

We have called this fallacy " mechanistic," meaning thereby that it treats the various components of a social situation, or of any organized system, as though they were detachable, isolable, homogeneous, independently operative, and therefore susceptible of being added to or subtracted from the causal complex, increasing or decreasing the result by that amount. But even a slight acquaintance with mechanism itself should teach us to avoid this fallacy. We find writers who tell us that juvenile delinquency is due so much to this factor and so much to that and so much to this other. But no mechanic would make the mistake of saying that the carburetor contributed so much and the ignition system so much and the gasoline so much to the speed of the car.[30] If a car is an organization of parts and

---

[30] It is of course another matter altogether to attribute to a change in any one factor, given the other factors as before, a difference, under stipulated conditions, in the result, say in the speed of the car. An important distinction between a mechanical unity and an organic or a social unity is that we can often change one factor in the former while keeping all the others wholly or practically unchanged.

materials that interdependently determine its functioning, at least no less so is a society. Moreover, the conditions to which social phenomena are responsive belong to a variety of different orders, so as to make the comparative rating of factors within the causal complex even more incongruous. When we are faced with the problem of multiple order causation we must proceed upon entirely different lines. In due course we shall deal with it. For the present a simple illustration may suffice. Various studies have been made of fatigue as a cause of industrial accidents.[31] These have led in turn to researches into the causes of fatigue in industrial operations. Evidences have been adduced to show that, besides the physical factors lying in the nature of the work itself and of the working conditions and besides the physiological factors of the health and strength of the workers, there are also psycho-sociological factors, described in such terms as " morale," " emotional adjustment," " co-operative and non-co-operative attitudes," and so on.[32] The issue here raised is that the valuations and attitudes of the workers are *interactive* with the physical conditions in the causation of fatigue and that therefore neither set of factors can be independently assessed. If this is so for a localized physiological phenomenon such as industrial fatigue, how much more should we pause before attempting to attach any independent or absolute rating to the numerous factors involved in the wide-ranging social phenomenon of crime!

---

[31] For example, Emery S. Bogardus, *The Relation of Fatigue to Industrial Accidents*, Chicago, 1912.

[32] An account of the conclusions to this effect of the Committee on Elimination of Fatigue in Industry is given by Donald A. Laird, " Work and Fatigue," *Scientific American* (1930), Vol. 143, pp. 24–26.

REFUGES OF THE SOCIAL SCIENCES

I

WHAT CAN WE KNOW THAT IS NOT CAUSALLY KNOWN?

THE PERPLEXITIES of social causation have fostered a tendency to resort to modes of explanation that avoid or seem to avoid the causal challenge. This tendency has particularly marked attempts to explain the large-scale phenomena of social change. In this chapter we shall consider the most characteristic and the most prevalent of these attempts. But first we shall raise the preliminary question, already implicitly answered in Part One: In what sense, if any, is it possible to explain things without reference to causation? Is causal explanation only one of several ways of explaining things? What kind or degree of knowledge can we attain that dispenses altogether with causality?

Whenever we seek to explain anything we relate it to other things: we assign it to some order of things, we place it in some rank or station or category, we compare it with other things, considering wherein it resembles them and wherein it differs from them. We investigate how it has come to be what it is, relating its present state to its past states. We consider its various aspects, properties, parts, or functions, examining their relation to one another, their interdependence within the unity of the whole. All our investigating is a search for relationships and all our science is the knowledge of systems of relations. The more we know, the more widely and the more fully do we apprehend things as related to others and things as themselves systems of relations. Thus the data of perception are brought into the realms of knowledge.

So our preliminary question becomes: Can we apprehend relations that are not, explicitly or by implication, causal relations? This question goes too deep to be adequately answered here. We are postulating relations between things, not merely between our ideas or mental images. We are assuming a real world, not a phantasmagoria. Suppose, then, we are engaged in the simplest act of knowing, in discerning any kind of resemblances and differences between things, between any things in the universe. We may observe that a cloud is " very like a whale," and that is in some sort knowledge. It would certainly be difficult to claim any causal relationship between a whale and a whale-shaped cloud. We may observe that a particular species of mushroom is shaped like a parasol. No one would suggest on that score a causal connection between mushrooms and parasols. But science is not concerned with resemblances of this kind. It does not classify its phenomena on the basis of such resemblances. If we ask why not, the answer is obvious. Science is interested not in superficial resemblances between things, but in resemblances that reveal like processes of development or continuous structural types, or that can be traced back to a single origin, or that in some way can be utilized to organize the data of science in an articulated scheme of orders and categories. Science is not interested in superficial differences between things, but in differences such as represent variations of a structural type, or distinguish one order or suborder or class of things from another, or raise problems concerning the adequacy, inclusiveness, or exactitude of the systems already constructed. In short, science is interested in how things belong together, and it studies and classifies resemblances and differences from this point of view. Everything from a galaxy to an atom is conceived as system, as system beyond system and system within system. Let us go one step further — let us make explicit the hypothesis that at once vitalizes the scientific pursuit and finds progressive support in all scientific achievement, namely, the hypothesis that *things belong together in systems because it is their nature to do so.* When we have taken this step we have reached the causal significance of the relations the knowledge of which is scientific knowledge.

The position thus reached we shall not endeavor to explore. Our subject is social causation, and we have here a special set of conditions that invest our data with their own kind of causality. They fall within social systems, and social systems are in part directly constructed and in large part the resultant of innumerable smaller constructive activities of individuals and groups. Whatever else these activities are they are means-ends activities. They incorporate aspects of objective, motivation, and design. The relations they create and the relations they sustain are immersed in their own causality. We can superficially describe them, we can superficially classify their phenomena as we might classify together animals and animal-shaped clouds, but we cannot comprehend their nature except in so far as we penetrate the causal nexus between social structure and the social being.

It is thus not unreasonable to conclude that all relations between things, if not themselves relations of causation, at least have somewhere a causal ground. Consider, for example, the difference between correlation and causal relation. Correlation, as we have already pointed out, is not a relation between things at all. The relation between quantitative variables is a mathematical relation, a relation of index numbers that *may* lead us to discover a relation of things. Correlation as such has no dynamic significance, any more than have the resemblances between animals and clouds. We seek out correlations in our search for knowledge of the relations of things. We count the instances of a certain phenomenon or we measure some property of a class of things. Then we count the instances of some other phenomenon or measure another property of the same things or the same property of another class of things. Correlation is simply the correspondence between the fluctuations of our numbers or measurements for the two (or more) groups, taken over a period of time or over an area of their spatial distribution. If the correspondence is close, whether directly or inversely, we want to know why. Does it mean that the correspondent variables are interdependent either on one another or on conditions common to them both? The prospect of an answer to this question alone sustains the scientific quest of correlation. We look for correlations only where we suspect they may be causally significant. We do not suspect a connection between the climate of Jupiter and the fashions of Western civilization. We may suspect a connection between sunspots and harvests. We certainly suspect a connection between temperature and industrial productivity. Such considerations determine the amount of effort we bestow on the discovery of correlations and the amount of study we devote to them after their discovery.

We are not contending that all knowledge, or even all scientific knowledge, is exclusively the apprehension of causal relations. We can appreciate the unity or coherence of things, even as we appreciate their resemblances and differences, without express reference to the causal implications of unity or coherence. We can have perspectives and reflections and intuitions that contemplate the sheerly existent, the enduring, even the timeless. We can apprehend the contours of things, their configurations and symmetries, their qualities of every kind, without examining the causal conditions on which these properties depend. We can follow the historical sequence of events as a series of vicissitudes happening to men and nations, with only a surmise of the causal links that bind them together. Often, in fact, the causal scheme of things is too complex, too obscure, or too deep for us to fathom, and we have to content ourselves with descriptive recognition, just as we watch the waves of the sea without reckoning the forces that determine their shapes and their motions. But such knowledge is not only very partial, it also contains glimpses of an unexplored causality; at the very least it contains the postulate of causation. It takes things together because it presumes, without knowing how, that they belong together. Science, however, engages itself in the endless task of learning *how* they belong together. And social science takes up a variety of the endless task, which introduces other forms as well of the eternal question: *Why?*

II

CHANGE AS PERIODICITY

No " explanation " of social change has had so continuous and so wide an appeal as that which views it as a form of rhythmic motion, the successive stages or recurrent patterns of which constitute the main theme of human history. This conception has pervaded alike popular reflection and philosophical theory. In its broadest and most ancient form it appeared in the doctrine of the ages of man, looking back to an age of gold that in the fulness of time would return. It animated the theories of the successive rise and fall of civilizations and of the stages through which each passed from birth to death. From the time of Plato

to our own days this doctrine has been variously em-
broidered according to the fancy of poet or philosopher,
among the more recent exponents being Nietzsche, Pareto,
and Spengler. Historical evidences have been massed to
support it, and quite recently statistical techniques have
been vigorously employed to confirm it.[1] Social scientists
of every kind, economists, political scientists, sociologists,
anthropologists, have traced the short-time and long-
time oscillations, waves, cycles, and spirals of numerous
social and cultural phenomena — business activity, employment, population growth, systems of government,
opinions, creeds, fashions, inventions, and so forth. The
total picture thus presented is one of an endless procession
of cycles and epicycles, constituting the intrinsic rhythm
of social change beneath all the commotion of its confused
surface manifestations.

Most of these descriptions of social change present it as
conforming to one or other of two main rhythmic patterns,
which we may distinguish as the wave pattern and the
closed curve pattern. There are, of course, other types,
such as the continuous upward spiral congenial to views
of human progress prevalent in the late eighteenth and in
the nineteenth century. But the wave pattern and the
closed curve pattern have been dominant throughout the
history of thought. Each of them is revealed in various
aspects of human experience, and the tendency to redis-
cover them in the processes of social change comes very
easily to us.

The wave pattern is represented by the motions of the
breath, by the beating of the heart, by the periodicity of
organic processes of every kind, by the alternation of light
and darkness, by the recurrent seasons, by the ebb and
flow of the tides, and by myriad other phenomena that

[1] P. Sorokin, *Social and Cultural Dynamics* (New York, 1937), Vol. III.

pulsate or recur with a regularity of succession far greater than that of the sea-waves, from which the pattern takes its name. The search for similar periodicities in the institutions as well as in the fortunes of men and peoples is never entirely unrewarded, for in the unstable balance of human affairs there are ups and downs without end. But this intriguing search is beset by two great temptations. One is the temptation to impose a simple symmetry on the facts, by simplifying or smoothing them, even by selecting them, to fit a repetitive rhythmic pattern. The history of the investigation of the " business cycle," for example, offers many illustrations of the seductiveness of this temptation. The other is the tendency to assume that the discovery of symmetries and periodicities is the discovery of a " principle of order " in the phenomena themselves.[2] The wave-like motion may be intrinsic to the phenomena, as in the pulsations of light, or it may be extrinsic, as are the symmetries we can trace by drawing the contours, in any direction taken at random, of a line of hills. These patterns do not reveal the eruptive forces that created the hills or the erosive forces that moulded them; no more may superficial symmetries in the succession of human affairs reveal the dynamics of social change. It is perhaps not without significance that some of the leading representatives of the undulatory theory of social change have been strong believers in the essential sameness of the fate and fortunes of mankind throughout the ages. It is the doctrine put forward by Machiavelli when he declared that " the world has always been the same and always contained as much good and evil, though variously distributed according to the times."[3] It is the view of Pareto, who thinks of social

---

[2] Thus, for example, A. L. Kroeber postulates a " principle of order in civilization " on the strength of certain periodicities in dress fashions, *American Anthropologist* (July-September, 1919), Vol. 21, pp. 235–263.

[3] *Discorsi*, Book II.

change as a protean scheme of oscillations, in which now dominant elements become recessive and now recessive elements become again dominant. " And so the pendulum continues swinging back and forth from one extreme to the other, indefinitely." [4] Revolutions come and go, élites are dethroned and others take their place and are dethroned in turn. There are endless variations of the recurring tides, but the tides forever recur. Since there is no direction, no evolution, no genuinely creative or constructive processes, since there is little that is inherently different or essentially new, the problem of causation can be largely ignored. The determinant factors are constant and are given from the first. These constant factors are merely reshuffled and recombined.

The doctrine of the closed curve dispenses much more radically with the specific investigation of causes, since it assumes a generic causal principle of a type that is peculiarly screened from investigation. We think in terms of the closed curve whenever we envisage the history of peoples, races, civilizations, institutional systems, as conforming to the curve of the individual organism, that is, as presenting the successive stages of birth, growth, maturity, decline, and death. From this point of view we do not look upon an unbroken sequence of ups and downs, retreats and advances, recovery after decline, the reassertion in new guise of constant factors. Instead we have the picture of determinate beginnings and endings, of determinate life-histories each self-enclosed, each endowed with its own germinal energy, each having an allotted span and following an allotted course. The contrast between the two patterns may be exhibited graphically as follows:

---

[4] *The Mind and Society* (New York, 1935), edited by A. Livingston, Vol. IV, § 2340.

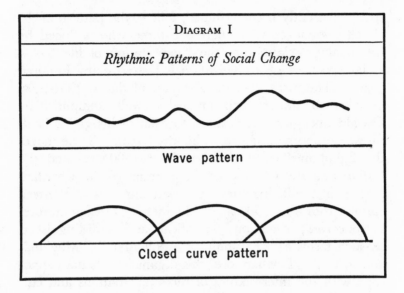

DIAGRAM I

Rhythmic Patterns of Social Change

Wave pattern

Closed curve pattern

The application to social unities of the concept of the closed curve rests on a tempting analogy. All the time things change and pass, in the social sphere as everywhere else. It is easy to think of all this changing and passing as evidence that social unities and organizations are also subject to the fate that befalls the individuals who compose them. There is, of course, no logical ground for the supposition that a unity must follow the course to which its units are predestined. The trees fall and the forest remains. The generations pass and the nation lives on. The individuals perish and the race endures. Sometimes forests and nations and races also perish, but where can we find clear evidence of a law that prescribes this mortality? No doubt if we make the span of time long enough *the conditions* become at length unfavorable to the continued existence of any form or order of life that previously favorable conditions have sustained. But this is an entirely different consideration from that which ascribes an organic being to these forms and orders of life, such that their life span, inherently predetermined, follows the pattern of the closed organic curve. There are those who, seduced by this analogy, claim that the " expectation of life " of a social epoch or of a civilization is just so many hundred years.[5] The gross liberties of historical dating that must be taken to support such notions are well exemplified by Oswald Spengler, who assigns to each of his great " cultures " a lifetime of fourteen hundred years. So he makes the Egyptian " culture " end about 1800 B.C., and the Indian and the Chinese at the opening of the Christian era! It also suits his purpose to date our present Western culture from about 900 A.D. The identity of each culture, so conceived, is tenuously mystical, and is distinguished by such terms as " Faustian," " Apollonian," " Magian," and so forth. Furthermore, this organicist schema cannot cope with the intermixture of races and nations and cultures, with the endless fusions of the old and the new, with the secessions and the reunions and reformations of groups and cultural elements, which characterize the processes of civilization but are totally inconsistent with the compact unity of a strictly organic structure.

With these and various other difficulties of the closed curve theory we are not here concerned.[6] Our point is that it evades the issue of causation. Since all the stages of a culture, society, or social organization succeed one another, from birth to death, in a predetermined course, the environmental factors are ignored or at best subordinated. The germinal life-structure accounts for the process of

---

[5] For example, Oswald Spengler, *Decline of the West* (New York, 1926), translated by Atkinson; W. M. Flinders Petrie, *The Revolutions of Civilizations*, London, 1911.

[6] The writer has dealt with them in other works, particularly *Community* (New York, 1928), Book III, Chap. II; *The Modern State* (Oxford, 1926), Chap. X; *Society: Its Structure and Changes* (New York, 1931), Chap. XXV.

development. If a society or a civilization declines, it is because its vital energies are spent, because it has reached the stage of senility, because " societies, like individuals, have a natural self-poisoning function." If it revives, it is only the recovery from a temporary sickness, and the final outcome cannot be stayed. From this point of view the vast transformations of social life responsive to the technological control of environment are merely episodes in the fulfilment of a culture, merely expressions of its stage of expansion. To Spengler, for example, the great city and its modes of activity and of thought represent that period in the life-history of a culture in which its original cohesion and vitality are being dissipated; they are expressions of ageing, relative to each particular culture, with no enduring or cumulative effect on the social history of mankind.[7] For thinkers of this school there is indeed no history of mankind, only the histories of the successive cultures as they rise and flower and fall.[8] Spengler insists that every significant culture scheme reveals the character or " soul " of an organic unity occupying some area of the earth for some fourteen hundred years — unless it untimely dies. Here we have perhaps the extreme example of the dogmatic neglect of causality that is always fostered by the closed curve theory.

III

EXPLANATION BY ORIGINS

The doctrines we have just been considering frequently dispense altogether with causal investigation; there are other doctrines that invoke causality but ignore or set aside the crucial issue of social causation — the relation of the phenomena of social change to the complex interplay of various and diverse conditions. The latter tendency we

---

[7] Spengler, op. cit. Vol. II, Chap. 4.
[8] Spengler, op. cit. Vol. I, Chap. 1.

find in many theories that account for social phenomena by appealing to their presumptive origins. Such origins may be conceived of as organic impulses, inherent in the biological or psychological constitution of man, as when a social formation is traced back to some particular instinct, emotion, or native disposition. Incidentally, this mode of explanation may be combined with a periodicity explanation, as in the doctrines of Pareto. Again, the origins may be presented anthropologically, as primary or nuclear situations whence later or more complex institutional systems are derived. The two modes of explanation are not far apart and they easily merge in one another.

The first mode is illustrated by Herbert Spencer's derivation of religion and of religious institutions from the fear of the dead or of ghosts.[9] Sumner hazarded a number of similar guesses, explaining, for example, that ceremonial originates as a form of propitiation.[10] To this author, hunger, love, vanity, and fear were the four main impulses from which, singly or in combination, social institutions took their start. According to Thorstein Veblen vanity and emulation were the source of fashion.[11] One school of anthropologists has attributed the formation of the family to the operation of male jealousy and possessiveness, while another derives it from the maternal need of protection.[12]

Sigmund Freud developed a remarkable variation of this mode. The originating factor is no longer " instinct " but a psychical complex, itself determined by an early

---

[9] *Principles of Sociology* (American edition, New York, 1900), Vol. III, p. 21.
[10] W. G. Sumner and A. G. Keller, *The Science of Society* (New Haven, 1927), Vol. II, p. 279.
[11] *The Theory of the Leisure Class* (New York, 1922), Chaps. I, IV.
[12] For the former claim see E. Westermarck, *Short History of Marriage* (London, 1926), Chap. VIII; for the latter, R. Briffault, *The Mothers* (New York, 1927), I, Chaps. III–VI and *passim*.

type-situation in which the " libido " is canalized, suppressed, or deflected. To one of these complexes, the " Oedipus," in which the nascent sex impulse is blocked by the father and vents itself in anger and hate towards the paternal relationship, he attributed a major role. In one work he went so far as to designate a supposititious primal patricide as the " inexorable criminal act with which so many things began, social organization, moral restriction, and religion." [13] His conclusion was in fact all-embracing. " In closing this study I want to state that the beginnings of religion, ethics, society, and art meet in the Oedipus complex." [14] While in other works these sweeping attributions were somewhat more qualified, they remained characteristic of the Freudian system.

The second mode of appeal to origins takes some simple or primitive form of social relationship, presumptive or evidential, and finds therein the core of the most complex institutions of an advanced civilization. This mode is frequently applied to class systems, political institutions, ecclesiastical institutions, and so forth, usually with some accent of evaluation, favorable or condemnatory. Herbert Spencer claimed that " ceremonial forms are naturally initiated by the relation of conqueror to conquered." [15] Marxist and other writers have maintained that the state began with the domination of one man over others or of one group over another group and that it has taken its essential character from this relationship. The state was originally, said Karl Kautsky, an instrument intended to guard the interests of a dominant group.[16] The state was originally, said Franz Oppenheimer, a social institution

---

[13] *Totem and Taboo* (New York, 1932), p. 237.
[14] Ibid. p. 260.
[15] *Political Institutions* (New York, 1882), p. 310.
[16] *The Class Struggle* (Chicago, 1910), Chap. IV.

imposed by victors on vanquished.[17] That original establishment still *defines* the state. The acceptance by Marxist writers of this definition of the state proved very awkward for them when they came to contemplate a state that *ex hypothesi* embodied another set of principles.

This second mode is often associated with evolutionary theories. For example, various theories of the evolution of religion present some one feature or aspect of religion as primordial or aboriginal, and regard it as playing a decisive role in the development of the whole religious system. Some have held that religion developed out of magic, there being in particular an evolution from the magical spell to the religious prayer. Some have found the primary religious expression in the sacramental meal, others in the propitiatory offering or sacrifice.[18] More broadly, the sociological school of Durkheim, Lévy-Bruhl, and Hubert and Mauss have viewed the evolution of religion as the process in which an early sanction or consecration attached to " collective representations " was elaborated and adapted to changing social situations.

In criticizing the various theories that explain later or more developed institutional systems by appeal to their supposed origins, whether psychological or anthropological, we are not casting doubt on the interest and value of research into the earliest knowable types of social situation or of social behavior. Much illumination has come to us and no doubt much more awaits us in the pursuit of this fascinating subject. But there are important cautions we must observe before we apply this knowledge to the interpretation of historical or contemporary changes and formations.

---

[17] *The State* (New York, 1926), Introduction and Chap. I.
[18] Cf. W. Robertson Smith, *Religion of the Semites*, Third Edition, New York, 1927; E. Durkheim, *Elementary Forms of the Religious Life* (London, 1915), translated by Swain.

The nexus between an early stage and a later one may not be a simple matter of growth, maturation, inherent development, or readaptation to external change. We cannot assume the organic analogy. The dynamic of social institutions or social systems is not, as it were, internal to them. For these social phenomena are sustained by group attitudes and interests operative so long as the phenomena themselves endure. Whenever they change, the social phenomena, from the simplest relationships to the most complex institutional systems, also undergo change. Furthermore, these group attitudes and interests do not create social institutions in the void but as responsive to environmental conditions of various kinds, themselves always changing and in turn reacting on the psychological factors. Present social institutions therefore depend on the interplay, *in the present*, of these complexly co-operating determinants, and are expressive alike of their continuity and of their change.

From this point of view neither mode of explanation by origins, nor yet any combination of the two, can satisfy us. The anthropological mode cannot carry us over the road from the primitive to the later scheme of institutions. If, for example, there is a transition from the magical spell to the religious prayer — though this itself is a very conjectural claim — we still cannot explain, by examining the earlier form, why the later form arose. If the earliest family was matriarchal that knowledge — itself also dubious — would not enable us to understand why the patriarchal family became dominant in many parts of the earth. The mud hut does not explain the skyscraper, even if there is in some sense an evolution from one to the other. A causal explanation must deal with the contemporaneous conditions, whatever light may be thrown on them from the knowledge of earlier conditions.

The evolutionary approach is beset by other dangers. The seemingly simple often hides the complex. We do not distinguish aspects so well in the smaller or more primitive pattern. We are apt to assume that they are absent when they are merely inconspicuous or undeveloped. The difference, for example, between the magical and the religious principle is more easily discerned at more advanced stages of culture. At the less advanced the magical element may predominate but it by no means follows that the religious is entirely absent. At the less advanced stage of religious institutions the sacramental meal or the propitiatory sacrifice may be the most obvious rite but it may be pervaded by a penumbra of attitudes that later manifest themselves in other rites. The discovery of origins is often elusive. The beginnings of many things cannot be dated. We cannot strictly say that they begin at a certain stage of culture or of civilization. They emerge rather than begin. This is what evolution properly means. If so, it may be vain to look for a *specific* origin or original form. If a thing evolves it cannot be dated. We can date events or laws or constitutions, the collapse of power systems, and so forth. Within limits we can date specific fashions, modes, styles, customs, and the rise of power systems. But we cannot date custom itself or ceremony or the family or the state. And we cannot, without arbitrary discrimination, derive such undatable and permanent phenomena from any one of their manifestations, however early or primitive these may be.[19]

Similar arguments may be directed against the resort to psychological origins. We shall have occasion at a later

---

[19] The more scholarly studies of "origins" fully accept these principles. We may cite, as examples, R. H. Lowie, *The Origin of the State*, New York, 1927; G. Landtman, *The Origin of the Inequality of the Social Classes*, Chicago, 1938; Paul Radin, *Primitive Religion*, New York, 1937; S. H. Hooke, *The Origins of Early Semitic Ritual*, London, 1938.

stage to show the hazard and the insufficiency of causal explanations that rely solely on subjective factors.[20] If this is so where we are dealing with situations immediately presented to us it holds still more forcibly when we are adventuring into " the dark backward and abysm of time." The naive assurance of our adventurers is undisturbed by the conflict of their various claims. What they take for simple may still be very complex — as well as very unexplored. Motives like " fear " and " vanity " are not simple homogeneous impulses, even when entertained by children or by savages. Institutions that abide through time are not the sheer embodiment of some one attitude or emotion that we can single out from the personality of the individuals who maintain them. Institutions are group responses to group conditions. The responses and the conditions are alike complex and complexly related. When I run it is I, not merely my legs, that run. When a man prays, it is he, not merely his fear, that prays. And if prayer becomes the habit of one man or the custom of many men, there must have been various considerations that prompted the formation of the habit or the custom. There is a congeniality of the group and the institution that is overlooked in these simplifying guesses about origins, but even if they were correct they would not suffice to explain the maintenance, the present existence, of the institutional scheme of behavior.

IV

THE KEY CAUSE

Of all the devices by which men have evaded the full problem of social causation the most prevalent by far is that which designates some one factor or complex of factors

---

[20] Chapter Seven. We leave for examination in that chapter the particular difficulties of the Freudian variety of the appeal to origins.

as peculiarly, exclusively, or dominantly determinant. We delight to simplify our problems, we delight to establish order by assigning priority, and we delight to have in our hands a key that will open any door. The whole history of social theory can be cited in evidence. Successive schools of thought have been distinguished one from another mainly by their discovery of a different key cause.[21] Every possible factor has been invested with that role. Sometimes the factor in question is merely prepotent over others, sometimes it is supreme and exclusive. Sometimes its dynamic range is limited to one order of phenomena, sometimes its range is universal over human affairs.

The sovereign factor may be specific or general, simple or complex, concrete or abstract, external to humanity or working in its blood or its brain. Some have found it in the sheerly environmental: to H. T. Buckle and to E. Huntington civilizations rise and fall in accord with conditions of climate and soil, while some economic theorists, such as W. S. Jevons and H. L. Moore, have maintained that sun-spot cycles or weather cycles dominate the fluctuations of prices and initiate corresponding variations in the whole scheme of business activity.[22] Others have found the key in some inborn quality of men or groups of men, in differentiated heredity, stock, race: sometimes it is the exclusive heredity of intra-communal families or groups, a theme expounded from the time of Plato to the present day; sometimes it is the inclusive heredity of peoples or races, also an ancient doctrine that received fresh stimulus

---

[21] The critical survey by P. Sorokin, *Contemporary Sociological Theories* (New York, 1928), affords particularly good corroboration of this point.

[22] H. T. Buckle, *Introduction to the History of England*, recent edition, New York, 1925; E. Huntington, *Civilization and Climate*, New Haven, 1924, and *World Power and Evolution*, New Haven, 1919; W. S. Jevons, *Investigations in Currency and Finance*, London, 1909; H. L. Moore, *Economic Cycles: Their Law and Causes*, New York, 1914.

from nineteenth century developments, and in the commotions of the twentieth has been elevated by at least one state into the first article of a political creed. In this version, first explicitly elaborated in the modern world by Gobineau and then Germanized by Houston Stewart Chamberlain, the dynamic factor became not race but superior race, so that its final and might-bearing prophet could announce: " Everything that we today admire on this earth — science and art, technique and inventions — is only the creative product of a few peoples and perhaps originally of *one* race." [23]

Apart from these polarities of limitless imputation there have been numerous attempts to attach the role of key cause to particular principles, activities, or conjunctures. The most famous of these attempts is doubtless the " economic interpretation of history " according to the special formula announced by Karl Marx and Friedrich Engels. It is the doctrine that the mode of economic production or the primary relations of the economic order determine the general character of the whole social structure, and that as this foundation changes so do all the expressions of human life, its cultural styles, philosophies, and faiths. [24] For others the changing scheme of productive activity, viewed technologically rather than economically, has been the artificer of the various processes of cultural change — a tendency encouraged by Thorstein Veblen when he derived the institutional order from the habit-forming lores and

---

[23] A. de Gobineau, *The Inequality of Human Races* (New York, 1914), translated by Collins; H. S. Chamberlain, *Foundations of the Nineteenth Century* (London, 1911), translated by Lees. The quotation is from Adolf Hitler, *Mein Kampf* (New York, 1939), unabridged translation, Vol. I, Chap. XI, italics as in original.

[24] Karl Marx, *Critique of Political Economy* (New York, 1904), translated by Stone, Chap. I; Marx and Engels, *Selected Correspondence*, New York, 1934; F. Engels, *Socialism, Utopian and Scientific*, Chicago, 1908.

skills of the work-a-day life.[25] Others, as we have already seen, have made some imperious urge, some instinct or some complex, the master inspiration of human activities. Some have found the key to social change in science, some in religion, some in dynamic reason, the dialectic of Hegel. Some have followed the ancient line of Heraclitus, discovering again that strife, war, conflict of any sort, was " the father of things."[26] A modern historian has found in the " challenge of hard conditions " the driving force in the rise of civilizations.[27] Some writers explain all social and cultural phenomena as the expression of a few human desires or wishes, of psychical factors however named. An opposing school transfers the onus from factors of individual consciousness to those of " collective consciousness." Another opposing school abjures the resort to consciousness altogether, and maintains that all phenomena, social or other, are alike what it designates as " physical."

This summary list could be extended indefinitely, but it is large enough for our present purpose. We do not propose to examine the grounds of these endlessly conflicting imputations. All of them omit or " reduce " or devaluate some aspects or elements of the presented totality within which the causal nexus obtains. Sometimes this is done on metaphysical grounds, as by the physicalists who would translate into physical terms the data of consciousness and are apt to dismiss from scientific discourse the language of " motives and goals." But metaphysics of this sort does not help us to discover why a man quarrels with his wife or why a war occurs. Whatever the causal role of purposes

[25] *The Instinct of Workmanship* (New York, 1914), Chap. I; *The Theory of the Leisure Class*, First Edition, New York, 1899; *Imperial Germany and the Industrial Revolution*, New York, 1915.

[26] For a list of modern philosophers and sociologists who have expounded this doctrine see P. Sorokin, op. cit. Chap. VI.

[27] Arnold J. Toynbee, *A Study of History*, London, 1937.

and valuations may be they cannot be dismissed as non-existent. Sometimes the exponents of key causes rely on correlations and concomitances between the chosen factor and the various conditions alleged to be determined by it. This is the type of evidence offered, for example, by such environmentalists as Huntington, when they show that a particular range of climate is associated with a high level of civilization. But they do not reflect on the fact that a high level of civilization is correlated with other things than climate. Even were Huntington's correlations much more firmly established than they are, we would still ask the question: Why dwell so exclusively on one only of the favoring circumstances when many others are clearly involved? Are we to say that, because all the life we know exists between the temperature ranges of minus 50 degrees F. and plus 150 degrees F., the main determinant of organic life is therefore temperature? The tendency to ignore alternative correlations is peculiarly characteristic of many advocates of key causes. But there are many others who do not offer us even a decent show of evidence. The racialists make grandiose claims and practically never cite, unless to dispute them, any facts or considerations that run counter to their theories. The economic determinists present a dogma and not a reasoned conclusion. In all the voluminous writings of Karl Marx there is nowhere any attempt to test the doctrine of the " materialistic interpretation of history." Constantly we are bidden to view events and situations in the light of the doctrine. We are told, for example, that " the ideas of freedom of thought and of religion express only the dominance of free competition within the sphere of knowledge." [28] The analogy is ingenious, if left as such. The " only " turns it into a dogma. It forbids us to view a many-angled situation from any angle but one.

---

[28] *Communist Manifesto.*

Sometimes the advocates of key causes make concessions, but in such a way as to assign an inferior causal status to all other factors. They admit that there are " conditions " without which the key cause would not function. Or they admit that, besides the key cause, other causes operate as " secondary factors." The latter is the line of defence adopted by the Marxists. They do not deny that political and cultural factors have some efficacy, but it is the efficacy of the created " reacting back " on the creator.[29] The economic or " material " factor is still fundamental, primary. But obviously, if various factors are interactive, their relationship can in any particular instance be discovered only by rigorous investigation and it may be entirely different in different instances. The hypothesis that it is always the same, that it is always the relation of a dominant factor to subsidiary ones, is not ranked by the Marxists as a hypothesis but always as an *a priori* truth. The evidences that apparently are in conflict with it are not examined but are given a coloration congenial to the doctrine. We turn on what the economic historian G. Schmoller called a " dry light," and then what seemed a struggle for religious liberty becomes a scramble for colonies or a protest against taxation or a class uprising. The most precarious of all imputations, the imputation of motives, is resorted to with complete assurance, although the least reflection tells us that in everyday affairs motives are often obscure and mixed and hard to disentangle. But this is a subject that will meet us again.

To criticize at any length the numerous expositions of key causes would take space and time we can better bestow on the central problem they alike evade. In every problem

---

[29] This interpretation is made in various letters of Engels in the Marx-Engels correspondence. See, for example, the letter of Engels to Schmidt, 1890.

of social causation we are confronted with a variety of factors or determinants. How are we to deal with them, how are they bound together in the social nexus? The problem is presented to us on two levels. Those who postulate key causes present it — and claim to solve it — in abstraction from particular situations or conjunctures. They assert the *universal* priority of one factor over others, as though it had some inherent efficacy, some predetermined status before which, on all occasions, the other factors make obeisance. Whatever factor they exalt to this status — whether it be religion or political power or reason or the sex drive or education or geography or technology or economic relationship — the same unwarranted principle animates the doctrine. The factor is detached from the conjuncture in which alone it has dynamic virtue and is erected into thinghood as an independent and integral cause. On this level the only answer is the logical exposure of the dogma that falsely claims to be science.[30]   Then we can descend to the other level, the level of particular situations. Here we are confronted with the variety of aspects that define a situation, the variety of conditions that contain it. If we call these aspects and conditions "factors," let us remember that in the causal process they are always interwoven and that we cannot isolate them severally within that process in order to study the causal efficacy of each. Since they are always interwoven, how can we claim that some one thread, no matter which, in the growing, changing pattern controls the further weaving? Even to speak of the "factors" as interwoven is to assert of each a degree of independence that simplifies and mechanizes their causal interdependence. Viewed apart from its relation to the rest

---

[30] A good example of such logical exposure is Max Weber's critique of R. Stammler's work, *Wirtschaft und Recht nach der materialistischen Geschichtsauffassung*, in *Archiv für Sozialwissenschaft und Sozialpolitik* (1907), Vol. 24, pp. 94–151.

every factor of the socio-psychological complex, whether named "economic" or "political" or "religious" or "sexual" or whatever else, becomes unreal or at least undynamic. What we strive towards, as conscious beings, is some state of conscious being, and none of these categories refers to that state in its wholeness, but only to some mode of attaining it or at most to some aspect of it. We abstract our categories from the wholeness of experience. We do so either for purposes of intellectual analysis, for the understanding (and therewith the misunderstanding) of situations; or for purposes of practical control, for the direction of our energies through the development of techniques and organizations. Thus these categories, our "factors," are modes of reference to experience but are not to be regarded as separable components that somehow make it up.

PART THREE

ANALYTIC APPROACH

CHAPTER FIVE

QUEST OF THE SPECIFIC WHY

I

THE WHY OF EVENTS

OFTEN the questions we ask are not aimed at the heart of the matter we want to know. This is as true when our interest is a practical one as when it is of an intellectual nature. Before we embark on any enterprise, before we conclude a deal of any kind, we ask a series of questions, such as may enable us to assess its merits and to clarify the nature and scope of our commitment. But often, especially if it be a new enterprise, we fail to ask just the right questions, and in the light of later experience we say, " If only I had thought to ask about this or that! " So it is when we undertake various kinds of causal investigation. It is easy to ask why, but not always easy to ask the specific why, the why that is pointed towards the mark. In treating certain subjects no small part of our effort should be devoted to the preliminary framing of the apt questions. To this problem the present chapter is addressed. We will take up in turn a number of areas of causal investigation, and though these are far from covering the whole ground they may suffice to show the character and the importance of this preparatory stage of every enquiry into causes.

Our starting point is the position that any effective causal enquiry should be addressed to a specific difference between comparable situations. If we ask why this thing happened or why it happened so, we are at the same time asking why that other thing did not happen or why this thing did not happen otherwise. Unless we have an alternative and comparable situation before us — in actuality where we can experiment, in conception where we cannot experiment — we cannot rule out the irrelevant concomitants of our phenomenon or pursue the quest for the particular nexus in which our phenomenon is bound. We have suggested, for example, that it is vain to ask so broad a question as: What is the cause of crime? It would seem equally vain to ask: Why is there a higher crime rate for the inhabitants of New York City than for, say, the Basutos? Perhaps it is no less vain to ask the causes of war, unless we limit our quest to a particular civilization. Again, it is not helpful to adduce a general cause for a specific phenomenon, as when, for example, a study of the University of Berlin explains the crime statistics of Sachsen-Meiningen by reference to the density of population, and the fluctuations of the population.[1] These are not specific causes of the specific phenomenon. Greater density of population, says the author, leads to more social intercourse and thus gives greater occasion for crime. Crime is no doubt a variety or an aspect of social intercourse, but our understanding is not much advanced when we are told that where there is more social intercourse there is also more crime. There are many such pseudo-explanations in which the phenomenon under investigation is not properly specified or in which the purported causes are not specifically related to the phenomenon.

Before, then, we can effectively pursue a causal investigation we must prepare the ground as follows: (1) We

---

[1] W. Weidemann, "Die Ursachen der Kriminalität im Herzogtum Sachsen-Meiningen," *Abhandlungen des kriminalistischen Seminars*, University of Berlin, 1903.

must ascertain that the phenomenon itself is clearly identified. (2) We must apprehend it as belonging to a situation that with respect to this phenomenon stands in contrast to another and comparable situation. The two situations must constitute a single frame of reference. What is to be explained is *one* thing or *one* system of things, with reference to some other thing or some other system of things, or some other state of the same thing or system, where the latter stands in sufficiently clear and effective contrast with the former. It is not the scale of the difference that determines whether it is a proper subject for causal investigation, but the adequate identification of it within a relevant frame of reference. It is just as legitimate to enquire why the universe is expanding (if there is satisfactory evidence that it is expanding) as to ask why a toy balloon explodes.

In this chapter we shall be concerned mainly with the initial identification of the phenomenon. In the field of the social sciences there are special problems of identification, and many investigations into causes fail to take due account of them. Sometimes the phenomenon is not sufficiently demarcated or it is not identified by reference to any coherent system within which it falls. We shall therefore examine various types of social phenomena, in order to show how the question of causation should be clarified and focussed as a preliminary to fruitful investigation. Let us begin with the category of *events*.

By event we mean a single manifestation, representing a unique historical moment, dated in time and space. An event thus offers an obvious antithesis to a process, since the latter is continuous through time and need not manifest itself in any event or series of events. The process works its way " underneath," the event " breaks out." An event is a salient occurrence, an eruptive phenomenon. It emerges from the context of more ordinary or more regular proceedings. It is something that goes on the record. It is a revelation of hidden forces, possibly a culmination, turning-point, or overt beginning of some movement of human affairs. Often it comes to disturb or disrupt some equilibrium within which it occurs.

For our immediate purpose we may distinguish two types of event. An example of the one would be the birth of a great man, of the other the act of an assassin. The former is an event not as such, but in the light of later developments. If the potential great man had died in infancy, his birth would not have been, for the larger record, an event. (At the first it is still, of course, an event for the family group within which the birth takes place.) An event is a significant occurrence, but in the first type the significance is not contemporaneous with the occurrence but accrues to it only in retrospect. We might even say that it is an event only because of later events. Hence any event in the full sense belongs to the second type. The act of the assassin is itself salient, as such has immediate repercussions on the established order, as such has a place on the record. It is with events in the latter sense, unique and dated occurrences that claim significance by their direct and immediate impact, that we are here concerned.

The causal interpretation of an event, so defined, has quite different implications from those that pertain to other objects of causal investigation. If, for example, we were dealing with a process, a movement, an institution, or anything whose very being involves either duration or change, we should have to view it as responsive to the selective patterning of persistent conditions. But an event has no time-depth. Events, the peculiar concern of the historian, alone do not require history for their causal explanation. We mean by this statement that everything necessary to explain an event is present in the sheer moment of its occurrence. If we knew the conjuncture of passions, ambitions, needs, opportunities, and so forth, in active being at the moment when a revolution or a war occurs, we should know all that we can know, or require to know, in order to explain its outbreak then and there. Of course we may also want to know why these passions, ambitions, needs, opportunities, arose — but these are not events. Our point is that, however far back into the past we may try to go to explain the developed patterns and the accumulated tensions of a social situation, it is only as these are given and operative at the moment of an event that they enter directly into its explanation. In this sense no research into the past, no digging down to the roots of things, no knowledge of what is not present here and now, will do anything to explain why an event is here and now occurring.

Let us then postulate that the why of events envisages only the time level on which they occur. This postulate liberates us from some of the difficulties attendant on other types of causal investigation. Moreover, the event is given to us as a single unique phenomenon arising within or breaking through a particular localized situation. We are not asking why wars happen, but why this war happened. We are not seeking what is common to many situations, but what is peculiar to this one. Only once does Caesar cross the Rubicon. When, as in this instance, the event is the single act of a man, or when it is the concerted single act of a group, there is only one causal question: Why did he — or they — do it? The why is as specific as the occasion. Why did Caesar cross the Rubicon? No preliminary investigation or analysis is necessary for the proper framing of our question. For what we are given is a willed act, and our quest is directed to its objective and to its motivation. How did Caesar view the situation as he took that fateful step? What were his plans, his ambitions, his hopes?

How did it fit into the scheme of his policies, as they were at that moment matured? The why is at least clear, whatever difficulties there may be in answering it. When, on the other hand, the event is a salient change in a situation, a crisis, a turning-point, a denouement, or any new condition brought about by the diverse actions of men, the implications of the question why are not so simple. It is one thing to ask: Why did this government declare war? It is another to ask: Why did this war happen?

The latter may be the more significant question, but, unlike the former, it is not self-explanatory. Are we seeking to find out who started the war, who mobilized first, who made the first declaration, who fired the first shot? But these issues may be quite subordinate — if indeed it is the outbreak of war that is our concern and not the mere technique of initiating operations. Are we, then, asking: Who was responsible for the war? But, as we shall see in a later chapter, responsibility is often an elusive thing, has different meanings according to the code by which it is adjudged, and anyhow is not a sufficient ground on which to answer the main question before us, since at best responsibility can be determined only after we know why the war happened. We are given a total situation in which a war breaks out. It is the kind of event that to an extreme degree disturbs the pre-existing equilibrium. Even if we could regard it as the inevitable outcome of the instability of that equilibrium, there is the implication that but for some precipitating factors in the total situation the warless equilibrium, however unstable, would have continued. The war certainly disrupts a multitude of non-violent processes of change inherent in the situation. So our question concerning the causation of the war should be directed to the discovery and characterization of those conditions within the pre-existing equilibrium that made its continuance precarious and of the manner in which certain precipitating factors conspired with these conditions to bring about the final disruptive event of war.

Here in brief is the schema for the causal investigation of any event, on whatever scale. We have an immediate situation that, by contrast with the emergent or salient event, is one of relative equilibrium. In other words, it is characterized by the continuity of processes rather than by the eruption of events. Within it are forces making for the maintenance of relative equilibrium; within it also are others making for the break-down of that equilibrium. Nevertheless it is maintained until some conjuncture arises — some accident maybe or seeming chance, some minor or local disturbance at some point within the larger system, some eddy in the tides of human passions, some stratagem, some new-born insight, some more conspicuous folly, in short some precipitant or complex of precipitants. This conjuncture enlists itself on the side of the innovating, unstabilizing forces, breaks the leash that restrains them — and so the event is born. How the precipitants co-operate with the forces congenial to them, so that from the breaking equilibrium the event leaps forth, is the specific problem belonging to this whole area of causal investigation. We shall not examine it more fully now, since it will be the subject of later analysis.

II

THE WHY OF SOCIAL PROCESSES

It is only quite superficially that history can be regarded as a succession of events. The event has a period of gestation. It is an expression, an outward thrust, of operations or forces that accumulate, undergo transformations, wax or wane, concentrate or disperse. Events are discontinuous, processes are continuous. The causation of events, as has been brought out in the preceding analysis, must be sought for not mainly in prior events but in the processes of which they are manifestations. We look for the causation of events outside of the events but for the causation of processes inside of the processes. To this aspect we now turn, premising that by social process we mean a system of social change taking place within a defined situation and exhibiting a particular order of change " through the operation of forces present from the first within the situation." [2]

The social sciences are deeply engrossed in the study of social processes. While this study takes a vast number of divergent directions we may distinguish certain broad types of investigation. One familiar type is that which centers attention on particular modes of dynamic relationship, particular ways in which people become associated or dissociated, singling each out for characterization either in general or as it manifests itself in localized instances. In sociology this procedure recalls such names as Simmel and von Wiese, and among Americans E. A. Ross, R. E. Park, and E. W. Burgess. These writers treat of competition, conflict, domination, submission, assimilation, amalgamation, indoctrination, and so forth, as distinctive forms of social process. Sometimes a sociologist makes a single process, so understood, the basis of his whole system, as Gabriel Tarde did in his book on *The Laws of Imitation*. One difficulty inherent in the work of all these writers is that social processes, if studied in this manner, are apt to be detached from the social structures that give them definition and specific quality. This detachment sometimes makes the treatment of processes arid or abstract or unconvincing, and from our point of view has the disadvantage that, by its lack of definite reference to structure, it makes causal investigation difficult except in general

---

[2] See the writer's book, *Society*, pp. 406 ff.

socio-psychological terms that do not go much beyond mere classification and description.

Another way of looking at social processes is to take some social group or complex of institutions and trace the transitions through which it goes, its formation, mode of growth, structure and functional differentiation, its changing objectives and interests, its shifting bases of authority or power, its internal conflicts, its increasing or diminishing cohesion, its transformations, and possibly its final dissolution. Here processes are referred to a particular social structure, such as a form of industrial capitalism, a feudal hierarchy, a religious organization, a class system, a doctrinal school, a political order, and so forth. The process is conceived of as the working out of certain potentialities inherent in the total situation or institutional complex. In a similar way people study the " process " of child development, of the acquisition of any art or skill, of the establishment of any habit or propensity, of numerous socio-psychological interests where the structural locus is the individual organism and not the social group or system. In fact, the study of processes, as above defined, constitutes a very large part of the total field of social studies. Some students again devote themselves to what they think of as *par excellence* " the " social process, seeking to distinguish the sheer effects or properties of continued social interaction, whether in a family, a small group, a neighborhood, or a larger community. This approach is characteristic of C. H. Cooley, who named one of his works simply *Social Process*, and it is very well illustrated in the book of Grace Coyle, *The Social Process in Organized Groups*.[3] The latter writer deals particularly with such subjects as " the development of *esprit de corps* " and " the process of collective thinking." A not dissimilar approach characterizes a con-

---

[3] New York, 1930.

siderable group of recent writers, among whom may be singled out M. P. Follett and John Dewey.[4]

A third type of investigation which may perhaps be included under this most inclusive rubric is that which traces, usually with the aid of numerical indices, the fluctuations of any social phenomenon, such as the standard of living, the volume of trade, the composition of population, the fortunes of political parties, the popularity of leaders, fashions and vogues, adhesion to a religious faith, and so forth. Some glimpses of the immense range of this search for trends, currents, or tides in human affairs may be had from a survey of the extensive volumes on *Recent Economic Changes* and on *Recent Social Trends* published under the auspices of committees appointed during his tenure of office by President Hoover. The character of these volumes, as well as of numerous other studies of lesser scale, is admirably calculated to reveal the need for a clear preliminary specification of the questions we set out to answer when we embark on the causal investigation of social trends.

For our interest in these trends surely goes beyond mere description, beyond mere measurement, beyond the plotting of indices and the finding of correlations between them. We want to understand them, to discover what forces promote and what forces hinder them, to follow their effects in the lives of men and in the whole moving system, to predict their further course and possibly to find means for their control. And none of these things can we do unless we look beyond indices and graphs to search for causes.

The causation of trends, or of processes of any kind, offers a very different problem from that involved in the causation of events. We saw that the whole causation of

---

[4] M. P. Follett, *The New State*, New York, 1918, and *Creative Experience*, New York, 1924; John Dewey, *Democracy and Education*, New York, 1923, and numerous other works.

the event is operative in the occasion of the event. But a process is continuous. Since therefore it cannot be explained by the conjuncture of forces at any one moment we must look for determinants that are themselves persistent, that work more deeply in the soil of society, that are congenial and understandably related to the direction of the process. We cannot any longer think merely in terms of casual conjuncture, or of precipitant and unstable equilibrium. If, for example, the process we are studying belongs to our first type, say the process in which domination and submission are reciprocally established within a group, we must view it as the shaping of a pattern of adjustment between the variant interests and attitudes of individuals or groups within a given situation.[5] Many dynamic factors meet, focus, clash, and co-operate in the shaping of the pattern. These have to be assessed at every stage of the process. If, again, the process under consideration belongs to the second type, and we are studying, say, the formation and development of some social organization, such as a church, we have to envisage, and verify in the continually changing scheme, the ramifying potentialities of the organization as these reveal themselves in its emotional and ideological appeal, in its direct or indirect provision of means to satisfy various more immediate interests of men who are already variously conditioned and indoctrinated, and in the cause-and-effect interactions of a growing establishment of authority or power. Finally, if our object of study belongs to the third type, whether it exhibit a cyclical movement, a trend, or any other configuration, we must look on the changing balance of various conspiring and opposing conditions and seek to penetrate beneath

---

[5] This is done, to some extent, in various sociological works, such as F. Znaniecki, *Social Actions* (New York, 1937), Chaps. VIII and IX, but seldom, if ever, with adequate statement of the nature of the causal problem.

that diversity so as to explain the convergence, the continuity of direction, the balance or dominance, revealed in the resultant pattern.

In every instance of a social process what we have before us is the continuous change of a dynamic system emerging from the interactivity of its components. This characterization suggests the initial steps in the framing of our questions when we set ourselves the task of explaining it. In the first place, what *is* the process? The precise reference of terms like "assimilation," "domination," "adjustment," and so forth, is by no means obvious or always clear.[6] Take "domination," for example. It has many shades of meaning, and the actualities it denotes may be classified under various categories, as has been done by Max Weber and others.[7] It may be exerted in diverse ways, some open, others disguised; some accepted, others resisted; some based on coercive power, others based on prestige or revered authority, and again others on self-interest or indeed on any combination of human attributes. What, then, is the process as a mode of change? From what, and towards what, and by what calculable degrees? No doubt something is always happening to "domination," but merely to list certain happenings — as some writers do — is not to define, still less to trace a process. And unless we make direction explicit how can we look for causes? What is the index of direction when we deal with anything so many-sided and so variable as domination? The pertinence of such questions is even more ap-

---

[6] One common confusion is that between the process itself and the condition that is established in the process. Thus "assimilation" may mean either the process in which a state of congeniality is attained between persons or groups or the condition of attained congeniality. "Assimilation" usually connotes process, whereas terms like "domination," though employed as belonging in the same category, usually connote not the process but the condition.

[7] Max Weber, *Wirtschaft und Gesellschaft*, Part III.

parent when we turn from our first to our second type of process. Writers of the Cooley school speak of " the " social process. There is here the implication that there is one specific process of socialization. This position may perhaps be justified when the reference is to the socialization of the child, to the process in which he is inducted into the life and folkways of the group. But when we apply it to beings already in this sense socialized it loses clarity and takes on divergent meanings. Von Wiese defines socialization as " the process by which ethically sanctioned intragroup and intergroup bonds are established." [8] This already suggests the danger that becomes very manifest in the work of Cooley, the danger that we will interpret socialization as the process of acceptance of those social norms which we ourselves approve or emphasize. So the term becomes clouded with the subjectivity of individual judgment.

We are saved many of these embarrassments when our project belongs to the third type, that of the trend or pattern of variation exhibited by any social phenomenon susceptible of measurement by some quantitative index. If indeed the subject itself has a quantitative character, such as the price level or the volume of trade, the mobility of labor or the cost of living, the membership of a church, or the " gainful employment " of women, our objective is already sufficiently defined and we can turn at once to the problem of attacking it. But often our index at best reflects or represents the changing character of a phenomenon that it cannot directly measure. It is one thing to measure changes in the cost of living and another to measure changes in the mode of living. It is one thing to trace the decline of an industry and another to trace the decline of a religion. According to the character of the phenomenon

---

[8] *Systematic Sociology* (edited by Becker), p. 367.

our index may be reasonably representative or only dubiously symptomatic. There may be a choice between one index and another, and we may arrive at very different conclusions according to our choice. For example, in one chapter of *Recent Social Trends* we are led to infer, on the ground of a large and rapid decline in the circulation of religious periodicals, the decline of religion in the United States, while in another chapter we are told that during the same period the number of church members kept pace with the increase of population while " religious bodies have made far more impressive gains in wealth than in membership." [9] If, then, it is religious change we are seeking to measure, *what precisely do we mean by that*, and what index will serve to represent the pattern of change we are out to discover? Obviously, wherever the object of our investigation has manifold aspects, as have all cultural phenomena, we face the challenging preliminary task of discovering the relevant questions concerning the character of our objective and its relation to our data, before we can intelligently address ourselves to any problem of causation.

The nature of this task we shall now seek to reveal more intimately by an analysis of certain cases from two welltrodden fields of causal investigation.

III

THE WHY OF STATISTICAL FACTS

By a statistical fact we mean a fact concerning the prevalence or frequency of some phenomenon that characterizes not all but some only of the individuals or units within a given system and that therefore is discoverable only by the use of statistical methods. Here our immediate interest

---

[9] Recent Social Trends, Vol. 2, Chap. XX, " Changes in Religious Organizations," by Luther Fry, with which compare Vol. 1, Chap. VIII, " Changing Social Attitudes and Interests," by Hornell Hart.

is not an event or a process but a summation of separate instances or cases belonging to the same category. We are concerned with the incidence of a phenomenon as measured by an index or rate. There is an initial problem peculiar to the study of these statistical facts. The index or rate is not an objectively presented datum. It is derived through two processes both of which are outside the control of the investigator and both of which are usually subject to variation. The first is an *official* process of definition prescribing the criteria for inclusion in the category. Some statistical facts, such as those relating to crime, are being redefined almost continuously. Other statistical facts, such as those relating to the categories of disease recorded in medical certificates, are apt to be redefined with the progress of science or of technology. The second process is the registration of the instances. The recording is done by numerous persons of varying competence. Considerations other than that of scientific impartiality may also enter in, as, for example, in the records of suicide. Similarly, the position and attitude of parents may be factors in deciding whether their children appear in the court records as delinquents. Sometimes utilitarian considerations are effective in limiting or extending the roll-call of cases. It is quite possible, for example, that an ostensible increase in the incidence of mental disease may be at least in part due not to the actual occurrence of more cases but to the increase in the number of beds available in mental hospitals. The investigator into the causation of statistical facts must always be on his guard against the social conditioning of the record itself.

Most frequently the causal investigator of statistical facts is concerned with the question why the number of instances occurring at a particular time or in a particular social group varies from the number occurring at other times or in other groups. The challenge to causal enquiry may be a trend or a cyclical movement or any other pattern of change. But the data are elicited by statistical methods — in the simplest form by mere counting — in such a way that the computed number is either exhaustive of or representative of the total number of instances of the phenomenon falling within the time-space limits of the investigation. The number or series of numbers is thus a purported fact about a social group. It is the presupposition of this type of causal enquiry that somewhere in the multifarious interactions of group life, or in the dynamic processes to which the group as a whole is subject, lies the secret of the changing rates or indices, whether they refer to one in a hundred thousand of the population or to nine out of every ten. We shall not at this stage enter into the major problems involved in the interpretation of statistical data. We are directing our attention solely to the preliminary requirements, in terms of our criterion, that every investigation of statistically determined facts ought to meet. One or two examples should suffice for this purpose.

1. Some considerations already adduced regarding investigations into the causes of crime apply equally well to the study of other phenomena that occur *The Causation* sporadically in human society. We have *of Suicide* suggested the futility of any enquiry into the causes of crime as such. The objective lacks form and clarity; it is not attached to any specific social order; there is no significant *difference* that gives it pointedness and direction. Crime as such is hopelessly relative. What evokes crime under one set of social conditions does not evoke it under another. Since there are innumerable sets of conditions the attempt to locate causes common to them all is vain. Instead, we should investigate, say, the causes of an increase or decrease of crime in a particular community during a particular period, or the

causes of a greater or less frequency of crime in one community as contrasted with another, or the causes of an increase or decrease of crime under particular conditions such as a depression or a war or a religious revival, or the causes of the prevalence under certain circumstances of particular categories of crime, and so forth.

Similarly it would not be very profitable to enquire why anyone anywhere commits suicide, which is equivalent to asking why any human being prefers to end his own life rather than to live on. The vast multiplicity of conjunctures, relative to the endlessly variant mental states of human beings, renders any such enquiry fruitless. Even the listing of a group of dominant " causes " must be artificial and unilluminating, whether they are derived from investigations of the circumstances under which a number of suicides take place or from the prior testimony of those who commit the act. We may list, for example, economic misfortunes, sex maladjustments, ill health, and so forth, but since we have sufficient evidences that multitudes of people are subjected to these conditions without exhibiting the least disposition towards suicide, the alleged causes carry as such no conviction. We may list instead certain mental conditions or attitudes that we find frequently associated with the tendency to suicide, such as a sense of inferiority or impotence or inadequacy, a state of depression or melancholia, morbid fears and obsessions. But while these conditions are important manifestations for the study of suicide they cannot be simply set down as its causes. They are the inner aspect, perhaps sometimes merely the reflection, of a relation between the individual and his environment. Moreover, for this investigation the momentary act of self-destruction is not our whole concern. That act is the end of a process, and the significant object of study is the process that terminates thus. From this point of view these mental conditions should rather be thought of as characteristic involvements or stages of the whole phenomenon of suicide and hence as data of the problem we are seeking to solve.

We turn therefore to our initial criterion. A causal investigation becomes pertinent whenever there is a challenging *difference* to be explained. We find, for example, that the suicide rate is distinctively different, over large areas or within a whole civilization, for different groups or categories of human beings. We find that there are relatively constant and characteristic rates, in a given society or a given stage of civilization, for religious, cultural, occupational, demographic, and other categories. Thus the rates differ for Protestant and Catholic groups, for the married and the unmarried, for whites and negroes, for urban and rural divisions, and so forth. These diversities present a ground for effective investigation. We have at once significant uniformity and significant difference. The uniformity, the attribute of being Catholic or married or rural, frees us from the embarrassment of the endless diversity of individual situations. The difference, lying between groups themselves sufficiently similar in other respects to give point and challenge to the causal enquiry, focusses attention on the drastically limited universe of conditions with respect to which the contrasted groups are alike and different.

The statistics of suicide rates are primary data for such investigations.[10] The statistician provides us with differential rates according to categories of *presumptive* significance. He does not classify his units according as they are blonde or dark-haired, short or tall, stout or thin, and so forth,

---

[10] See, for example, E. Durkheim, *Le Suicide*, Paris, 1912; M. Halbwachs, *Les Causes du suicide*, Paris, 1930; Ruth S. Cavan, *Suicide*, Chicago, 1928; L. I. Dublin and Bessie Bunzel, *To Be or Not To Be*, New York, 1933. The last-mentioned work has a useful bibliography and a careful compilation of statistical data.

though he might find differential rates characterizing these categories and conceivably they too might be significant. His primary classifications are not constructed with special reference to the phenomenon of suicide but are those that are equally employed for many other purposes — classification on the basis of locality, nationality, age, sex, marital condition, income level, and occupation. But classifications along these lines may suggest others of a more specific nature. The differential rates for localities may, for example, reveal contrasts arising out of conditions that vary for different areas. Which categories, then, are most significant? This the statistics themselves may not tell us. We find, say, that the frequency of suicide is higher among the unmarried than among the married.[11] We cannot simply on that score conclude that marriage is a factor dissuading from suicide. It may be that some conditions operating to prevent marriage or to dissolve marriage are also such as increase the chance of suicide.[12] Or we find that suicide is more prevalent among Protestants than among Catholics, sometimes the rate for the former being two or three times as high as the rate for the latter.[13] But we cannot immediately conclude that the difference of religion explains the differential rates. It may be that other conditions characterizing the groups with Protestant affiliations are more conducive to suicide than the corresponding conditions of Catholic groups. If we go back to the middle of the nineteenth century the statistical evidence shows that the suicide rate for Jews in Germany was generally as low as and often lower than that of Catholics, whereas in the first decade of the twentieth century the

---

[11] See, for example, Dublin and Bunzel, op. cit. Chap. XI.

[12] Cavan (op. cit. p. 320) shows that in Chicago divorced males have the highest suicide rate; next, but at a considerably lower level, come widowed males, and next divorced females.

[13] Cavan, op. cit. p. 118.

Jewish rate in all areas exceeded even the Protestant rate.[14] Such facts warn us against premature inferences regarding the causal role of religion. Once again, to take Durkheim's famous example, we find that more people commit suicide in spring and early summer than at other times, but it by no means follows that the climatic factor as such determines, or even affects, the differential rate. With the coming of spring and summer, human activities, contacts, and modes of living change. It may be that the onset of these changes somehow operates to increase the rate of suicide.

These examples admirably illustrate the need to make our why more specific. We begin by asking: Why is there more suicide among the unmarried than among the married, among Protestants than among Catholics, among city-dwellers than in rural areas? We are not entitled to ask yet: Why does the unmarried status, Protestantism, or urbanism favor a higher suicide rate? What we should ask, on our march towards the ultimate specific why, is instead: What are the conditions associated with the state of being unmarried, or being Protestant, or being urban that are more conducive to suicide or less deterrent of it?

There are various ways of setting about this task. We can, for example, examine how the rates vary for subgroups within our categories, for, say, Protestants and Catholics in different areas, at different times, or under different social and economic conditions, thus acquiring a clearer perspective on the influence of religion. Another way would be to investigate whether there is any significant factor characteristic alike of unmarried adults, non-Catholics, and urban dwellers differentiating them from the married, Catholics, and rural dwellers. If we can discover any condition distinguishing the very disparate cate-

---

[14] Dublin and Bunzel, op. cit. pp. 118–123.

gories that exhibit a higher suicide rate, any condition understandably related to the greater frequency of suicide, that condition may very well furnish the clue we are seeking.

This was the method followed by Durkheim. He seized upon the hypothesis that the distinctive difference between the groups showing a higher suicide rate and those characterized by a lower one was the degree of social cohesion. Marriage, adherence to the Catholic faith, rural life, make for closer social cohesion than do the antithetical conditions. With much ingenuity he followed out and supported this hypothesis, embracing within its scope many facts that at first seem to belong to another order, and particularly the seasonal variations of the suicide rate. We cannot pursue his argument here. It is very possible that he overloaded his claim.[15] It is very possible that, because of certain postulates of his system, he underestimated the role of non-social factors, particularly of neurological and physiological conditions. But these deficiencies leave untouched the merit of his method. Few social investigations have so fully met the criterion from which we started. With considerable success he sought to relate a challenging difference (the frequency of suicide) to a relevant difference (the degree of social cohesion) in the various situations where the phenomenon occurs. Similar methods might well be applied from other viewpoints than that of Durkheim, involving other classifications of the statistical data. These will bring out specific relationships ignored by Durkheim. They will reveal the limitations of his social philosophy, but they will not detract from the value of his unusually clear perception of the nature of a causal enquiry.

---

[15] Cf. M. Halbwachs, op. cit. *passim*, and especially pages 85 ff. See also H. Alpert, " Explaining the Social Socially," *Social Forces* (July, 1939), Vol. 17, pp. 361–365.

The Causation of Prostitution

2. We will take as our second example a social phenomenon which, like the first, belongs to what is sometimes described as the area of social pathology. Prostitution resembles suicide in that, in a very broad sense, it proclaims its own "cause." The definition of the phenomenon is already a general statement of its causal basis. Suicide is the act of taking one's own life; the suicide prefers not to live — that is why he kills himself. Prostitution is the practice of absolute or relative promiscuity in sexual relations on the basis of payment. We may, then, say that prostitution results from the willingness of persons to make a living, or to make a profit, out of it. We could even say, as one author gravely puts it, that "sex is the cause of prostitution." But obviously such statements are no more than partial definitions or indications of the phenomenon to be explained. What is it, then, that we want to discover? Prostitution, like crime and suicide, occurs under the most diverse conditions and at nearly every stage of civilization. It would hardly be illuminating, and in any event it would be impossible, to give an exhaustive account of all the human conditions under which it is found. It would be a baffling and unprofitable task to survey these conditions in the hope of discovering some among them that might be universally associated with the occurrence of prostitution. We could indeed confine our attention to a single area, country, or civilization, and enumerate various "factors" of prostitution. This has been done not infrequently, and we are offered extensive lists of conditions under this vague designation, family conditions, economic conditions, educational conditions, neighborhood conditions, recreational conditions, political conditions, and so forth.[16] But these omnibus conditions are equally asso-

[16] See, for example, Howard B. Woolston, *Prostitution in the United States* (New York, 1921), pp. 300–301.

ciated with a thousand other phenomena. At best they describe the environment of prostitution — or rather one type of environment in which prostitution occurs with relative frequency.

We shall quote a typical example of the way in which, without further analysis, prostitution is explained. It is sufficiently characteristic of the prevailing mode of dealing with the causes of social phenomena to deserve citation in full.

" In modern society the most general cause of prostitution, that to which all the others may be traced, is the extreme poverty that sometimes obliges parents themselves to sell their children. More particularly, we must point to the vile influences emanating from the lack of proper education and the failure to set a good example, not only in working-class families but also in those which possess some degree of comfort but which conduct themselves in accordance with the widely accepted maxim, ' Since nature provides us with passions, there's nothing wrong in obeying, for their satisfaction, the instincts it implants in us.' We must adduce also the promiscuity that prevails in working-class environments or among low-paid employees, owing to the housing limitations consequent on high land values in the great cities or on the rapacity of certain landlords. Children sleeping in the same bed corrupt the morals of one another, and young girls become ready-made recruits for prostitution. The wandering habits of children without adequate supervision lead to the same results. So too does the bad habit of frequenting places that offer unhealthy seductions, taverns, low-class music-halls, and above all public dancing-establishments where, in the great cities, girls of twelve or thirteen years of age meet with prostitutes and pimps and soon learn to follow the same kind of existence. We should observe also the deplorable system prevailing in workshops, factories, and large stores, where sex promiscuity and pernicious examples produce the gravest disorders, where the bosses and often the customers demand shameful compliances from the young working girls dependent on them. Add to this the inadequate wages paid to women; the nefarious system of hiring out and subletting jobs, known in America and in England as the 'sweating system,' which drives thousands of girls to prostitution because they cannot earn enough for their subsistence; the abandonment by their seducers of the girls they have seduced, once they become pregnant; the immorality of those middle-class householders who abuse their domestics; the levity with which nursemaids are dismissed for insufficient reasons; the want of sympathy for erring women or girls who, when their lapse is known, are harshly repulsed and refused employment, so that they are driven to vice to earn a living; the refinement of immorality and laziness that impels parents to hand over their daughters, husbands to deliver to prostitution their wives, and wives to prostitute themselves voluntarily in order to augment or to maintain their standard of living, to procure fashionable adornments above their condition, to buy jewels or furnishings that appeal to their vanity or caprice. We should refer also to the exploitation of women by unscrupulous go-betweens or the parasites of prostitution; to fake employment bureaus engaged in the white-slave traffic which with the bait of jobs as governesses, companions, teachers, and stenographers, supply numbers of Belgian, Dutch, and Austrian women for vile locations in Egypt, Turkey, America, and Australia. Then there are the keepers of 'houses of tolerance,' who make game of police regulations by bringing into their establishments minors and unwitting children; there are go-betweens and pimps, whose greed and vice lead them to incite to prostitution as many girls as they can.

Finally, we must mention a quite modern evil, the system of standing armies that constrains thousands of men, in the period of their greatest vigor, to share the demoralizing life of the barracks where they must live, for the most part, as bachelors. They are impelled to satisfy as best they can their instincts and their appetites; some frequent houses of prostitution, others endeavor to seduce the women they meet. On the other hand the same system deprives, for a longer or shorter time, thousands of women of their natural protectors, of their bread-winners, so that through sheer poverty they are driven to prostitution." [17]

Now as a summation of a variety of conditions making for prostitution the above-quoted statement will do as well as any other. But that is just the trouble. Other lists include " factors " omitted here, omit " factors " included here. What is more significant, they vary considerably in the emphasis they place on one or another type of cause. Professor Woolston, in the passage already referred to, admits that some of his " factors " are merely contributory circumstances, while others are " more strictly causal." But the basis of this distinction is nowhere clear. Few if any of the writers on the subject offer any explanation of how they arrived at their particular selection of causes or at all approach the initial problem: What is meant when we speak of the causes of prostitution? Many of the causes put forward are conditions characteristic of a particular civilization. They are characteristic, say, of France but not of Argentina, of the United States but not of China, of industrial civilization but not of feudalism. But prostitution may be no less prevalent in the social systems that our attributions do not fit. It is as indigenous to China as to any part of the Western world and to feudalism as to in-

---

[17] Translated from *La Grande Encyclop'die* (Paris, 1886–1902), Vol. 27, p. 815.

dustrialism. Almost the only feature common to the various explanations is the role of destitution — economic privation or economic exploitation. But this cause is implicit in the generally accepted definition of the phenomenon. It needs no elaborate enquiry to show that the women who give themselves promiscuously in return for payment are mostly under economic pressure. But even so there are forms of prostitution where the economic urge is absent or unimportant, as in the temple prostitution of ancient Babylon, Egypt, and Arabia. It is, moreover, exceedingly difficult to maintain that the amount of prostitution varies with the degree of economic misery. Besides, the amount of prostitution is a matter of demand as well as of supply. In many primitive communities, where marriage is practically universal and takes place at an early age, prostitution is scarcely known. In the present stage of Western civilization there is some evidence that, for certain classes at least, prostitution is on the wane, a situation that may well be associated with the development of contraceptives on the one hand and a correspondent change of sex mores on the other. The economic ground has reference solely to the supply side, and if it is true that, with respect to the causation of this social phenomenon, the demand evokes the supply more than the supply evokes the demand, all such explanations fail to get to grips with the problem.

Nor is our knowledge of causation advanced by those writers who find the main cause of prostitution in the " lack of ethical training," in " bad home conditions," " the failure of parental responsibility," " vicious neighborhoods," and so forth. In effect all they are saying is that prostitution is a deplorable condition and would not exist except for deplorable conditions. A moral judgment, no matter how much we may agree with it, cannot be a substitute for the proper study of causes. Scarcely less defective

is the conclusion of those who find a main cause of prostitution either in "mental deficiency" or in "abnormal
sex impulse." They too cannot have faced the prior question concerning the nature of the causation they attempt
to ascribe. While they must know that the amount of
prostitution varies greatly under different social conditions
they make no attempt to show that there is a corresponding
variation in the amount of "mental deficiency" or of
"abnormal sex impulse." Since prostitution is a phenomenon found in the most widely different types of
society our search for causes can make little headway unless it introduces the comparative method. Once again we
must remember that *the search for causes is the search for
differences within comparable situations.* To find the difference
— the more or less, and the variant traits of the more and
the less — and to establish the comparability of the situations is often no small task, but it is the preliminary requirement that we must meet if our causal investigations are not
to begin, and end, in obscuration and confusion.

IV

THE WHY OF RESPONSIVE ATTITUDES

We turn to another type of investigation that is often
infected with a kind of initial ambiguity not associated
with statistical facts as such. The statistical fact is a datum.
It is not in itself a matter of degree, still less a matter of
opinion. The preliminary difficulties it presents to the
enquirer into causes are mainly those of delimitation, of
interpretation, of reference to the dynamic reality. But
there are other subjects within the range of the social
sciences that are not clearly denoted or identified by the
terms we use for this purpose. For example, many studies
have been made of "assimilation," but they have used that
term in various and confusing ways, and sometimes with-

out any specific indication of the nature of the process so named. The difficulty is particularly great when we seek to study processes involving changes of social attitudes and social relationships. We cannot dismiss this type of investigation from our reckoning. Probably it excites more intense interest than any other kind. Probably the discovery of the causation of phenomena falling into this category would have more far-reaching influences on everyday life than any other advance of knowledge. The lack of objective identification does not exclude the category from the range of scientific enquiry, though it makes investigation more difficult and far more precarious. We may legitimately ask concerning the conditions of social well-being, of solidarity, of social harmony, of cultural advance, of the vitality or decadence of national life, of contentment and unrest, of affection and animosity, of any or all of the complicated interdependent emotional states or attitudes manifested within or between social groups. But in pursuing such questions the primary problem of making our why specific is heavily embarrassed by the elusively subjective quality of the field of interest.

Since numerous studies are undertaken in this field without adequate recognition of this formidable difficulty it may be well to state its character in more precise terms and with reference to a particular example. The example we are choosing is one in which a peculiarly elusive subject is attacked, but the embarrassments that beset it are present to some degree in many other studies undertaken by social psychologists and sociologists. It is, moreover, a subject that has recently received no small amount of attention. We refer to the study of the conditions of " marital adjustment " or " happiness in marriage." [18] Let

---

[18] A selective list of recent studies devoted to the subject is as follows: G. V. Hamilton, *A Research in Marriage*, New York, 1929;

us consider what the peculiar problems are that beset the initial setting-up of any investigation along these lines.

In the first place, no matter what terms we use to identify or to describe the phenomenon, it remains somewhat ambiguous and indeterminate. The term " adjustment " has a specious neutrality, but there are many varieties and degrees of adjustment between personalities. Those who use the term have not infrequently to resort to more colorful but not more specific language, such as " compatibility," " accord," " marital happiness," " success in marriage," " marital satisfaction," and so forth. Observe how different it would be if the subject we are investigating were, say, the factors determining a particular size of family. Then we should have no difficulty in ascertaining whether in any instance the object of our enquiry was present or absent. We should not need to go around asking near neighbors or intimate friends their *opinion* as to whether the family consisted of three children. There would be no particular reason, even were the facts not obvious, why the parties most directly concerned should conceal the truth.

K. B. Davis, *Factors in the Sex Life of Twenty-two Hundred Women*, New York, 1929; R. L. Dickinson and L. Beam, *A Thousand Marriages*, Baltimore, 1931; G. Bernard, " An Instrument for the Measurement of Success in Marriage," *Publications*, American Sociological Society, 1933, Vol. 27, pp. 94–106, and " Factors in the Distribution of Success in Marriage," *American Journal of Sociology* (1934), Vol. 40, pp. 49–60; L. M. Terman and P. Buttenwieser, " Personality Factors in Marital Compatibility," *Journal of Social Psychology* (1935), Vol. 6, pp. 143–171, 267–289; L. M. Terman, " Methodology and Results of Recent Studies in Marital Adjustment," *American Sociological Review* (June, 1939), Vol. 4, pp. 309–324; H. R. Mowrer, *Personality Adjustment and Domestic Discord*, New York, 1935; E. W. Burgess and L. S. Cottrell, *Predicting Success or Failure in Marriage*, New York, 1939; E. L. Kelly, " Concerning the Validity of Terman's Weights for Predicting Marital Happiness," *Psychological Bulletin* (March, 1939), Vol. 36, pp. 202–203; C. Kirkpatrick, " A Methodological Analysis of Feminism in Relation to Marital Adjustment," *American Sociological Review* (June, 1939), Vol. 4, pp. 325–334.

There would be no reason why they should enter into collusion on the matter or why one member of a pair should hesitate to give a frank answer lest the other member learn of it and be aggrieved. They would have no difficulty in deciding what it was the investigator wanted to know. Nor would the investigator need to interpret the responses given to him.

In all these respects the situation is reversed when the question is one of " adjustment " or " happiness." Professor Clifford Kirkpatrick relates an instance in which " one highly intelligent co-operator trained in psychiatric work sent blanks to a couple who had been given a rating of ' well-adjusted.' " " Shortly afterwards, the husband informed the investigator of a contemplated divorce." [19]

In the second place, the postulated situation is one involving a harmony of responsive or reciprocal attitudes. We are not asking whether A is "well-adjusted" and B " well-adjusted " but whether A and B are "well-adjusted" to one another. But their adjustment to one another may obviously be dependent on conditions not peculiar to the marital relationship. They may depend on the temperament or the individual history of either party, on a whole series of life chances that affect them independently, so that the failure of adjustment may not spring from factors directly relevant to the marital union. Conversely, individuals can be " well-adjusted " or " maladjusted "

---

[19] " A Methodological Analysis of Feminism in Relation to Marital Adjustment," loc. cit. p. 333. Burgess and Cottrell express rather complete confidence in the results they obtained from the rating of marital adjustment in terms of the responses given by the marriage partners severally and by an outsider. They used a five-point scale, " very happy," " happy," " average," " unhappy," " very unhappy." They claim that, when certain methods are employed, " happiness ratings appear to be reliable and stable on a five-point scale " (op. cit. p. 43). " The general conclusion is that the score is reasonably dependable though necessarily crude " (ibid. p. 74).

under the most diverse conditions and so a married pair may preserve an appearance of inter-adjustment because of stabilizing forces, such as religion, success otherwise attained, and so forth, that operate on each of the parties and cloak a defect of functional harmony in the union itself. On this account it would be a less hazardous enterprise to enquire into the causes that disturb or disrupt inter-adjustment than into those that maintain it. Or, if we are using the most elusive word " happiness," we might with somewhat more confidence confine our causal enquiries to the causes and conditions of " unhappiness " than to those of its dubiously presumptive antithesis. Certainly no physician would venture to investigate the " causes " of health, after the manner in which our psychologists and sociologists investigate the causes of marital happiness. He would study the causes of particular forms of ill-health, because ill-health can be divided into specific categories, whereas it is less easy, if indeed at all meaningful, to speak of categories of healthiness.

But even if we limit ourselves to "maladjustment" (or to definable " unhappiness "), the conjuncture of conditions is so endlessly complex and variant as to make the quest very problematic. The assumption that by segregating and weighting individual " factors " we can arrive at " causes " may itself be quite misleading, since each factor may depend for its efficacy on a total situation and it is the combination of them, the subtle, particularized coincidence of moods and situations, on which the outcome of disrupted adjustment hangs. If therefore the investigator assumes that specific factors are correlated meaningfully with the instances of maladjustment or adjustment he may be led, by what seems to be a valid statistical process, to unwarranted conclusions. Even the discovery of high positive or negative correlations between certain specific evidences and his cases of maladjustment may have little significance. These evidences may themselves be merely symptoms or sequelae of the break-down of the marital relationship. Or, again, they may be significant for a group or class characterized by one set of mores and be without significance for a group or class with a typically different social background.

A review of the conclusions arrived at by a variety of investigators appears to support our argument. Thus, while some, like Harriet R. Mowrer, place much weight on the pre-established personality traits of the marriage partners; and others, like Katherine B. Davis, on conditions of physical health; and others, like E. L. Kelly, on the radiation of the happy type of individual temperament into the happy marital relationship; there are some, notably Dickinson and Beam, who deny that health, character, and extrinsic conditions have any important bearing on marital adjustment and find instead that the dominating factor is that which pertains to the marital relationship as such, the " total satisfaction " attained through the sexual act. But if we accept this position, there still remains, as these authors recognize, the question whether the degree of sexual satisfaction is not itself a reflection of the congeniality of the whole marital situation. The difference, according to the authors, between the maladjusted and the adjusted, is " merely a state of mind which means entire acceptance of marriage or of life." [20] This " state of mind " is revealed and focussed in the sexual relation, but the authors give ample evidence that the lack of sexual satisfaction is due to a " psychic handicap." [21]

We do not raise these difficulties obstructively, with any desire to slight the valiant pioneering work of a number of

---

[20] Op. cit. p. 233.
[21] See, for example, op. cit. Chap. IX, on " Dyspareunia."

skilled investigators in this difficult terrain. Researches like those of Dickinson, Hamilton, Kelly, Davis, Terman, and Burgess and Cottrell have certainly thrown much light on the nature of the problem. But we believe that, for the understanding of the causation of marital adjustment, the difficulties encountered along the various approaches to the problem have been underestimated and the prospects of conclusive results have been over-rated. Much interesting information has been gathered by the researchers, but exceedingly little definite knowledge concerning causes. If this is so, it should lead us to a far more careful analysis of the nature of our task. In so doing we should evince a greater interest in the subject than in the methodology; we should be more concerned to get at the truth than to get results. We should not feel that we have made as yet any contribution whatever to the discovery of causes when we have found correlations for specific " factors " in our inevitably limited and selective list of cases. We should not rest on exact symbolic statements or measurements without seeking to find out what, if anything, they mean. We should avoid the appearance of achievement that is apt to accompany such conclusions as that the factor F is found in 64 per cent of the instances of well-adjusted marriage or that the correlation between F and the number of instances is plus .58 with a sigma difference of .062.

It does not lie within the scope of this work to give a detailed analysis of any one causal investigation. At the present stage particularly our attention is devoted to those preconditions of specific formulation that must be met if causal enquiry is to be effectively pursued. We will therefore confine ourselves here to a few suggestions, based on the preceding discussion, regarding the manner in which, when dealing with a subject such as " happiness in marriage," the question of why can be so stated as to avoid ambiguities and prepare the way for a direct attack on a clearly defined problem of causation. We may observe in passing that some of the studies we have cited are not directly or fully addressed to this issue. Thus the work of Dickinson and Beam is put forward as " a treatise on *diagnosis*, a medical study of symptoms of disorder." [22] Again, the methodical investigations of Burgess and Cottrell are pointed to the discovery of an instrument of prediction. While they have elaborated a technique for measuring " adjustment in marriage " their professed objective has been to derive therefrom a " prediction scale," a preoccupation probably inspired by a broader interest in prediction as a function of the social sciences. But strictly considered, the interest in prediction is not identical with the interest in causation, since often prediction may properly, and indeed adequately, be based on symptoms or signs that themselves leave us in ignorance of the causes of the phenomena they proclaim.

While the suggestions that follow are immediately relevant to the example we have chosen they are meant to indicate the general lines along which any investigation of this type, and especially those that deal with the congruity or conflict of attitudes, can be limited or defined so as to conform to our primary criterion.

Obvious as is the ambiguity of terms like " adjusted," " well-adjusted," " happy in marriage," " satisfied," and so forth, some investigators are content to carry on as though the difficulty were either irremediable or negligible. Some think that by examining the responses to a series of questions or by noting various circumstantial evidences they can infer the degree of " happiness " or " adjustment " of the subjects. Others take refuge in the *cul-de-sac* of

---

[22] Op. cit. Introduction, p. xx. Italics in original.

" operationalism." In other words they take certain items, traits, data of some kind or another that can be counted or possibly weighted, that lend themselves to something that may be called measurement. Thus Clifford Kirkpatrick tells us that, faced with the lack of precision in such concepts as " marital adjustment," he adopted an operational definition. " Any investigator undertaking to measure or classify marital adjustment is confronted with difficulties and dilemmas. The way out was to define 'marital maladjustment' as that quality in a marriage which causes one close friend to classify the couple as maladjusted. Marital adjustment was crudely defined in a similar way." [23] But surely if we do not discover what leads close friends (who as a class are themselves as variant as other human beings and may not be resting their opinions on any one " quality in a marriage ") to characterize couples as maladjusted or adjusted, we are not very likely to discover the causes of the " quality " they so designate, still less of the quality that we ourselves as investigators must have in mind if we are to investigate it at all.[24]

---

[23] C. Kirkpatrick, " A Methodological Analysis of Feminism in Relation to Marital Adjustment," *American Sociological Review* (June, 1939), Vol. 4, pp. 331–332.

[24] A note on " operationalism " may be in place here. Professor Kirkpatrick is by no means an extreme " operationalist," since he is as genuinely interested in the subject he is investigating as in the methods by which he investigates it. The complete operationalist, according to Professor George Lundberg ("The Thoughtways of Contemporary Sociology," *American Sociological Review* (1936), Vol. 1, pp. 708 ff.), defines his subject by his measurements or "operations". We are informed that this is the way physical science proceeds, but even here Professor Lundberg reduces a useful principle to an absurdity. " Space *is* that which is measured with a ruler; time *is* that which is measured by a clock; force *is* that which makes pointers move across dials " (p. 711). This of course is a specious half-truth. Space is that which is measured by a ruler — not with a metronome, the ruler being chosen because it is already a *spatial* unit. Time is that which is measured — not by any clock, but by the kind of clock that measures time. Force is that which makes pointers move across dials — when the movement of the pointers is so controlled as to be determined by force. In the

On one point we agree with the operationalists. We believe that when a subject is as ill-defined and elusive as that of " marital adjustment " we should not forthwith proceed to study its causes. " Adjustment " means such different things to different people. The investigator must

---

same spirit Professor Lundberg applauds the definition of intelligence as that which the intelligence tests test. Is it unreasonable, then, to ask, " Very well, but what is that? " Presumably the testers have some notion of what they are testing when they construct their tests. Presumably some tests are better than others for the purpose they have in mind, though all tests are equally good for testing " that which they test." Of course, if the testers were to come out and say, " We are not measuring intelligence, but only that which we measure," nobody would object and nobody would care. Every different test would measure a different *that which*, and there would be as many objects of research as there were variant researchers, and the more they differed the less they could possibly disagree, and everything would become perfectly " objective " and perfectly meaningless.

A like criticism is relevant to the work of the keen critical mind who is largely responsible for the adoption by some social scientists of the principle of operationalism, namely, Percy W. Bridgman, author of *The Logic of Modern Physics*, New York, 1927, and of *The Intelligent Individual and Society*, New York, 1938. As he applies the principle in the latter book, it becomes more and more clear that every meaning becomes personal, and peculiar to every operator, leading to a kind of anarchistic relativity that in the end must confound the very medium of communication he still employs, like the most of us, to convey his own meaning.

Operationalism can, however, be understood in a less absolute and more defensible sense. When the phenomenon we are investigating is not susceptible of exact delimitation by means of any available indices universally present where or in the degree in which the phenomenon is present, we may resort to the best approximations to such indices that we can devise so as to make its investigation feasible. We do not abandon the quest because we cannot wholly control it. We do not even simplify it — what we simplify is the methods by which we follow it. We admit that these methods are crude or insufficient, but we use them because we have as yet no better ones. We seek to refine them as our experience grows, and we constantly refer back to the original problem to correct or qualify such conclusions as we attain by methods that are confessedly inadequate to embrace the full range or import of the phenomenon to which they are applied. In so doing we proceed on the common-sense assumption expressly and dogmatically rejected in the metaphysics of Professor Lundberg, that a phenomenon can be recognized and approximately identified before we set about to investigate its nature or in any sense to " measure " it.

define it so that there can be no question as to what *he* means. He cannot get round his difficulties by assuming that there is one quality of marital relationships called " adjustment," with an absence of that quality called " maladjustment." He cannot assume that one set of " factors " denotes its presence and the absence of these same factors its absence. He cannot therefore convincingly construct a continuous linear scale ranging from the zero of maladjustment to the 100 per cent of perfect adjustment. Nor can he assume that there is one norm of adjustment, with deviations from it in different directions. Anyone possessed of considerable social experience will reject a methodology based on such assumptions. What way, then, remains open?

We suggest that two ways remain. One is to take only sufficiently overt and comparable signs of maladjustment, such as constant bickering, admitted continuous aloofness of either spouse from the other, resort of either spouse to a physician, legal or other professional adviser on the ground of dissatisfaction with the marital relationships; to define the kind or degree of maladjustment under consideration by the presence of these signs; to uncover by numerous case-studies the variety of conditions under which these signs emerge, and thus to make the problem of causation reasonably specific and subject to possible attack along various lines, such as are discussed elsewhere in this work. Investigations so conducted would doubtless have more likelihood of success if the cases selected were representative of some one social category, defined by social status, income level, education, national origin, or other attribute.

The second way is a longer and perhaps more difficult road, but one that has rich and scarcely at all explored possibilities. It also involves a wide use of case-studies. Here the preliminary objective would be to discover and analyze types of maladjustment. There are, to begin with, certain fairly obvious types of maladjustment, or of situations in which maladjustment occurs, such as the marital relationship where one spouse is habitually dominating or exacting while the other is not inclined to submissiveness, or the various conflict relationships in which the presence or influence of a third party is congenial to one of the spouses and uncongenial to the other. There are, again, various types of maladjustment directly associated with or responsive to the nature of the sexual union, as the medical and psychiatric evidences abundantly reveal. No doubt also typical patterns of maladjustment can be found belonging to different periods of marriage duration — some may be characteristic of the first few months of marriage and others of marriages that have lasted fifteen or twenty or thirty years — and so with various other features of the marital situation, such as income level, the degree of economic independence of the wife, and so forth. Once more there are certain external phenomena, such as physical or occupational mobility, so frequently associated with the definite break-down of marital relations that the nature of the association would well repay intensive study. The clarification of typical situations along these and other lines would prepare the way for specific questions of causation that we can scarcely raise until such preliminary work is accomplished. Some of the most expert case workers are impressed by the need for the development of this method of study.[25] It would certainly provide a useful check on the assumptions that underlie the methods generally followed by sociologists at present when they list a series of particular traits or items and seek to associate them causally with the complex phenomenon they are investigating.

---

[25] See, for example, Ada E. Sheffield, *Social Insight in Case Situations*, New York, 1937.

CHAPTER SIX

CAUSE AS PRECIPITANT

I

EQUILIBRIUM AND PRECIPITANT

IN CARRYING through the initial clarification of the causal quest, to which the previous chapter was devoted, we have to take into account not only the particular character of the subject-matter but also the particular purpose of the investigation. The purpose sets appropriate limits to the range of causes with which we need to be concerned. Suppose, for example, that we are setting out to investigate an unemployment situation. Our object may well be to discover some way of controlling it, to reach some conclusions as to measures that would at least diminish the volume of unemployment. Again, we may be seeking for certain controllable factors, political or economic, so as to suggest means of preventing the recurrence of similar situations in the immediate future. Given such an objective, we shall concentrate attention on those conditions associated with the unemployment situation that seem in degree amenable to experimental control, such as speculative production, seasonal variations in production, the balance of saving and spending, the interest rate, and so forth. Of course all such investigations involve some hypothesis regarding the relation of the controllable factors to the total situation, but they may confine themselves to an examination of the implications of the hypothesis and to proposals for carrying out a practical test of it. In effect they envisage a new factor that at some stage can be introduced into the situation and offer evidence for the assumption that such and such a factor — a law, a monetary device, a type of economic reorganization, or what not — would modify the total situation in the desired direction. Or, again, we may be investigating means, not for the direct control of the phenomenon itself, but for the control of its consequences. We may be studying means by which the impact of unemployment upon those subjected to it may be most effectively lessened, as through unemployment insurance. This too is a causal investigation, and like the previous ones it proposes to introduce a new control factor into the unemployment situation.

A practical investigation into causes thus limits itself to, or at least concentrates attention on, the question of controls. A theoretical investigation is concerned with the more inclusive problem of causation. While the one seeks to manipulate, to utilize, to direct, or to prevent the phenomenon, the other seeks to understand it. Obviously the two types of investigation are not opposed but interlinked. The inclusive theoretical enquiry often leads us to practical means of control. The practical enquiry aids us in some measure in the larger quest for causes. Yet not infrequently we may discover agencies of manipulation and control where our understanding of a phenomenon is very incomplete. We may discover, by experiment or accident, how to cure a disease, even though its etiology remains quite obscure. We can learn to utilize a power, like electricity, though its nature remains mysterious. In everyday life we are forever endeavoring to control what we do not understand. The urgency of need will not wait for the difficult and often baffling quest for causes. We are faced with alternatives and must decide. Every law that is passed is such a decision. It is the new factor introduced into the situation for the purpose of control. Its effects are often different from those intended by its authors, simply because when we introduce a new control we do not merely add a new factor, we change the relation to one another of all the pre-existing conditions affected by it. Social control without social understanding is on that account most precarious. We discipline children, only to find that their unanticipated reaction defeats our aims. We pass a law to prevent the consumption of alcoholic liquors, only to find that the custom of convivial drinking digs new and deeper roots in the social soil. We pass a law drastically increasing the penalties for minor crimes and find, to our surprise, that the amount of major crime is thereby increased. When it comes to customs and valuations, human society — or human nature — is not a mechanism that can be confidently controlled by the operation of certain external levers.

Wherever, in the more practical or in the more theoretical type of investigation, we distinguish some factor that is introduced from the outside, or else emerges from within, so that it evokes a series of repercussions or reactions significantly changing the total situation, we may call such a factor a *precipitant*. The search for precipitants in this sense is one of the favorite forms of the limited causal quest. We have above suggested the role it plays in investigations directed primarily to control, but it is no less prominent in many forms of investigation devoted primarily to the business of understanding. We will begin with a few of the more common applications of this concept.

Often we envisage a situation as dependent on the balance of two opposing forces or on the equilibrium of a number of forces. The balance or equilibrium is unstable, temporary, precarious. One of the simplest of cases would be where public opinion is nearly equally divided in favor of and against a particular policy. Some event, some accident, some act of leadership, may decisively turn the scales. In a larger sense we may think of one set of forces making for the perpetuation of an established order and another making for change or revolution. The forces of change are held in leash by the resisting forces. Again, some event, a war, an invention, the rise of a new prophet, a local outbreak of the suppressed forces, may be conceived as destroying the pre-existing equilibrium. Some writers actually go so far as to interpret all change along similar lines. Thus the German legal philosopher Binding maintains that " the causation of a change is identical with a change in the balance between the restraining and the promoting conditions," and adds that " man is the cause of an effect in so far as he causes any superiority of the promoting over the deterring conditions." [1] But what right have we to assume that equally matched opposites meet in every situation until some precipitant overthrows their balanced neutrality? Why should change advance by a series of jumps and halts as disturbances successively interrupting states of equilibrium? The conception arbitrarily denies the reality of genuine causal *process*. It is more pertinent to enquire under what conditions and with what limitations the principle of precipitant and preceding equilibrium is justified.

The nature of this problem is best seen in the field of economic analysis, which from the time of Adam Smith has been generally dominated by the concept of a static or a moving equilibrium. The adherents of " equilibrium economics " tell us how things " normally " behave, how prices " normally " correspond to costs, how wages and

---

[1] Karl Binding, *Normen und ihre Übertretung* (Leipzig, 1914), Vol. II, pp. 472–510.

profits are " normally " determined, how the balance of international payments is " normally " adjusted, how interest rates are " normally " related to the volume of savings, and so forth. They provide us with equations and functions showing the " normal " interdependence of economic factors. They admit that in practice things do not happen quite that way, that the market does not always behave as a market should, that a purely competitive equilibrium is actually a rare phenomenon. They admit, with Adam Smith, that the market price may not be the " natural " price, or, with Ricardo and John Stuart Mill, that the temporary value is not the " permanent " value, or, with Karl Marx, that the " absolute general law of capitalist accumulation " is modified in its working by many circumstances.[2] They admit that there are " disturbing causes," " discrepancies," " interferences," " random factors." But they add that, in spite of all obstacles, prices are always tending towards " this center of repose and continuance," as Adam Smith put it. Or they tell us that they are concerned with the " long run," not with the " short run " effects, that they are dealing with the " ultimate causes of large economic phenomena."[3] They tell us, with Alfred Marshall, that their conclusions are " subject to the condition that *other things are equal*, and that the causes are able to work out their effects undisturbed." The same author points out that this limitation holds generally for scientific laws. " Almost every scientific doctrine, where carefully and formally stated, will be found to contain some proviso to the effect that other things are equal: the action of the causes in question is

---

[2] The references are to Adam Smith, *Wealth of Nations*, Book 1, Chap. VII; D. Ricardo, *Treatise on Political Economy*, Chap. I; John Stuart Mill, *Principles of Political Economy*, Book III, Chap. I; Karl Marx, *Capital*, Vol. 1, Part 7 (Modern Library edition), p. 707.

[3] F. W. Taussig, *Principles of Economics* (Third Edition, New York, 1922), Vol. 2, Chap. 52, pp. 222–223.

supposed to be isolated; certain effects are attributed to them, but only *on the hypothesis* that no cause is permitted to enter except those distinctly allowed for." [4]

The conception underlying these statements is that there is a relatively independent economic system, operating through forces intrinsically belonging to it. These forces make for a continuous adjustment or equilibrium of the various parts of the system in relation to one another, but this equilibrium is constantly being affected by extraneous impacts, so that the inherent economic causes are not " able to work out their effects undisturbed." Now there is no dispute on the point that every change in any economic factor involves a readjustment of all the other factors. If the price of one commodity rises the prices of other commodities are affected in various ways. But we cannot tell how these other prices will respond, we cannot tell even whether they will rise or fall, if we depend on any process of economic analysis that does not get to grips with the actual situation in which the change occurs. And when we do face the situation we nearly always discover a complex pricing pattern that looks mightily different from that which would correspond to the operation of the postulated economic causes. [5] That the causes thus postulated do operate we are not questioning. What we question is the validity of a method that attends to these alone, that assumes that all other determinants merely modify in a temporary manner and to a limited degree the normal course of events, and that accepts the faith in the long-run triumph of the particular causes they invoke.

The economists of the Marshall school do not think in terms of equilibrium and precipitant, but only of equilib-

---

[4] Alfred Marshall, *Principles of Economics* (Eighth Edition, New York, 1925), Book I, Chap. III, pp. 36–37. Italics as in original.

[5] See, for example, the price studies contained in Walton Hamilton and others, *Price and Price Policies*, New York, 1938.

rium and disturbance. For them the equilibrium is fundamental, has its maintaining forces within it, and recovers
from the constant impacts that it undergoes. The latter
are merely interferences, causing deviations and oscillations,
never the essential phenomena of the economic life. The
proponents of this doctrine do not consider seriously " the
possibility that our economic mechanism is so kinetic that
the rate at which new disturbances occur is habitually
greater than the rate of adjustment to such disturbances." [6]
Still less do they admit the implication of the fact that this
economic mechanism is in important if always changing
respects a *politico-economic* mechanism. They attach little
significance to the complicated structure of usages and
dominations that ramify in every economic area and make
the pricing system of nearly every industry so different
from any that could be deduced from consideration of the
few simple economic motives that are the only causes they
" distinctly allow for." Nor can they on these assumptions
account for the cumulative character and the historical
direction of economic change.

It is not surprising, therefore, that this type of economic
analysis often conveys the impression of remoteness from
economic actualities. The disturbances appear to be more
than disturbances, they appear to be precipitating something new and different. The resort to the proviso, " other
things being equal," seems rather formal and inadequate.
Some new disturbing factor often seems to " escape from
the compound of *ceteris paribus*." [7] The position is effectively stated by Wesley Mitchell. " One who turns from
reading economic theory to reading business history is
forcibly impressed by the artificiality of all assumptions of
a ' static ' or even a ' normal ' condition in economic

---

[6] Barbara Wootton, *Lament for Economics* (New York, 1938), p. 75.
[7] Ibid. p. 73.

affairs. For, despite all efforts to give technical meaning to these ambiguous terms, they suggest the idea of an unchanging order, or of an order which economic principles are always tending to re-establish after every aberration. But a review of business annals never discloses a ' static ' or ' normal ' state in either of these senses. On the contrary, in the real world of business, affairs are always undergoing a cumulative change, always passing through some phase of a business cycle into some other phase . . . In fact, if not in theory, a state of change in business conditions is the only ' normal ' state." [8]

There need be no objection to the endeavor of economists to show what would happen in particular situations " on the hypothesis that no cause is permitted to enter except those distinctly allowed for." There need be no objection to the postulate that, *as a first approach* to the understanding of economic causation, we regard human beings as actuated by rational self-interest, defined in purely economic terms, so that they delicately weigh comparative utilities and comparative costs, so that they judiciously discount present satisfactions for future satisfactions, so that they always buy in the cheapest and sell in the dearest market, and so forth. The study of causation is so intricate that any first simplification may be permissible, as a step on the road to a fuller understanding. The objection is to the conclusion that this first step brings us anywhere near our goal. There may be some areas of economic activity with respect to which an explanation in such terms needs only a moderate amount of correction; there are many others with respect to which it is, by itself, most misleading. For the " other things " that are told to stay equal may not be merely " other " things, they may belong to the very essentials of the situa-

---

[8] Wesley C. Mitchell, *Business Cycles* (New York, 1913), p. 86.

tion, while the " free competition " on the assumption of
which the analysis mainly depends may be conspicuous
only by its absence, or may be so limited and distorted that
the assumption becomes worse than useless.

With the many problems involved in this type of causal
analysis we cannot deal within our limits. What we are
chiefly concerned to point out is that, as a device for inter-
preting social and economic changes, the concept of equilibrium and disturbance is less serviceable than the concept
of equilibrium and precipitant. The former never introduces us to any vital source of change, it always minimizes
change in favor of the *status quo*. But since, as we have seen,
it is precisely the difference, the contrast, between social
phenomena or social situations that we must seize upon if
we are to make any effective advance in our causal enquiries, we cannot expect much enlightenment in that
regard from a viewpoint that looks on change itself as the
incidental and temporary interruption of a persistent order.
It is quite otherwise when the change-provoking factors are
thought of as precipitants. For now we need postulate no
self-maintaining order, we are committed to no doctrine
of permanence, to no distinction between primary and
secondary causes. All that is implied is a condition of
things that endures, for no matter how short a time, until
some intrusive or explosive factor converts it into another
condition of things. It may be that we are dealing with a
relatively closed system, or a system that slowly changes,
or with a mere moment of seeming inertia. Then something decisive occurs. A class order that has been dominant
for centuries is overturned. A mode of production that has
been long established is in a relatively brief period transformed into another. A political party that commanded a
majority allegiance is suddenly overthrown. A leader, a
general, a popular hero, falls from his eminence to oblivion

or disrepute. In all such situations we usually conceive
that some one factor has intervened, has emerged within or
thrust itself into the total situation, in such a way as to
bring about a state of disequilibrium, a change of direction,
or a realignment of forces.

Innumerable changes occur that seem to conform to this
pattern. But an immediate caution is necessary, for a
danger besets this mode, as indeed all other modes, of
isolating a factor as distinctively causal. It is the danger
of attaching an undue weight or role to the designated
factor. We omit for the present any consideration of the
evidence required to assure us that a particular event, or
some narrow conjuncture of events within a total changing
situation, effectively disturbs or disrupts a pre-existing
equilibrium. We will assume that the designated factor
does function as precipitant. A single thrust may set a
landslide moving. A spark may set a whole forest afire,
with all its entailments. The mistake of a general may lose
a war and thus have far-reaching repercussions on a whole
civilization. One invention may revolutionize an industry. "A grain of sand in a man's flesh, and empires
rise and fall." These things are in the record. But there
are empires that do not fall because an emperor dies and
there are wars that are not lost because a general makes
a mistake and the thrust sends the landslide moving only
because the conditions are all prepared for it. The situation may be ripe for change, and for change only in the
particular direction congenial to the complex of forces controlling it. The landslide would have happened sooner or
later apart from the particular thrust, or from any thrust
at all. The appeal or the manifesto that seemed to change
the fortunes of political parties may merely accentuate or
bring to light the till then inarticulate but deeper-working
trends of public opinion. The storm may shake from the

trees only the ripe fruit or the dead leaves. A student of social revolution remarks that " personal conflict between revolutionaries has often precipitated the decline of their movement, pre-determined by more deep-seated causes." [9] If the foundations of the revolution had not been undermined the personal conflict between revolutionaries would not have given impetus towards its disintegration.

On the other hand there are events, intrusive forces, interventions, discoveries, even accidents, that in the light of our best knowledge still appear decisive, changing the direction of the whole stream of human affairs. If, to take a much quoted example, the Persians had defeated the Greeks at Marathon, the history of civilization would doubtless have been a quite different story. And there are frequent instances in which a single event has a train of consequences so dependent upon it that we cannot assume they would have been brought about apart from this event. The act of an assassin at Sarajevo precipitated a world war. Who can say with assurance that this kind of war would have occurred, sooner or later, had there not been this event? And even if the absence of the particular precipitant should only have delayed such a war, who can affirm that it would not have followed an entirely different course, had it broken out at some different time?

It is apparent, then, that the role of the precipitant may vary enormously in significance, and that in each instance we can assess its causal importance only if we understand the whole dynamic system into which it enters. The causal efficacy we impute to any factor must always be contingent not only on the other factors but also on the dynamic interdependence of them all within the total situation. It is only as a temporary heuristic expedient that we can select

---

[9] Boris Souvarine. *Stalin* (New York, 1939), p. 284.

any item as " cause " and speak of the rest as " conditions." The need for this caution will appear more fully as we proceed with the discussion of various selective factors as causes.

II

ROLE OF THE PRECIPITANT

In everyday speech we constantly attribute definitive causality to some act or event, to some person or thing. We say that this general defeated the enemy, that this statesman won an election, that this business leader built up a new industry. We say that this proclamation ended slavery, that this new constitution united the country, that this manifesto created a new party, that this book revolutionized men's thoughts on this subject. We say that the automobile causes so many deaths per annum, that the radio reduces cultural differences between regions, and so forth. The factors thus singled out fall into various categories. Among these we want to distinguish more precisely the type we have called the precipitant, leaving the others for later consideration.

We have seen that it is the perception of difference that prompts our causal enquiries. We do not usually raise the question why so long as things pursue what we regard as their normal or typical course. It is the exception, the deviation, the interference, the abnormality, that stimulates our curiosity and seems to call for explanation. And we often attribute to some one " cause " all the happenings that characterize the new or unanticipated or altered situation. Somewhat more strictly, we mean by " precipitant " any specific factor or condition regarded as diverting the pre-established direction of affairs, as disrupting a pre-existing equilibrium, or as releasing hitherto suppressed or latent tendencies or forces. The presumption is that a system is operating in a manner congenial to its self-perpetuation, until something intervenes; that a system is relatively closed, until something breaks it open. The " something " is then a precipitant.

This conception is one of the ways in which we seek to understand the problem of continuity and change. We postulate a social law roughly corresponding to the physical law of inertia, to the effect that every social system tends to maintain itself, to persevere in its present state, until compelled by some force to alter that state. Every social system is at every moment and in every part sustained by codes and institutions, by traditions, by interests. If a social order or any social situation within it, suffers significant change we think of some insurgent or invading force, breaking as it were this " inertia," the *status quo*. The simplest form of the concept is that which we considered in the previous section, where change is thought of as the disturbance of a persistent equilibrium. The defect of that concept was not its postulate of an equilibrium, but its unwarranted assumption that a single type of equilibrium, determined by relatively simple forces, was fundamental and permanent so that any change affecting it was incidental, alien, or extraneous. It is more in keeping with the historical record to think in terms of a constant tendency towards equilibrium, beset always, even in simple or primitive society and still more obviously in the higher civilizations, by forces threatening to unbalance or disrupt it. So the nature of the equilibrium is itself forever changing. The competitive system as conceived by Smith and Ricardo was an imperfect equilibrium on one level, preceded and succeeded by other imperfect equilibria. But because they represented it as adequate and perfect in its kind they could not conceive of its being substantially modified or transformed. They were construing what Max Weber has called an ideal type as though it were the social reality.

The concept of the ideal type in fact serves our purpose better. It claims no permanence and therefore admits the role of the precipitant. In his doctrine of the ideal type Weber gave theoretical formulation to a principle that is implicit in nearly every attempt to depict an historical situation or a social system. We conceive it as an understandable *order* of things. But in its full actuality every historical stage is embarrassingly complex and in numerous details refuses to fit into any neat conceptual frame. Our comprehension of it is inevitably partial, inadequate, and selective. One mode of comprehension is in terms of the typical ways of behaving, the generally accepted norms of action, which are at the same time attributable to the acting individuals and reflected in the institutional structure of the system. Individuals may frequently violate these norms but they tend to act in accordance with them, and it is this tendency that gives the system its typical form and quality. From this tendency we derive the " laws " of the particular order or historical stage. Such laws, says Weber, " are typical *chances*, confirmed through observation, of a course of social action that is to be expected given certain conditions and that is *understandable* in terms of typical motives and typical meaningful intentions of the acting individuals." [10] He cites as an instance Gresham's Law, that " bad money drives out good money " or more strictly that " the overvalued currency goes out of circulation." The " law " rests on the assumption that, given two monetary units of different value in the same market, men act with economic rationality, and the assumption is confirmed by experience, since the " good money " does

---

[10] *Wirtschaft und Gesellschaft* (Second Edition, Tübingen, 1921), Chap. I, § 1.

actually disappear from the market. Sometimes, of course, men do not act as economically rational beings. In so far as this happens the ideal type is not in correspondence with reality, but it is still serviceable. " The use of these ideal types enables us to understand the *real* economic behavior though it is also, in part at least, determined by traditional restraints, emotional impulses, misapprehensions and intrusions of non-economic purposes and considerations. The ideal types enable us to understand economic behavior, first *in so far as*, in a specific instance or on the average, it is actually determined by economic rationality, and second, as facilitating, by reason of the divergence of the real course of action from that corresponding to the ideal type, the disclosure of the *actual* economically non-rational motives."[11]

With the complexities and ambiguities of Weber's doctrine of the ideal type we need not here concern ourselves. [12] For our purposes we shall use that expression in a relatively simple sense. We are always seeking to grasp each social situation, each historical moment, each period or even epoch, as something coherent, as somehow a unity of elements. We think of, say, mid-fourteenth-century Florence or early eighteenth century Boston or the pre-Civil-War South or even the Middle Ages, as a distinctive social entity, with characteristic thought-forms, modes of living, norms of behavior. Every historian, biographer, and novelist endeavors to depict historical situations in such wise that they take on this distinctive character. Often the picture is ridiculously oversimplified and thus falsified, but as we learn more or learn better we continue to view the situation as having some coherence, no matter how many exceptions or contradictions we may find; as possessing

---

[11] Loc. cit.
[12] See A. von Schelting, *Max Webers Wissenschaftslehre* (Tübingen, 1934), pp. 329 ff., and T. Parsons, *The Structure of Social Action*, pp. 601 ff.

some essential quality of its own, no matter how subtle or difficult to render. In short, we are always pursuing the type, the comprehension of many particulars within a unity, though each type is finally a unique instance. Otherwise we cannot apprehend a social situation. We deal with its aspects and its details on the assumption that they belong to or within a whole. It is the same mode of apprehension we employ in knowing our fellow-men. Each, in so far as known, becomes for us a personality. Similarly each social situation is invested with the equivalent of personality. We understand its activities, its events, its manifestations of every kind, to the extent in which they are typical — or atypical — for it.

A social situation, so conceived, implies a system of sustaining forces. It is possible only on the postulate that certain forces are dominant and others incidental, weak, or absent. A feudal economy, for example, is not conceivable where there is much mechanization, much mobility of labor, much economic competition, or much levelling of class distinctions. A slave economy is scarcely conceivable where the division of labor is highly specialized. A caste system seems incompatible with the absence of both racial distinctions and religious orthodoxies. Each instance of any of these systems implies a more particular conjuncture of congenial forces. The importance of this viewpoint for the whole attack on the problem of social causation we shall consider at a later stage. Meantime we refer to it merely as providing some justification for the conception of cause as precipitant. The challenge of causation is aroused when a situation ceases to conform to our expectancy, when it no longer reveals, as before, its typical activities and its typical chances. Then we must presume that the hitherto dominant pattern of sustaining forces has suffered a serious change. And we look for some intruding force. We perceive that the " other things " are not " equal," and, taking more or less for granted the forces congenial to our " ideal type," we attribute the change to one or more " uncongenial " factors.

The validity of this attribution is dependent, unless our precipitant is clearly an external factor introduced into the situation, on the validity of the assumption that the total situation is a coherent, self-maintaining unity. The risk of the ideal type approach is that it may discount or ignore the tendencies to change already present in the situation. This risk is not absent from the treatment of the subject by Max Weber. He takes the position, for example, that the Protestant ethic was in a special way the solvent of the traditional restraints on business enterprise and monetary acquisition and thus a primary cause of the rise of capitalism in Western Europe and in America. But it might easily be claimed that the rise of the Protestant ethic itself, with its stern individualism, its " worldly asceticism," and its doctrine of stewardship, was the expression in the religious sphere of a pervasive change of social attitudes corresponding to and causally interdependent with a changing socioeconomic order. Unless this claim can be refuted — and I do not see how a claim of this sort admits of definite refutation — we cannot establish the fundamental role in the process of social change attributed by Weber to the Protestant sects.[13]

Moreover, while a particular complex of social attitudes may enter very significantly into the causal process, it is difficult ever to assign to a factor of this sort the salience and immediate causal decisiveness suggested by our term

---

[13] For the doctrine here referred to see Max Weber, *The Protestant Ethic and the Spirit of Capitalism* (London, 1930), translated by T. Parsons; also T. Parsons, op. cit. Chap. XIV; A. von Schelting, op. cit. pp. 281–309, and H. M. Robertson, *Aspects of the Rise of Economic Individualism*, Cambridge, England, 1933.

" precipitant." These qualities are more appropriately looked for in the *event*, the dated conjuncture of forces that perceptibly disturbs or disrupts a pre-existing order or coherence. A war, a revolution, a bold stroke of policy, a drastic new law, a quarrel between leaders, the assassination of a ruler, are obvious examples of precipitant in this sense. Any of these may, under certain conditions, decisively disrupt the going system, and yet, any of them may reasonably be regarded, at the hour of its occurrence, as not inevitably the outcome or expression of the conditions or forces inherent in the particular system it disrupts. There is an element of conjuncture, if not of sheer chance, in the mode and time of the occurrence. The most indubitable type is that in which the decisive factor comes wholly or essentially from outside the affected system. A war, for example, might precipitate important changes in the economic employment of women, in the credit structure of a country, or even in an artistic style. The settlement of missionaries or of traders among a primitive people may initiate profound changes in the life of that people. Again, wherever a system is relatively closed, that is, when it rigorously clings to pre-established lines and resists all innovations or new adaptations, it is likely that significant change will await the impact of some definite precipitant and be more drastic or shattering when it occurs. A caste system, for example, is usually broken open only by some powerful intrusive factor, such as revolt, invasion, a new gospel appealing to the masses, or the introduction of an externally developed industrial technique.

Another type of situation for the understanding of which the concept of the precipitant is serviceable is that in which any one of several potential developments seems to hang on the turn of events at a particular moment or even on some chance happening. Perhaps the best field for illustration is the personal life-history, since examples occur in the life of every man. If A had not gone to this party he would not have met Miss B, could not have married her, and his whole story would have been different. If C had not travelled on the same ship with D he could not have recommended D for this position, and the subsequent events, so profoundly important for D, would never have occurred. If this sensitive boy had not injured his eye in an accident he would not have become morose and brooding and probably would not have turned into a delinquent. The instances in which a particular act or event seems to determine the further history of the individual life are endless. A man loses his job, through no failure on his part. The loss of employment preys on his mind, intensifies a nervous condition, stimulates inter-family conflicts, and leads to a complete breakdown of health and morale. Many of the personal tragedies of everyday life seem to stem from some precipitating event.

There comes also into consideration a causal factor that is the antithesis of the precipitant. If some action or event thwarts or balks the operation of the intrusive factor we may speak of it as an anti-precipitant. If the boy with the injured eye had at the crucial moment found some wise counsellor he might not have followed the road to delinquency. Or if skilful treatment had been applied so as to heal or to conceal the injury the boy would not have developed his sense of inferiority. Again, we may take an illustration from the larger field of history. For this purpose Weber's instance of the battle of Marathon will serve. Had the Persians won that battle they would in all likelihood have dominated Greece. Had they dominated Greece they would probably have introduced their own system of controls, political and religious, and thus counteracted the characteristic Greek tendencies towards city-state autonomy and intellectual liberty. By defeating the Persians the

Greeks saved their own distinctive social order at a relatively early stage in its development.

We have now suggested the general conditions under
which it may be legitimate to single out some causal factor
and invest it with a decisive role as precipitant. But much
discrimination is needed lest we make this or any other
type of causal imputation too absolute or too detached.
Every alleged cause is relative to a whole dynamic system
and can be properly assessed only in the light of our comprehension of that system. On this point we shall here
content ourselves with two further comments.

First, in assigning the decisive role of precipitant to any
act or event we are in substance claiming to know, not only
what actually happened, but what *would have happened* had
not this act or event occurred. Like every causal imputation, this is an inference, not a datum. Sometimes the inference may be extremely obvious. If the missionaries and
the traders had not come the native customs would have
endured. If the gun had not been fired the man would not
have been killed. But often it implies an intimate knowledge of the situation in which the change takes place. It
implies that we know, not merely the immediate operation
of the forces inherent in the situation, but the mode in
which, but for the precipitant, they *would have continued* to
operate. This implication is most evident where the precipitant does not come from outside but emerges within
the situation. It may be said, for example, that the appeal
of a leader turned the tide of opinion in the direction of his
policy, but to validate the statement it is not enough to show
that the tide actually turned after his appeal. It must be
shown, as being at least highly probable, that the prevailing
conditions of public opinion were such that, but for the act
of the leader, the tide would not then — or soon thereafter — have changed in this direction. Again, we find in

the history books frequent statements like the following: "The war of secession altered profoundly the governmental ideals and methods, the economic life, and the whole social structure of the United States." The claim is that, but for the war of secession, the political, economic, and social conditions of the United States would not, in the period that followed, have undergone profound changes or else that the changes they might have undergone would have been vastly different from the actual changes. The obverse of this claim is made when we designate a factor as antiprecipitant. The battle of Marathon prevented a profound change, so Max Weber's argument runs, in the course of Greek history, permitting the forces inherent in the cultural situation of Greece to fulfil themselves.[14] The problems here suggested we shall discuss in a later chapter.

Second, the act or event we single out as the precipitant is still inextricably bound up, with respect alike to its own initiation and to its causal operation, with the whole moving dynamic system. It would be meaningless to define the precipitant as that without which the change would not have taken place. Without any one of a thousand things and without the express interaction of them all the change would not have taken place. On this ground we might even deny that what we have called the precipitant has any more causal significance than any of the numerous other factors involved. This position is taken, for example, in the following passage from Tolstoi's novel, *War and Peace*. He is talking of the war of 1812 between Western Europe under Napoleon and Russia under Alexander.

"If Napoleon had not taken offence at the request to withdraw beyond the Vistula, and had not commanded his

---

[14] *Gesammelte Aufsätze zur Wissenschaftslehre* (Tübingen, 1922), pp. 276–277. See also A. von Schelting, op. cit. pp. 255–257, and T. Parsons, op. cit. pp. 610–613.

troops to advance, there would have been no war. But if all the sergeants had been unwilling to serve on another campaign, there would have been no war either.

" And the war would not have been had there been no intrigues on the part of England, no Duke of Oldenburg, no resentment on the part of Alexander; nor had there been no autocracy in Russia, no French Revolution and consequent dictatorship and empire, nor all that led to the French Revolution, and so on further back: without any one of these causes, nothing could have happened. And so all those causes — myriads of causes — coincided to bring about what happened. And consequently nothing was exclusively the cause of the war, and the war was bound to happen, simply because it was bound to happen. Millions of men, repudiating their common sense and their human feelings, were bound to move from west to east, and to slaughter their fellows. . . .

" The acts of Napoleon and Alexander, on whose words it seemed to depend whether this should be done or not, were as little voluntary as the act of each soldier, forced to march out by the drawing of a lot or by conscription. . . .

" The historian who says Napoleon went to Moscow because he wanted to, and was ruined because Alexander desired his ruin, will be just as right and as wrong as the man who says that the mountain of millions of tons, tottering and undermined, has been felled by the last stroke of the last workingman's pickaxe. In historical events great men — so called — are but the labels that serve to give a name to an event, and like labels, they have the least possible connection with the event itself." [15]

But the fact that numerous other conditions are equally

---

[15] *War and Peace* (Carleton House edition), Part IX, Chap. I. We deal later with the type of " determinism " and historical " fatalism " that in the above-quoted passage receives illicit support from the principle of the " multiplicity of causes."

necessary for the result affords no ground for the denial of the distinctive role of the precipitant. The point is obvious enough when our precipitant is itself such an event as a war. The author of the passage before us is thinking, however, of such salient or decisive actions as might be said to precipitate the war and is denying our right to assign them any special causal importance. The act of an emperor, he suggests, was of less moment than the acts of " millions of men in whose hands the real power lay." These other acts were of course equally necessary for the total determination of the phenomenon, but it does not follow that they were equally important for the understanding of the phenomenon. From the latter point of view we are justified in concentrating attention on the plans and ambitions of a few dominant men, no matter how dependent their policies were on the whole system to which they belonged. In the first place their acts were the specifically initiating acts. What the sergeants and the peoples did was use and wont. They were the instruments of policy, not its causes. Their causal role was as a function of the established order wherein soldiers obey their generals and peoples respond to the demand of their governments. Soldiers and peoples have done so through ten thousand wars. They do it in peace as well as in war. Their doing so throws no particular light on *this* war. The intrusive precipitating factors were what Napoleon did and what Alexander did. As such they are legitimately singled out — provided we do not assume their detachment from the whole scheme of things.

The proviso is essential. To explain social change we must always relate events to the order in which they occur. We must furthermore see the event as the culmination of a process or a new stage in the process. We cannot therefore turn history into a succession of events. If we seek to do so we ignore the deeper-working processes of change. For any mere moment of change we may content ourselves with the schema of precipitant and pre-existing order or equilibrium. But the order that is reasonably postulated for the comprehension of any single moment of change cannot be taken as the mere background of a *succession* of events. For the dynamic order is changing in response to its inherent forces and on the phenomenal level of events we cannot grapple with its changes. Since this point is of primary importance for our later construction we must deal with it more fully.

III

CRUCIAL EVENT AND CAUSAL CHAIN

We think of one act or event as plausibly the cause of other acts or events, and in the preceding section we have suggested the limits within which, for any given moment of change, it is legitimate to think in this way. We may, however, be tempted to extend this simple type of explanation to include a whole series of events. We may think of one event precipitating another, and this in turn precipitating a third, and so on. This is the concept of the causal chain, and since it is rather freely applied in various types of exposition, and especially in historical narrative, it deserves particular analysis.

At the outset we should distinguish the causal chain from other linkages that are not strictly causal. For example, in a logical chain we have a train of inferences, each dependent on the preceding. The proof of a mathematical theorem is a *logical* chain, as a series of successive steps leading to a demonstration. But, as we have already shown, no causality is implied in a chain of reasoning. We show, for example, by a few simple steps that if the sum of two angles of a triangle is equal to the sum of two angles of another triangle, the third angles are equal. But what we offer are reasons, not causes. Similarly one clue may lead to another, and so to the detection of a crime, but the clue as such is in no sense a cause of the crime. There is another type of chain that also lies outside the strict causal category, viz., the free schema of means-ends leading to some goal.[16] We seek D in order to get C, and we seek C in order to get B, and we seek B for the sake of A. A value relation links A to D, and at each step it enters into a process of teleological causation. But D cannot properly be said to cause C and C to cause B and so forth. Again, we seek D for the sake of C, but we may achieve D and find that it does not after all bring us C. The connection is hypothetical, and this applies particularly to any final end that we seek, or *believe* we seek — such as happiness, security, comfort, distinction, and so forth — through some series of activities conceived as means. A genuine causal chain does not depend on ambiguous hypotheses or invalidated beliefs. It is a succession of causes and effects, in which each succeeding effect becomes causal to that which in turn follows it.

Let us take a simple illustration first. A doctor is summoned to a patient who must have a certain serum without delay. But a storm has arisen which blows down a large tree, which blocks the highroad, which prevents the doctor from proceeding further, which delays the arrival of the serum, so that the patient dies. Here we have a putative causal chain, of the form $GFEDCB — A$, linking the storm G to the death of the patient A.

Can we, then, say that the storm was the cause of the death of the patient? Had it not been for the storm his death probably would not have happened. That is true,

---

[16] We characterize this schema as " free " simply to avoid the confusion of it with the mechanical sequence presently to be considered.

just as it is true that had it not been for certain other conditions present in the situation of the patient his death would not have happened. These other conditions we may regard as pre-established and by ignoring them on that account attribute specific causality to the storm. It is the precipitant overthrowing the prior operative system. But then even with the storm the death of the patient might have been prevented. The blocking of the road closed one contingency, but several others may still have remained open. For example, the doctor might have telephoned to the patient and suggested another available source of the serum, or he might have turned back and driven to the nearest airport and hired a plane, or he might have summoned assistance and arranged to have the obstacle removed, perhaps at the cost of neglecting his other engagements, and so forth.

Observe that in this instance the crucial events regarded as causes are assigned this role because they are represented as interferences with normal conditions. The chain of causes was a linked series of such interferences. The storm was an interference in this sense. The blocking of the road was an unanticipated disturbance of the usual mode of travel. A storm is, however, " normal " *under its own conditions*. The fall of a decayed tree is also " normal " under its own conditions. What was not normal, that is, not in accordance with the regular course of things, was the conjuncture that the storm should have felled a tree that blocked the roadway. This was the specific interruption of the regular operative system.

Our illustration already suggests limits to the applicability of the principle of a causal chain. A somewhat fuller analysis will reveal how serious these limits are. We shall distinguish three types of causal linkage for this purpose, which we shall call respectively physical sequences, historical sequences, and mechanical sequences.

1. By physical sequences we mean a chain of single causes of the form *GFEDCB — A* in which each link is a natural phenomenon, or in other words lies wholly *Physical* outside of the teleological realm, such as the first *Sequences* two items in our previous example, the storm and the fall of the tree. It is at once obvious that the principle of a causal chain, in the sense defined, has little or no significance here. A single phenomenon may be " abnormal," if we mean thereby that it intrudes on a relatively constant system or disturbs a relatively constant equilibrium — collisions of stars, earthquakes, hurricanes, lightning bolts, organic monstrosities, and so forth. But no chain of " causes " in this sense is likely. The fallen tree is not the starting-point of a series of " abnormalities " in nature. The organic monstrosity does not initiate a series of others. The causal sequence of single events, the chain *GFEDCB — A*, in which each event is salient, precipitating a fresh disturbance of an established equilibrium, is itself " abnormal." It seems, on closer scrutiny, rather like an application to nature of what we loosely imagine that we find in human experience. In fact, many of the natural events we regard as disturbances are so from the point of view of human systems. The tree falling in the forest is " normal," the tree falling on the highroad is " abnormal." Man has set up within or upon the order of nature a vast number of temporary operative systems, subject in their degree and after their kind to disturbances from within and from without. The tree falling on the roadway was a disturbance from without, but the internal equilibrium, the social operating system, is itself always of precarious stability. For one thing, it exists on the basis of an elaborately constructed interdependence, involving the consentience of large numbers in an institutional order and their co-operative activity towards its maintenance. But this order is subject to frequent disturbance. The

myriad changes and chances of human affairs forever play upon it — changing interest, changing distribution of power, changing leadership, changing attitudes, changing experience; and because it is so elaborately interdependent these changes have repercussions throughout the system. The equilibrium of nature is self-restorative to an extent far from being attained in the equilibrium of society. It is therefore in the social area that we can more plausibly speak of a chain of causes, in the scheme of a series of determinate single events that lead from the relative point of origin G to the relative result A.

▾

2. Let us examine what is meant by an historical sequence. First let us offer a schematic example. The *Historical* head of a government of country X chooses as *Sequences* his adviser a statesman who has a strong dislike of a neighboring country Y (G). This statesman persuades the ruler to put up a high tariff against the goods exported by Y (F). The government of Y demands the removal of the tariff (E). The ruler of X refuses (D). The refusal is made a *casus belli* (C). The commander in chief of X loses a great battle through mistaken strategy (B). A revolution follows in country X and the ruler is deposed and executed (A).

By an historical sequence we mean simply a succession of causally linked events within any social system. Obviously these events need not be of the kind that are significant for history, understood as the larger record of human affairs. An example such as the following would serve our purpose equally well. A business man loses an important contract G. Consequently he goes home in a bad temper and is surly to his wife F. In a fit of nerves she leaves him, taking the car to drive to her mother's home E. Driving badly in her excitement she runs into another car, injuring two people D. The police bring charges against her C. Her mother, hearing of it, has a heart attack B and dies A.

Here we have a series of events which exhibits the character of a causal chain. Each event precipitates in some manner the next one, so that there is an historical sequence linking G to F, F to E, E to D, D to C, C to B, and B to A. But two points should be noted. In the first place the selected sequence is not the only one that leads to A, and therefore its causal adequacy is impugned. In the second place no genuine causal sequence can be simply a succession of *events*.

These points are easily established. It can be shown in several ways that the historical series, presumably entitling us to say that G is the cause of F, F the cause of E, and so on, does not therefore entitle us to say that G is the cause of A.   Suppose, for example, we extend our first series back to N, adding a sequence N to H, say a chain of events leading to the seizure of power by the ruler of country X. N cannot in any significant sense be regarded as the cause or even as a cause of A. To reduce the chain to an absurdity, we could equally well claim that the marriage of the ruler's mother was a cause of his deposition and execution, since that event also is the relative initiator of a chain of events leading to H, the appointment of the ruler. Clearly there are many sequences that lead to A, and their number increases in a kind of geometrical ratio, the more links we add to the chain. From every link in the chain a different regression, or several of them, could be established. For example, an alternative sequence could be traced through B, the error of the commander in chief, back to the events leading to his appointment or even to those that inspired his error.

The historical sequence, in short, has causal significance only for immediately successive links, not at all for the relation between remote links.[17]   Often an historical narrative conveys a false suggestion of causal determinateness, because it emphasizes a particular sequence, one out of the many equally available. To explain the event A, it selects, say, a spectacular event D, and thus concentrates attention on a particular series $DBC — A$. That the implication of causality is misleading becomes obvious if we present even a much simplified diagram of the various sequences that lead from the level of the event D to the event A.

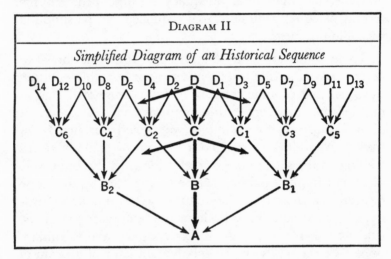

DIAGRAM II

Simplified Diagram of an Historical Sequence

All our D's, not only our central one, are links in causal chains that lead to A. Why, then, do we give prominence to one out of the many? Why, to return to our first example, do we make our D the rejection of a proposal from country Y by the ruler of country X? That event did not inevitably lead to a declaration of war, still less to the defeat of country X. It would not have done so apart from various other events — *or apart from a whole set of conditions that are not events at all.* The only plausible answer is that the event

---

[17] The question of responsibility is a somewhat different one and will be the subject of later consideration. See Chapter Eight.

selected for inclusion in the historical sequence is presumed to be one that specifically disrupts a temporary equilibrium, whereas the other events on the D level are presumed to have no such efficacy. The selected event is thus thought of as peculiarly the precipitant of a group of events on the C level, including the central C, which is thought of as playing the same role with respect to the B level — and so to the end of the chain.

Even without further analysis it should be obvious that the selection of a series of precipitants, for the presentation of an historical sequence, is necessarily precarious. We can readily discover here or there some one crucial event, but it is likely to be the outcome of a considerable conjuncture of impacts rather than of some one preceding crucial event. And its repercussions spread through a whole series of changes even if these again should in turn evoke a new precipitant. Consequently, a historical sequence, or any array of historical sequences, is apt to become highly artificial and unsatisfactory if presented as an explanation of social change. This is the more so since the events adduced as precipitants of change are commonly, almost inevitably, those of a revolutionary, catalytic, or catastrophic character. If great social changes are indeed associated with slowly maturing processes, such as the decay of traditional mores, the rise of new social classes, the spread of a new religion, or if, again, they are the accumulation of adaptations progressively made to technological changes, themselves developing from small beginnings, or even if we are content to regard them as the concreted products of numerous particular reactions to occasional precipitant events, then the historical sequence is bound to give us a distorted picture of the situations it purports to explain.

The problem of historical narration is here raised, and we may touch it in passing. History, as a mode of knowl-

edge, is concerned peculiarly with the time order of significant events, set against the background from which the
events emerge. The problem does not attach so obviously
to the specialized histories that are the record of particular
aspects of human affairs, medicine, science, engineering,
government, law, and so forth — since these find their
scope and definition by reference to the subject-matter in
view — but to history in the generic sense, whether the
history of a people, of a period, of a " civilization," of a
country, of a locality. What, then, does history mean?
What does it set out to do? How can it present the significant record of any community? In the endless vicissitudes
of human affairs what is significant and for what? We can
answer only in terms of our variant valuations, so that some
value assumption underlies every historical narration. But
this is only the beginning of our problem. Let us take value
assumptions for granted, whether they are explicit or, as
more frequently, only implicit in the historian's mind.
These values obviously inhere not in the events but in the
situations to which the events contribute, in the changing
condition, the striving, the enjoying, the suffering, in short
the experience of the human group. If we were justified
in regarding events as the chief determinants of these situations, then the task of the historian would be somewhat
lighter, since his record is largely a concatenation of events.
But if the secret of change lies as much, or even more, in
slow or cumulative processes that only now and then break
into decisive events, then the business of writing history
becomes profoundly difficult and uncertain — if indeed its
object is not merely to register changes but to interpret
them, to show their relation one to another and to bring
out their significance in the life of the community.

History is engrossed in the time order of change, and
this time order is most readily construed as a succession of

conspicuous events. History is generally conceived as a story, a narrative, say the story of a people, and the narrative form inevitably emphasizes the succession of events. The interest of a narrative moves from one salient, dramatic, disturbing, or novel occurrence to another. While the technical historian is largely engaged in the discovery, verification, and reorganization of evidences relating to great or even to obscure occasions, the synoptic historian travels down the stepping stones of events, pausing on each to assess its significance. Thus we often have the semblance of a causal interpretation, such as we get on a smaller scale in a biography. But in both cases the semblance may be in part illusory, for as we have seen the causal validity of the historical sequence, and therefore its adequacy for purposes of social interpretation, is tantalizingly limited.

▼

3. From this digression we turn to our third type, the mechanical sequence. Here we seem to get nearest to a strict chain of causes. A button is pushed. It *Mechanical* closes an electric circuit that operates a starter *Sequences* that sets an engine in continuous motion, involving an elaborate series of successive operations, each dependent on the preceding. Here G may be said to cause F and F to cause E and E to cause D and so down to A. But what is A — the end of this causal chain? In the case of a running engine, apart from the starting impulse, the operations repeat themselves indefinitely, so that we have a circular chain. But there is an end-product that is not part of the circle and that is its teleological cause. The prior causal chain has been contrived to effect this end-product. The chain is a chain because of a predesigned system of adaptations. The same principle is apparent in a non-circular mechanical sequence, as when the pulling of a trigger leads to the firing of a shot. The mechanism,

including the stored and specially adapted motive power, is a pattern pre-arranged to ensure that *A* will happen if *G*, the first act in the causal chain, is performed. In causing *G* to happen we *will A*. The mechanical sequence exists only where there is, outside of it, an objective.

Here we come close to a profound problem. The mechanical sequence is a system of closely interdependent pre-- adaptations. But we find something analogous to it in nature. In the first place organic processes, such as the process of digestion, might be compared to mechanical sequences, except that the transitions are so fine and imperceptible that no mechanism can be conceived as running so smoothly. These organic processes are thus entirely unlike a series of determinate events, a chain of causes as here discussed, each " precipitating " the next. But nature does yield us many examples of quasi-mechanical adaptations, such as the mode in which orchids are fertilized by bees. These adaptations are so suggestive of purposive contrivance that sometimes it is difficult to describe them without using the language of teleology. Nevertheless all that we can say is that these pre-established adaptations operate *as though* they had been somehow designed. The study of purely " blind " forces, such as hereditary variation and natural selection, reveals in part how they may have come about. For the rest all we have a scientific title to claim is that nature is such as to produce everywhere wonderful and exquisite examples of inter-adaptation. But this is a way of restating a problem, not of solving it.

CHAPTER SEVEN

CAUSE AS INCENTIVE

I

SOME TYPICAL ATTRIBUTIONS

No MODE of explanation of the behavior of men and groups is more frequently employed than that which singles out some *incentive*. By incentive we mean any subjective factor regarded as initiating and directing a course of action *meaningfully associated* with the subjective factor. Whenever we explain human behavior in terms of " drives," " urges," " instincts," " emotions," or " motives," we are appealing to incentives in this sense. The meaningful association is for the agent himself. It exists where the action is implicitly or explicitly purposive.[1] The agent has some awareness of the dependence of the action on his " urge," or of the mode in which the action is prompted by it, or of the degree in which the action serves to fulfil it. We are here excluding from the category of incentive the stimuli of merely reflex actions, hormones and other chemical determinants of organic processes, and so forth. Of course our incentives are bound up with our physico-chemical constitution, and immediately with our hormones and glandular secretions, but, no matter how themselves conditioned or determined,

---

[1] The position here taken is that the incentive is a psychical phenomenon and that the purposive is the best *indication* of the psychical; see, for example, John Laird, *Problems of the Self* (London, 1917), Chap. VI.

they fall within our definition only as they manifest a psychical aspect.

Since this subjective or psychical aspect is a primary datum of the behavior of social beings we immediately face the question: How far and under what conditions are we justified in singling out a particular subjective attribute as the explanation of individual or group activity? In all our social activities we are immersed in means-ends relationships. How, then, are we justified in isolating and accentuating, under the guise of incentive, one side, and indeed one aspect of one side, of the universal interaction of subject and object, so as to make it the explanation of the total act? The concept of incentive, as we have defined it, includes no reference to means, to external goal, to any non-subjective element. We are not thinking of such explanations of behavior as attribute it to things like money or position or security or fame. When we name such things we designate objectives and merely suggest, in the most general way, the psychical aspect (the desire for money and so forth). When on the other hand we attribute an act to a particular emotion, drive, or instinct, to the sexual impulse, to fear or anger or revenge, we are denominating only the subjective factor. The distinction we have already drawn between objective and motive comes into operation here. For when we specify an objective, for example money, as the cause of an act we tend to think of the external or environmental factor as the " stimulus " and the act itself as the " response." But when we specify an incentive, such as passion or ambition, we focus our explanation directly in the subjective. The incentive is thus either a motive, in the sense already defined, or else some subjective impulse that may be otherwise defined but contains an element of motivation.

We return to our question: Under what conditions do we single out incentives as causal explanations and how far are we justified in so doing? Let us consider some typical usages, beginning with more simple and limited applications and advancing to those of wider social range and greater theoretical amplitude.

▼

1. In certain situations the external side of behavior is given or obvious or taken for granted. We do not need to ask the *what* but only the *wherefore*. Until we know the latter the act is void of meaning for us; no judgment can be passed upon it. The significance of many things done lies not in the doing but in the reason for the doing. The significance of many things said lies not in the saying, not in the overt sense of the words, but in the hidden thoughts that inspired them. The incentive is never given, it is always only inferred. The same external act of another may evoke in us love or hate, joy or sorrow, approval or condemnation, according to the way we read its motivation. In this problem everyone is engrossed who seeks to explore human nature or explain social actions — the novelist, the dramatist, the biographer, the historian, the anthropologist, the social psychologist, the sociologist, the social philosopher. With this problem, with the intent behind the act or the gesture, everyone is concerned whose business it is to assess or evaluate conduct — the judge, the novelist, the religionist, the instructor of the young, and in fact the vast majority of men and women as self-appointed guardians of the mores. To get at and to utilize incentives, to touch the hidden springs of favorable response, is the main business of everyone who seeks to control or manipulate human beings — the politician, the propagandist, the advertiser, the fashion creator, the merchandizer. Thus in a great many situations the only problem is that of the hidden incentive, and the discovery of incentives appears, then, to be all that is necessary to explain individual or group behavior.

2. In certain situations we conceive of the external act as completely at the mercy, so to speak, of the internal urge. In such cases the objective is merely incidental. Where it can be said to be present at all its attainment is mainly or wholly subservient to the prior urge. An angry man pounds his fist on the table or knocks over a chair. The act serves merely as a vent for his anger. Under the spur of revengeful emotion a man kills or injures someone who has wronged him. The agent scarcely looks beyond the immediate satisfaction in what he does, beyond the release of the urgent tension. The type of act called by the French *crime passionel* falls generally within this category. Again, if a man is suffused with any strong feeling, whether gratitude or benevolence or jealousy or envy, and takes whatever way is immediately available to express it through external manifestations, we may reasonably attribute such action to the promptings of his particular feeling. We may observe that while the number of *objectives* that may be adduced in explanation of human activities is practically endless, the number of the subjective urges commonly adduced for a similar purpose is quite limited, even though there is little agreement among psychologists as to precisely how many there are. On the other hand any subjective urge, such as revenge, sexual desire, maternal love, and so forth, may manifest itself in a great variety of external acts. Wherever we think of an act as primarily the expression of an urge, as the manner in which, given the occasion and the opportunity, the urge seeks its immediate satisfaction, we explain the act in terms of an incentive.

▼

3. The same principle is invoked not only for the explanation of specific acts, but broadly for the explanation of types of action or of human behavior in general. Certain psychologists have derived all social actions from an original equipment of "instincts," ranging from two or

three to a dozen or even a score. While this method may serve for the *classification* of animal activities, most of which can be made to fall under the categories of mating activities, parental activities, and activities of self or group preservation, it becomes increasingly precarious, even for the mere purpose of classification, as we pass to the complex life of civilized man. Where there is much variation in behavior it is no longer satisfactory to subsume it under the concept of " instinct." Apart from other difficulties involved, there is the initial obstacle that " instinct " is only a name for uniformities, not a clue to differences. Some impulses are more important or more universal than others or more obviously associated with organic mechanisms. But no one knows how to draw the line. If we call parental care instinctive, we may have to admit on the same grounds an instinct of curiosity or of imitation or of workmanship or of speechmaking, and so on until we have the most embarrassing array — embarrassing because when we limited ourselves to two or three they seemed to explain something but when we number them by the hundreds we know that they explain nothing. Accordingly this mode of explanation has fallen out of favor.[2]

The quest for subjective causes has in recent times taken diverse directions. Some have followed Jung in seeking for psychological types such as his " extravert " and " introvert," referring to each type a characteristic mode of behavior.[3] Others have followed Freud in his far-reaching attempt to unmask one basic drive, that of the sex impulse.

---

[2] See, for example, L. L. Bernard, *Instinct: A Study in Social Psychology*, New York, 1924; John Dewey, *Human Nature and Conduct* (New York, 1930), Chap. VI; P. Sorokin, *Contemporary Sociological Theories* (New York, 1928), Chap. XI; and for a somewhat less drastic view, Morris Ginsberg, *Studies in Sociology* (London, 1932), Chaps. VI and VII.

[3] C. G. Jung, *Psychological Types* (New York, 1923), translated by Baynes.

Others have substituted for instincts, as determinants of behavior, a list of " wishes " or " propensities " or " dispositions," such as the " four wishes " of Thomas and Znaniecki — " response," " recognition," " security," and " new experience." [4] One of the most elaborate attempts along this line is that of Pareto, who presents a curious list of six classes of " residues," which he defines as " manifestations of sentiments and instincts." [5] These residues are the relatively constant elements, the " principles " or determinants, of the various explanations and rationalizations that human beings offer for their " non-logical conduct." The classes are named respectively " instinct for combinations," " group persistences," " need of expressing sentiments by external acts," " residues connected with sociality," " integrity of the individual and his appurtenances," and the " sex residue."

Each of these schemes of causal imputation has its own peculiar difficulties, but these need not be discussed here. Our special concern is a difficulty common to them all. How can they validate the selection, from the complex totality of human nature, of certain specific traits, attributes, propensities, as *constant* causal factors, operative either singly or in specific combinations? It is noteworthy that nearly every exponent of the subject offers a different list and that the basis of classification is nearly always obscure. How, for example, can we relate Sumner's list of four basic incentives — hunger, love, vanity, and fear — to the list of four offered by Thomas and Znaniecki — response, recognition, security, and new experience? Each seems capricious in the light of the other. The terms used are often vaguely inclusive, so that the most diverse actions

---

[4] *The Polish Peasant* (New York, 1918), Vol. I, Methodological Note, pp. 72–73, and Vol. III, Introduction.
[5] *The Mind and Society* (New York, 1935), edited by A. Livingston, Vol. I, § 306, §§ 798–799, Vol. II, *passim*, and Vol. III, Chap. IX.

may be subsumed under any one of them. At best they denominate different aspects of a total personality active always as a whole, and the endless intricacy of aspectual relationships within the personality renders the classification of little service in causal explanation. The attempt to avoid this difficulty by making one fundamental urge cover a multitude of quite diverse manifestations, as Freud does for the sex impulse, runs into serious problems of another kind.[6] It must draw precarious inferences from mere analogies, extending the domain of sex to activities that seem quite remote from it. Thus we are told that the Marxist revolutionary is obsessed by an anti-father complex, that a people deprived of territory after defeat in war is the victim of a castration complex, and that a person who is incapable of sliding downhill on skis thereby indicates sexual frigidity. By a similar feat of imagination any strong impulse could be made equally inclusive.

4. In certain systems of philosophy the inspiration of all human conduct is conceived as being the quest of a subjective state called " pleasure " or " happiness " or merely " satisfaction." The doctrine of psychological hedonism was formulated in particular by the utilitarians, notably by Bentham and John Stuart Mill, and has been followed by various economists and sociologists. But, as has frequently been shown, its plausibility rests on a fallacy. We get satisfaction in the attaining (and in the seeking) of our objectives, but the objective must not be identified with the satisfaction it yields. If a man finds pleasure in the attainment of objectives, it is " only because he has previously desired them, not because pleasures are the objects de-

---

[6] See, for example, K. S. Lashley, " Physiological Analysis of the Libido," *Psychological Review* (May, 1934), Vol. 31, pp. 192–202; and Karen Horney, *New Ways in Psychoanalysis* (New York, 1939), *passim*.

sired." As the philosopher just quoted goes on to say: " The pleasure incidental to the satisfaction of an interest cannot be attained after loss of the interest itself, nor can the interest be revived by wishing for a renewal of the pleasure incidental to its satisfaction." [7] In any event, since the search for causes is the search for the differential factor of the specific act or type of act, the invocation of a universal incentive can scarcely play any part in causal explanation.

Reviewing this whole range of usages we are led to the conclusion that the attribution of certain relatively simple manifestations to a particular incentive, as discussed under 1 and 2 above, may adequately serve as a mode of causal reference. The infant cries for its bottle, the wild animal prowls the woods for prey. When we say it is on account of hunger we have sufficiently answered a particular why. Even in the case of the complex adult personality there arise conditions of overmastering organic need or tension whereunder a similar explanation may suffice. But for most situations this singling out of the subjective urge is not enough. The urge is the dynamic direction of personality. The classification of " instincts " or drives is differently constructed by nearly every classifier. The reason may well be that in the adult personality the incentive to action at any moment is a complex and endlessly variable impulsion of the dynamic self.[8] If so, we cannot pick out of a small list of designated urges any one, or even any two or three, as the precise determinant of behavior. Even where one can be regarded as dominant, it is so qualified by the total personality that it cannot as such be a sufficient explanation of the specific act. Moreover, we must interpret the complex and focussed motivations of human beings in

---

[7] T. H. Green, *Prolegomena to Ethics*, Book III, Chap. I.

[8] The point is well brought out by G. W. Allport, " The Functional Autonomy of Motives," *American Journal of Psychology* (1937), Vol. 50, pp. 141–156.

the light of the objective situations on which they are focussed and to which their complexity responds. We can no longer explain behavior by reference to the subjective alone.

But there is another and most obstinate difficulty that everywhere besets the appeal to incentive as causal.

II

THE IMPUTATION OF MOTIVES

Causal knowledge is always inferential, never immediate. The causal nexus, like every other relationship between data, is not itself a datum. It can never be vindicated by perception or by any of the devices that come to the aid of perception. The assertion of any relationship, no matter how simple or obvious, involves the appeal to reason, and its establishment is a scientific *construction*. We do not perceive the relationship of the earth to the sun or of a child to its mother, we only infer it. Some relationships are completely demonstrable, like the properties of geometrical figures; others are cumulatively demonstrable, we can approach ever nearer to full verification — or refutation — by means of scientifically attainable evidences; others again are of such a nature that complete demonstration is barred by a seemingly insuperable obstacle. To the last category belongs the imputation of motives. The peculiar feature of the imputation of motives is that we are asserting a nexus between an overt action and a purely subjective factor that cannot be exposed to any kind of direct scrutiny and that is not as such manifest in the action. If, for example, a man competes for a prize we can say with some assurance that the prize is his *objective*, but if we add that he seeks the prize in order to triumph over a rival or to recover from a former defeat we are precariously going behind the objective to assert a motive for it.

Several alternative motives in this sense or several different combinations of motives are equally admissible for the explanation of a particular action, in the sense that the action itself does not enable us to refute any of them. There are certain conventional symbols and gestures of motivation that are expressed or indicated by the agent, but even so they may be entirely deceptive. " One may smile, and smile, and be a villain." So when we impute motives we are inferring not simply a relationship between one datum and another — we are inferring a relationship (the causal nexus) between a datum (the overt act) and a postulate that is itself a highly precarious inference (the alleged motive). We should here observe, however, that the postulate is not the existence of motives but the presence of a particular motive within the scheme of a particular situation.

Confronted with this dark hazard one might easily conclude that the imputation of motives is a wholly unscientific business; that it represents what one writer roundly calls " the animistic, theological, cause-effect viewpoint "; that in all science, not alone physical science, " a generalized statement of *how* events occur is the only *why* we seek," so that we must relegate the quest for motives to the limbo of ancient superstitions.[9] But we are loth to accept this conclusion, for the simple reason that we cannot dismiss, as beyond scientific enquiry, any intelligible question concerning reality. That motives, as already defined, belong to the world of reality is established by the best of all evidences, that of immediate experience. We are all aware

---

[9] The quotations are taken from G. A. Lundberg, *Foundations of Sociology* (New York, 1939), p. 260. I fully accept the statement of this author that " motives and goals can be inferred only from behavior " (p. 286). But he begs the question when he suggests that there are no more scientific grounds for inferring motives and goals for human actions than for concluding that " it is the ' motive ' and the ' goal ' of lightning to thunder! "

that we have motives. We might even go so far as to suggest that the phenomenon of motivation constitutes an elementary distinction between animate beings and inanimate things. We cannot accept the intellectual asceticism of those who would rule out of the realm of science the study of motivation, since by that decree we should be denying to the scientist a vast area of human interests. Those who assert, as an objective against the language of " motives and goals," that the scientist is concerned only with the *how* of things are not really facing the issue. We are told by such writers that the *how* of behavior includes " *the conditions under which it takes place and the probability of its occurrence under those conditions.*" [10] Now among the conditions of human behavior are the subjective attitudes and impulses without which it would certainly not be human. To the agent himself these subjective urges are important as conditions and explanations of his act. For him they constitute its why. They at least appear to be determining factors, and that is why the term " why " is more relevant than the term " how." Or, if you prefer it, among the hows of behavior are certain factors that we distinguish as whys. There is an obvious distinction between asking why we did something and asking how we did it. To enquire why people make money is not to enquire how they make it. This why is intelligibly different from other conditions of the act. There is no human, and certainly no social, area of investigation to which this question of why, in one or other of its forms, is alien. We want to know not only how, but why, customs change, divorce increases, the birth-rate falls, conflicts arise, social movements grow and decline.

Those who abjure the language of " motives and goals " are apt to combine, sometimes indiscriminately, two con-

---

[10] Ibid. p. 286. Italics in original.

tentions for their position. They may claim that it is " un-scientific " to speak of motives at all, that such concepts belong to a scientifically outmoded, " animistic," " folk-lorish " manner of speech. Sometimes their claim is based on a materialistic or mechanistic metaphysics, buttressed by the fact that in mechanistic physics, their model for all the sciences, such language finds no place. But if motives and goals exist as data of experience, the claim comes perilously close to being a blind dogma. It would exclude from reality something indubitably present in human behavior. It is, of course, an interesting hypothesis that the apparent role of motives as determinants of behavior is a subjective illusion, but they do not investigate this hypoth-esis, still less establish it. And even were it established, these illusory motives would still remain among the " con-ditions " under which behavior takes place. It would be " animistic " thinking to assert that the lightning strikes a tree because it is angry with the tree. We should be ille-gitimately extending the concept of angry intention from the sphere to which experience entitles us to refer it. This illegitimate extension is the meaning of " animism." But what on earth does it mean to dub " animistic " the language of " motives and goals " when that language is applied not to the angry lightning but to the angry man?

The second contention is logically independent of the first. It is based on the peculiar difficulties involved in the discovery, identification, and attribution of motives. Mo-tives are hidden from the observer, they cannot be brought into the light of day. Even the agent's consciousness of them is elusive and obscure. Because of their baffling un-certainty, because they cannot be verified, because they cannot be examined, tested, " measured," they lie outside the area of scientific investigation. They may be fit themes for the novelist or the moralist, but the scientist should leave them severely alone, for he is concerned only with observable and verifiable facts.

For this second contention we have more sympathy. The difficulty we face in seeking to include motives within the range of scientific investigation is obvious and great, but the question is whether that difficulty is insuperable, so as to justify an attitude of complete scientific renunciation. The mere fact that an enterprise is difficult is an unworthy reason for abjuring it altogether. Let us, then, consider more fully the nature of the difficulty.

1. The first count is that the investigator can never observe or " get at " motives. They are the secret of the agent and since the same overt action may be inspired by any one of a variety of motives, or rather by any combination of a number of complex and elusive urges that together constitute the motive of the particular action, the external signs are quite inconclusive. They are often quite misleading. The agent has often a motive for hiding his motives. When he lets us into his secret, as it were, he may be concealing it the more. Even if he is genuinely attempting to reveal it he cannot offer us any proof. There is no way of " objectifying " the motive. It cannot be recorded, it cannot be expressed in precise, unmistakable symbols. It cannot be made amenable to tests of its presence or absence, still less of its quantity and degree.

2. The second count is that even the agent has no assurance concerning his own motives. He may confidently announce them to others — because their credence in his alleged motives helps him to gain his objectives, because the announcement contributes to his self-satisfaction or his social standing, because his interests persuade him that

such are his motives, because he wants to persuade himself
that his motives are what he declares them to be. He
" socializes " or " rationalizes " his motives, proclaiming
them the expression of certain simple attitudes of a kind
that are socially esteemed. It is so much easier to do this
than to state or even to discover what his actual motives
are. For motives are complex and elusive. Why should
one undertake the difficult business of fathoming them —
in so far as they can be fathomed at all — when it serves
our purpose so much better to resort to these conventional
and plausible simplifications? It is true that we often are
curious about the motives of others. Sometimes we even
expect them to answer questionnaires concerning the reason
why they got married or divorced, why they chose their
occupation, why they went to college, why they voted for
a certain candidate, and a thousand other things. And we
naively expect them to name one, or possibly two or three,
out of a short list of simple " reasons." But if we candidly
ask ourselves why *we* did any of the things in question we
are most likely to find that our self-examination reveals no
such clarity of motivation. Why did we go to college?
We went because each of us, being the kind of person he is
or was, just acted so in the light of the particular alternatives presented to him. To analyze a decision of this sort
is a difficult task, often baffling and sometimes repugnant
to us; but when we try it we learn at least how hazardous
this whole business is of naming and imputing motives.

As if these difficulties were not enough a modern school
of psychological analysis has advanced another that is even
more perturbing, since it threatens the validity of our conscious motives altogether. They tell us that the attitudes
and emotions we recognize in ourselves and believe to be
determinant of our actions are frequently not those that
really move us; that they are only a substitute or a mask

for our true motivations, which lie deep in our unconscious being; that because of early experience, indoctrination, and our built-up interests we have powerful inducements for suppressing the very awareness of these motivations and for resisting any exploration that might lead to our own enlightenment. We have, so to say, strong motives for ignoring our motives. It is true that this school has, on the basis of certain assumptions, devised its own techniques for the unearthing of the unconscious, but whatever we may think of these assumptions, the evidence adduced to show the deceptive character of our own beliefs concerning our motives sets up new danger signals for the investigator hot-foot for certainty in this world of elusive apparitions.

What, then, should we conclude? That we abandon altogether the quest of motivation? But in the arguments we have cited there is no suggestion that motives do not exist — and even as apparitions they call for investigation; and there is no demonstration that access to them is impossible, but only that it is difficult. Let us take the first count, to the effect that the outsider cannot get at motives. Obviously he can read motives only through their manifestations. Sometimes the signs are obscure and baffling, sometimes they are relatively clear. A man discovers that an acquaintance is the lover of his wife. Uttering words of anger and evincing the gestures associated with rage, he attacks the man. In a case of this sort, particularly if we know from other evidences the characteristics of the agent, we infer that he intended to do harm to his wife's lover and that he was animated by feelings of hatred and anger. We cannot demonstrate the conclusion beyond all possible doubt. In one instance out of many we may go wrong, even in reading such obvious and universally accepted signs. But why should it be unscientific to read the signs as care-fully as possible, to develop the logic of evidence and apply

it to situations, even though it yields not absolute certitude
but only some kind of probability? We may surely advance
towards truth by repeated approximations, each based on
partial evidence, as well as by adding one to another a series
of itemized and finally verified unit blocks of knowledge.
Some very important types of knowledge, some aspects of
all knowledge, we can attain only in the former way.
Moreover, as students of the social sciences we are not
dealing with individual behavior as such but with patterns
of behavior exhibited by many individuals. The case cited
above represents such a pattern. Since we have hundreds
of instances, we can discover with a high degree of assurance
typical social behavior under well-defined conditions. And
in this typical behavior we find quite recognizable motives
operative. The typology of social actions is a vast branch of
social science that is still very undeveloped and that is susceptible of far more scientific treatment than it is now receiving.

We conclude that it would be excessive and stultifying
scepticism to deny that motivation is sometimes clearly
revealed. " The burnt child dreads the fire." It is a simple
and common experience in the motivation of which there
is generally no ambiguity. Again, we all recognize in our
friends and acquaintances certain tenacious predispositions
that express themselves in many and various activities.
One man has a constant tendency to protect a sensitive
self-esteem, another has a powerful strain of sympathy for
the underdog, another takes himself for the hero of every
encounter. The recognition of motivation along the lines
of some established behavior pattern is often unmistakable.
Again, in every society, but most obviously in primitive
society there are sanctions and taboos that are known to
everyone. Where men, against their self-interest, conform
to the rules thus sanctioned, the motives for their so doing
are sufficiently apparent.

So far, in consideration of the first count, we have referred only to cases where the signs are clear or relatively clear. We agree that often the signs are utterly inadequate to provide grounds for reasonable inference. But the further objection that the agent, who alone has " inside knowledge " of his own motives, frequently misrepresents them with intent to deceive does not justify a purely negative attitude towards the task of investigation. We cannot assume that the deception is invariably successful. There are other evidences than the words and gestures of the agent. So far as the behavior of any one individual in any one situation is at issue, our inference may be quite conjectural and hazardous. But when we relate the single action of the individual to his other actions, to his life-history, and still more when we relate the action of one individual to the actions of others in similar situations, we may well discover a consistency of behavior that discounts the diverse allegations of plausible motives and enables us to discern with high probability, if we proceed far enough, the *characteristic* motivation associated with *types* of situation. We may find, for example, that a nationality group, suffering from exploitation by a dominant people, clings more strongly to its traditional mores than do the members of the same nationality where they are autonomous; or we may find that a racial group, suffering discrimination on racial or other grounds, adopts more readily than do other groups a social philosophy subversive of the system under which it lives; such findings carry with them strong indications of motive, and if our examples are numerous enough it would be idle to deny that these indications have scientific value.

The misrepresentation of motives is a difficulty, not a total impasse. Sometimes the disguise is subtle, sometimes it is transparent. The following case may serve as an illustration. A certain petty official held a post in a municipal administration, several members of which had been convicted of corrupt dealings. A special prosecutor presented evidence that this official had been consorting with an array of thugs, racketeers, and convicts. The official, rather than submit to examination, resigned his office. He did so on the plea that if he defended himself the records of these people would be published. " Many of them," he declared, " are now leading decent clean lives, bringing up families the best they can, and the disclosure of their names can bring only shame and distress to their innocent ones. . . . I cannot and will not, no matter at what cost to me, cause any further suffering and humiliation to those people. There are but four weeks remaining to my term of office. It is too brief a time to justify all of the suffering and humiliation that might result from a public hearing." [11] To say the least, no investigator would be misled by such a plea. Nor would he entertain serious doubt concerning the motive that prompted this parade of motive.

We turn, then, to the second count, that the agent frequently mistakes and misinterprets his own motives. But this claim is itself a positive one. It has validity only in so far as motives are knowable. It can be advanced only by those who profess to be able to uncover the real motive behind the disguise, the genuine wish underneath the repression, the determinant urge back of the agent's false consciousness of his motives. In fact a characteristic of the various schools that dwell on the distinction between real motives and apparent ones is the assurance with which they undertake to reveal the former. Pareto has no trouble in identifying the " manifestations of residues " and in exposing the " derivations " that mask them, any more than has Freud in identifying a primary " libido " as

---

[11] As recorded in the *New York Times*, December 4, 1937.

the core of the most elaborate credos. In like manner the critics of " ideologies " assume the ability to penetrate behind the mental defences of those who proclaim them. Whether or not we share this assurance we must agree that only in so far as there is some ground for it can we reasonably assert that the agent either misapprehends or disguises his " real " motives, and that consequently the distinction thus drawn affords no argument for dismissing the possibility of scientific investigation.

We may note, however, in passing, that those who make the distinction as sharp and decisive as do the Freudians proclaim, in so doing, their possession of techniques enabling them to arrive at absolute certainty, particularly with respect to the hidden, disguised, or " unconscious " motives operative in individual behavior. We cannot accept so clear-cut a solution since all the investigator can do is to discover, examine, and organize the evidences that point to the presence of particular motives, thus revealing the grounds for an inference that can be no more than highly probable. If, as psychoanalyst or psychiatrist, he is engaged with problems of individual therapy, his diagnosis of motivation may be confirmed or corrected by the results of the treatment based on it. If, as social psychoanalyst, he is concerned with problems of group behavior, he can achieve the very considerable reinforcement of probability that comes from the study of the like behaving of many individuals. On this basis he can learn to predict with expertness how people will respond to similar situations as they occur; how, for example, a group of people of a particular culture will feel and act if they are treated thus and thus by another group. If this art is still rudimentary it is not because the evidences of motivation are lacking but because the scientific study of these evidences has gone so short a way. Nor is the sociologist any less scientific in drawing probable conclusions from such evidences than is the meteorologist who predicts what tomorrow's weather will be. The lapse from science appears when he claims unwarranted certainty and treats his inferences as though they were established facts. And, in spite of the remarkable and possibly epoch-making work of the Freudians, they have widely exposed themselves to this charge. Their certainty rests on a number of assumptions regarding the biological nature of man, regarding the dominance of a construct called the " libido " and of a few sex-rooted " complexes," regarding the causal role in adult behavior of a few experience patterns attributed to infancy and childhood stages, regarding the analogical reference to these patterns of a wide diversity of behavior manifestations, and regarding the translation of the same patterns into a wide diversity of social institutions.[12] Freud tells us, for example, that the rise of religion is due to the child's sense of helplessness and his longing for a father. But psychoanalytic pronouncements of this sort are merely suggestive hypotheses which should be stated and treated as such. Such hypotheses are not to be taken as demonstrated merely because they are in harmony with psychoanalytic assumptions. They should be checked as rigorously as any other hypotheses. In the literature of psychoanalysis there is all too frequently the contentment with the congenial guess, the acceptance of analogy as proof, the daring leap in the dark — the *salto mortale* of faith.

From this point of view some danger lurks in the very expression " unconscious motive." In what sense, if any, can we be said to have desires, feelings, attitudes, of the

---

[12] See A. Kardiner, *The Individual and His Society* (New York, 1939), Part III; Erich Fromm, " Über Methode und Aufgabe einer analytischen Sozialpsychologie," *Zeitschrift für Sozialforschung* (1932), Vol. 1, pp. 28–54, 253–277; Karen Horney, *New Ways in Psychoanalysis*, New York, 1939.

existence of which we are not even dimly aware? A particular biological tension stimulates appropriate desires, a particular nervous condition is reflected in correspondent attitudes; but does that justify us in treating the tension as desire and the neurosis as attitude? No doubt it is a matter of definition but there is a genuine risk of confusion if we use the same term for the phenomena of conscious life and for the organic conditions and processes that work below this level. The psychoanalysts are particularly interested in the *relation* between the two levels, which is all the more reason for keeping the terms distinct. In effect, when they speak of " unconscious motives " they constantly pass from one level to the other. We find at least three usages. (1) There are motives of which the agent is totally unaware, but which the psychoanalyst can infer from various indications, such as dreams, beliefs, fantasies, and "Freudian errors." For the organic tensions and strivings thus indicated it would probably be better to use some other language than that of motivation. It is not in question that motives, as phenomena of consciousness, express or reflect the organic constitution. (2) There are motives of which the agent is fitfully or dimly aware but without realizing their full significance. " Awareness of an attitude comprises not only the knowledge of its existence, but also the knowledge of its forcefulness and influence and the knowledge of its consequences and the functions which it serves."[13] But a dim light is still a light, and to suggest that we are " unconscious " of an attitude when we do not know " its consequences and the functions which it serves " is to employ a mode of speech that plays havoc with any distinction whatever between the conscious and the unconscious. (3) There are motives of which the agent is clearly conscious but which nevertheless have an entirely different

[13] Karen Horney, op. cit. p. 20.

character or direction from that which he ascribes to them.
" We may be disgruntled or depressed without knowing
why; . . . our interests, our convictions, our attachments
may be determined by forces which we do not know." [14]
But the fact that we do not examine our motives, could not
" explain " them even if we tried, and do not understand
what lies back of them, does not entitle us to call these
motives themselves " unconscious " or to call " motives "
the unconscious factors that may determine them.

To pursue these issues further is beyond our present
scope. It is obvious enough that the investigation of motives is a task beset by peculiar hazards. It is obvious that
the application of scientific method to this task is still, in
spite of the brave new leads of the psychoanalysts, somewhat rudimentary. But surely the moral is not that we
abandon the endeavor but that we make the fuller recognition of difficulties the basis for more thorough exploration.
We need in particular to extend the range of our enquiry
into motives. On the psychological side we have to study
more explicitly their relation to the types and varieties of
personality, to the developing interest-complexes dependent on the interplay between personality and environment,
to the impact on such interest-complexes of conjunctures and crises occurring in the individual life-history;
and we have to learn to read the indices of motivation
within the coherence of such total situations. On the sociological side we have to investigate the impulses generating
social movements of all kinds, the sentiments that characterize the various forms of group solidarity, the foci of emotional attachments under different social conditions, the
like responses of men within the same situation and in
similar situations, and so forth. There is a sociology of
emotion that is almost entirely unexplored and that might

---

[14] Ibid.

throw much light on the problems of motivation. And if there are some who still doubt either the importance or the feasibility of such investigations it may perhaps suffice to point out that the art of the manipulation and control of motives is already a large-scale enterprise, with its private practitioners and with what is still more formidable, its public agencies. If the art advances, applying its knowledge of motivation to ends that often are regardless of all truth, shall science, the truth seeker, abjure that knowledge altogether?

III

MOTIVES AND THE SITUATION

Many of the difficulties that beset the imputation of motives spring from the tendency to treat these elusive aspects of the dynamic personality as though they were detachable, independently operative determinants of individual behavior or of social organization. This tendency is conspicuous in the Freudian system. He presents us with a great drama of " instincts." He depicts a mighty struggle between instinct and civilization. He proclaims the constant warfare of Eros and the death-instinct. He describes a number of processes which the " libido " experiences, such as repression, transference, sublimation. His subjective forces advance, retreat, disguise themselves, recur, as though they kept a strange integrity not only within the confines of personality but also within the endless transformation scenes of environment. Personal development and social change alike seem to be merely superficial. All the traits of civilized man are phylogenetically determined. The entire institutional scheme is a vehicle of primary biological drives, and when it deviates from that function it becomes simply an agency of repression. Every stage of social development is characterized in terms of some dominant aspect of the " libido " of the individual, with special reference to sexually orientated complexes.

But when we turn to actual situations we find endless variations and complexities both in the pattern of individual behavior and in the institutional system. The dynamics of primal drives, maintaining their simple biological quality through all processes of differentiation, seems curiously inadequate to account for the differentiation itself. Recurrence and recapitulation cannot explain change but only the unchanging element within it. Even if the fear of incest were the origin of taboo, it would not account for the elaboration and endless variation of taboo systems. We have constantly, in the Freudian interpretation, to reduce the complicated to the simple — which leaves the complication still unexplained. Moreover, the reduction constantly invokes the act of faith, the acceptance of the original hypothesis as the major premise from which the conclusion is derived. Only so does Freud conclude, for example, that attitudes towards social authority reflect the guilt of some supposititious " primal parricide " ; only so does he identify thrift and orderliness as expressions of " anal eroticism." The dependence of the forms of authority or of order on the conditions of group life is not considered. If the family, for example, displays the most remarkable differences of structure under different conditions it would seem obvious that we must include in our explanation not only the universal " instincts " that manifest themselves in familial relationships but also the divergent situations within which specific modifications occur. If, again, the family is not a fixed determinate organization, but a changing structure within a larger changeful system, how can the appeal to " instincts " account for this ceaseless process ? We cannot make institutions the mere projections of instincts without denying the reality of institutions and without denuding history of significance.

This point is well stated by a critic of the Freudian dynamics.

" The motive for repression in the individual in our culture gives us no clue to the forces or motives that set the institution into motion. The institution is merely a part of the individual's environment, to which he must accommodate himself. These institutions are end results of instinctual or social conflicts established by necessity, force, or expediency; their origin is largely a matter of conjecture, for no reconstruction is possible without the aid of history. For this lost history, the theory of primal parricide is no substitute. The structure, tempo, and order of repression in the individual are entirely contingent upon cultural forces. These forces differ in different cultures. The individual is a finite being, and an organic unit with a fixed ontogenetic course; the group has no such organic unity, no such ontogenesis, and has no beginning and no end. Institution and repression are reciprocal influences and hence cannot be treated as identical even though they originate from the same source. The institution creates a force, repression is a symptom of its operation." [15]

Once again we see that the enquiry into causes can never be satisfied unless it comprehends the entire pattern of relationships within which the phenomenon of change emerges. In the pursuit of causation we are always led from the linkage of unit factors to the inclusive nexus — though, as we have already seen and will see more fully as we proceed, the comprehension of totality still leaves us far from the end of our quest. But without it we cannot

---

[15] Abram Kardiner, *The Individual and His Society* (New York, 1939), pp. 388–389.

even state the problem of causation. Here is the clear defect of the Freudian interpretation of society. It ignores totality — ignores environment, ignores history, practically ignores anthropology. We are not brought face to face with total situations, or even with total personalities, but only with persistent and scarcely deviating " complexes." It is the complex that is the subject of experience, rather than the person. It is the complex that is fulfilled or frustrated, not the person. The complex is insulated in the whole — or from it. In the Freudian construction the whole, the personality, does not bear upon the situation *in its specific aspect relative to the situation* but only through the agency of the designated complex. But this methodology does not do justice to the integrative and selective self. It is you, as a personality, that act in a situation, but the " you " that is evoked in action is neither the totality of your being nor yet any specific element of that totality — it is the self as focussed on and responsive to the situation, presenting a different *aspect* to every difference of situation. The whole self is involved, but it is not involved as a whole. We must know the situation before we can know how it is involved. The process of interaction, interadaptation, is missing in the Freudian causality. We are offered the parthenogenetic products of the complex, not the products of the relation of the self and the environment. Least of all are we presented with any genuinely social products. Authority, order, the class structure, the group unity, the group sentiment, appear as either specific complexes " writ large " or else as the defences and disguises of these complexes.

In a previous section we pointed out that for purposes of causal explanation we may concentrate attention on the subjective urge, provided the situation is obvious or already given, as when, for example, we are studying differences of response to like conditions. But the Freudians always concentrate attention on the subjective urge, with scant consideration even of the most unlike conditions. One result is that the specific incentive is often postulated *a priori*, rather than inferred from the historical evidences. This attitude allows the school to speculate freely on social origins where evidence is altogether wanting. The following is a characteristic statement: " One may suppose that the founding of families was in some way connected with the period when the need for genital satisfaction, no longer appearing like an occasional guest who turns up suddenly and then vanishes without letting one hear anything of him for long intervals, had settled down with each man like a permanent lodger." [16] All the other considerations and needs, economic, social, and cultural, that accompany sexual desire, blend with it, follow after it, are here without warrant subordinated, even though mating and the forms of family life are found not only over the whole range of humanity but also among the lower animals.

We have chosen the Freudian approach as an illustration of the dangers inherent in the isolation of incentives or subjective urges as causes. We have done so not because it is the chief offender but because we regard it as the most significant of the systems that err in this direction. It deserves very different consideration from that proper to the older instinctivist theories or to such loose deliverances as those of Gobineau, Spengler, or A. Rosenberg, which find in social racial instinct or soul the main determinant of social evolution or national achievement. Since these doctrines are wholly unscientific we need not consider them here. The Freudians on the other hand have developed a novel and powerful instrument of investigation, psychoanalysis, which is not dependent on the extravagances of

[16] S. Freud, *Civilization and Its Discontents* (New York, 1930), p. 65.

imputation indulged in by the founder of the school.[17] The identification of emotional-biological complexes, the discovery of the modes in which they mask themselves or build defensive structures around themselves, the application of such heuristic concepts as " ambivalence," " frustration," " emotional transference " — these and other contributions are notable achievements in the history of a science presenting peculiar difficulties to the explorer, the science of human nature. What gives this school its particular importance is that more than any other it has sought to penetrate beneath the immediate data of consciousness, not to some purely physiological or physico-chemical conditions but to the more inclusive and more persistent characters of the psyche itself. It has sought the deeper motivation behind the specious or superficial one. It has brought out much suggestive evidence of the manner in which mental states such as anxiety, jealousy, and the sense of offended or wounded selfhoods, permeate the whole being and are reflected in behavior that is seemingly motivated by quite other considerations. It has sought to relate the socialized, rationalized deliverances of the self to the psychical system of which they are the partial, interested, and often misleading expressions. Whatever its degree of success in other respects, there can scarcely be any doubt that it has staked a claim to an area rich in scientific promise.

It is easy to understand how in the first flush of exploration the leader and his followers unduly insulated the dynamic factors they pursued, spotlighting them, as it were, and leaving in obscurity the conditions with which they are bound up and ceaselessly interactive. But this phase passes. Motivations, subjective urges of all kinds, are the expression of felt needs. But needs vary with external con-

---

[17] See, for example, Karen Horney, *New Ways in Psychoanalysis*.

ditions, are responsive to them, in large measure depend on them. Where the sun is hot, human beings feel no need for warmth. Where food is plentiful they are not obsessed by the fear of hunger. Where men do not feel oppressed, they do not have the animus of the revolutionary. Where they are not menaced by social restrictions they do not magnify liberty. The expression of need is relative, never absolute. Sexual need finds different expression according to the cultural setting, according to the restrictions and permissions of the mores. Some of the complexes which play so large a role in the Freudian system seem to be absent from the mentality of certain peoples where the conditions do not predispose to them. It is claimed, for example, that the Oedipus complex is lacking among the Marquesans and the Trobriand Islanders.[18] The wide diversities of motivational systems as evidenced by anthropological studies reveal the necessity for conjoining motives with the relevant situations if we are concerned to discover their causal role.

---

[18] See Kardiner, *The Individual and His Society*, p. 246.

CHAPTER EIGHT

CAUSE AS RESPONSIBLE AGENT

I

THE PRINCIPLE OF RESPONSIBILITY

WE CONSIDER next a third mode of singling out a causal factor. This mode is one that raises some fundamental questions regarding the nature of social causation, questions that later on will occupy the center of our stage. It is obvious at the outset that when we impute responsibility to a person for an act or for its consequences we are making him a cause in a quite distinctive sense, in a sense that is not applicable to the other factors within the total causal nexus. We do not think of the responsible agent as merely co-operating with the other factors, as a mere part or aspect of a functional system. He is the author of the act, the engineer of its consequences. He is conceived of as cause in his own right, not as contributor only. For certain purposes he is conceived of as the initiator of the act, a first cause beyond which we do not need to enquire. We do not refer his responsibility back to a prior responsibility, as we refer causation back through an endless regress of causes. Here is a kind of imputation that might seem to contradict the very logic of causation. When we say that a criminal is responsible for a crime or a general for a defeat we are making him a cause in an absolute sense that looks quite incompatible with the ordinary implications of the scientific method.[1]

---

[1] See Paul Fauconnet, *La Responsabilité* (Second Edition, Paris, 1928), Chap. V, § 4.

This conclusion would indeed follow if we identified responsibility with causation, as some legal philosophers have tried to do. But when we say that a man is responsible for an act we usually mean that he is a cause *and* something more or something else. We mean that by virtue of his being a cause he is exposed to an evaluative judgment. Sometimes, of course, we use the word " responsible " in a looser way, applying it to any causal factor. But when we speak of moral, ethical, or legal responsibility we mean that the person, as causal agent, plays a role within a system of values. Responsibility is not what he does, but what he incurs by doing. It is only with respect to this something more or something else that the absolute quality of the imputation of responsibility has any *meaning* — whether it has any *validity* is a different question, which does not belong to this study. There are, in effect, three stages in the imputation of responsibility.

The first is the inclusion of the agent within the universal nexus of causation. He, or what he has done, is included in the sense that had it not been for him, or his doing, the event would not have occurred, the damage or the injury would not have followed. But this is predicable of countless acts to which no responsibility, moral or legal, is attached. Had he not, legally, sold a gun to the man who committed a murder; had he not, innocently, repaired the car in which the murderer, or perhaps his victim, drove to the scene of the crime; had he not, innocently, directed the criminal on the right road, the crime would not have happened. So the next stage is the imputation to the conscious agent of an attitude or disposition, perhaps we might say an *animus*, which makes not the doing only but the doer susceptible to a value judgment. If the vendor had been aware that the man to whom he sold the gun intended to commit a murder he would have already linked the purpose

of the latter to his own. This *animus* binds him in the teleological nexus relative to the act. This condition in turn
makes possible the final step in the imputation of responsibility, the investment of his causal role as conscious agent
with a moral or social significance that is not inherent in the
scientific datum but is derived from another order altogether. Let us consider each of these stages and the relation
between them.

▼

1. Where there is no nexus establishable between a particular person and an offending act, violated obligation, or
any instance of social hurt that evokes the demand for
penalty or sanction, there exists no ground on which to
impute responsibility to him. If someone suffers an injury
and instead of seeking out the author of it " retaliates " on
the first chance person he meets he is deemed a madman.
The issue is not changed by the fact that the ground of responsibility may be supposititious, imaginary, or magical.
Since responsibility is not something inherent in nature but
something subjectively attached to persons, the conditions
of its attachment must vary not only with variant valuations
but also with intellectual discernment. In primitive
thought the sins of the fathers are visited upon the children.
In the vendetta or blood feud revenge is taken on the kin
of the slayer. Among some Australian groups, when a man
has killed a member of a neighboring tribe and is sentenced
to death by an avenging party, his father or his elder
brother may be substituted for him.[2] Such behavior admits
of two alternative explanations, one that the family or kin
constitutes a single agency, the other that the directly
offending kinsman is actually punished by the hurt done
to those who belong to him or with him. The validity of

---

[2] A. W. Howitt, *Native Tribes of South-East Australia* (London, 1904),
p. 327.

either claim need not concern us, since the belief in a nexus, not the actuality of it, constitutes the first step in the imputation of responsibility.[3] In modern law the principle of vicarious liability depends on the doctrine of agency, though it does not ordinarily extend, as in primitive conceptions, to criminal responsibility.[4]

▾

2. When we impute responsibility to a person we are making him " answerable " for something he has done or failed to do. We assume that it was in his power, *had he been so minded*, to have done otherwise than he did. In other words, we attribute to him an *animus* relevant to the situation. In its positive aspect this animus is intention. Its negative aspects are negligence and omission. He neglected to do or omitted to do what, if he had been otherwise minded, he would have done. The responsibility itself is positive in all cases. Even omission is, for the imputation of responsibility, construed as a positive act. It is not merely " not doing " but " doing nothing." An obligation may be an obligation to do, no less than an obligation to refrain from doing. With the technical problems of the attribution of negligence or of omission we are not here concerned. The principle itself is clear. If A sees a burglar breaking into a house and could convey a warning to the police but fails to do so, he violates an obligation, he incurs responsibility. Or if, to take an example from a different category, B enters into a contract and fails to implement it, he violates an obligation, he incurs responsibility. In every such situa-

---

[3] The distinction may perhaps be made that all forms of *social* responsibility, including legal liability, are doubly subjective, since they depend (1) on the accepted nexus, whether it be real or imaginary, and (2) on the valuations associated with it. Whereas *moral* responsibility, as defined below, is subjective only under the second of these conditions.

[4] The term " liability " is used to signify the kind of responsibility that is formulated as a specific obligation, enforceable by legal or quasi-legal procedures.

tion there is, then, the assumption of *animus*. In primitive thought this assumption is directed to inanimate things as well as to the wholly unintended and the totally unforeseeable consequences of behavior. The knife as well as the slayer may be guilty. The man who owned the knife as well as the man who used it may be guilty. The man who through sheer accident injured another may be treated in the same way as the man who intended an injury. But it is because they extend the concept of animus beyond the range admitted by more advanced thought that such primitive peoples also extend more widely the principle of responsibility.

We have already had frequent occasion to dwell on the differential element introduced into the scheme of causality when the person or conscious agent is included within it. In fact, were it not for this differential element there would be no need to devote to social causation any special consideration or analysis. But up to the present we have on the whole been concerned with the *phenomena* of consciousness as they manifest themselves in causal processes. On this ground we distinguished objective, motive, and " design." In the last chapter we examined various aspects of the subjective urge or incentive, as a somewhat more inclusive designation of motive. But a subjective urge implies a subject, a motive a being who moves or is moved. Just as we attribute heat and light to the sun, so we attribute motive and objective to the conscious being. The decisive capacity of the conscious being to act along certain lines we call his *will*; the particular direction of his will we call his *intention*.[5] These are terms that, so used, have no application to inanimate things. They have no meaning outside

---

[5] Such terms as " intention," " purpose," " aim," do not convey the specific distinctions to which we apply our terms, " objective," " motive," and " design." We employ the former only where these distinctions need not be considered.

the teleological nexus. They signify the character of the conscious person as dynamic.

Many difficulties cluster around the concept of volition or will, and we must presently pause to examine the most persistent of the confusions attending it, that concerning the " freedom of the will." But there are certain primary differences between a willed or intended act and all other kinds of activity or happening. In the first place, when an activity is willed, intended, consciously undertaken, the agent has some kind and degree of foreknowledge of what he is about to do and some anticipation of a changed state of affairs as consequent on the doing. To will is to organize, control, predetermine an activity. Whether it is a matter of walking down the street, firing a gun, signing a contract, or what not, there is a prior conception or image, clear or dim, of the doing before it is done and there is some sense of the direction of a change in the situation dependent on the activity. We may distinguish two aspects of the anticipation of the changed situation. Often it is a change of the situation external to the doer that is the heart of intention. We want to make things different, whether it be by sweeping a room or by reforming the world. Sometimes, on the other hand, we are more engrossed in the subjective change, the change expected to accrue to us in the form of some satisfaction, release of tension, gratification of a dominant emotion, and so forth. The two modes of anticipation are, of course, combined and indeed inseparable, but the distinction has analytic importance. Often the satisfaction seems, as it were, a bonus on the attainment of that which we seek or intend; the objective occupies our intention, not some motive behind the seeking of it. The subjective satisfaction redounds from the accomplishment or achievement, and in the same manner it pervades the process of achieving — sometimes the approach to the objective yields a greater bonus than the final attainment of the goal — but in both cases the primary satisfaction comes because we are so minded, so constituted, as to *want* the thing we seek and not merely the satisfaction of having sought and found it. Sometimes, on the other hand, the accruing satisfaction dominates our intention, whether as positive future enjoyment or as the deliverance from some present sense of dissatisfaction, tension, malaise, or actual pain. Then the motive, not the objective, controls our behavior. The objective, or the completed externalized activity, becomes merely or mainly the accessible means whereby to attain a sought-for pleasure, to be rid of a gnawing ache, to accommodate the urge that we call ambition or revenge or resentment or jealousy or love.

The forepicture or anticipation involved in a willed act gives it a distinctive status in the realm of causation. The conscious agent envisages at least two alternatives. One is that which exists, endures, or comes into being if he does not intervene; the other is the situation as changed by his intervention. One is the course of events as it proceeds under the conditions external to his own activity or as persisting apart from some change from his normal procedure; the other is the course of events as deflected by that activity. In this sense the conscious agent may be said to *initiate* change, since his choice determines which of two or more potentialities will become actualized. This quality is enhanced in proportion to the command of means, the possession of power or knowledge. For knowledge directs the act to the focal point of effective operation, utilizing to that extent the causal mechanisms of nature, and power controls the wills of others, and the means of which they dispose, to the service of the owner of power.

Thus the conscious agent, as initiating and directing action, or in other words as willing, may be considered a causal factor in a quite distinctive sense. Not only can he intervene to change the course of events, he can do so in any one of several different ways. In other words the mode of intervention, within certain limits set by the situation and by the means he commands, is open, is not predetermined by anything external to himself. Within these limits he chooses in terms of his interests and attitudes.

▾

3. These interests and attitudes are valuations and belong within a realm of values. This is the ground for the attachment of responsibility. The particular act, the particular choice, is now viewed as it affects a value system. It may, for example, be prejudicial to the value system of the agent himself. He may feel, in the moment of choice, that he is doing that which he ought not to do or he may feel, after the act, that he was moved by prejudice or passion to do that which he ought not to have done. He adjudges his act by his own moral code and condemns it. The sense of " oughtness " or obligation, arising within a scheme of values and applied to the choice between alternatives of action, carries with it the concept of responsibility. The individual " answers for " his choice of alternatives before some seat of judgment. If the obligation depends on his own " conscience," his own personally accepted system of values, then the responsibility is strictly a *moral* one. If the obligation is imposed on the individual by the mores of his group or community, instead of being incorporated in his own morality, then we should perhaps distinguish the responsibility as a *social* one. This too is often called a moral obligation, but there is the difference that the bar of judgment is not that of the individual's own conscience but the operative moral code of his group, and the sanction attached to violation consists in the direct

reaction of the group.[6] This social responsibility is surely the most pervasive and deep-working of all the determinants of behavior and would be felt as the most tyrannical of all compulsions were it not that, through the processes of indoctrination and habituation, so much of it is translated by each individual into his personal morality as well. Over against this form we may set *legal* responsibility, where the obligation is imposed by law and the immediate sanction is applied by a judicial and executive agency established for the purpose.

It appears, then, that the concept of responsibility assumes authorship and *selectively* attaches a valuational quality to it. The weight of responsibility assigned to different acts, as well as the selection of acts as subject to the onus of responsibility, is always changing within every society. Thus responsibility is never a mere corollary from authorship. While the imputation of responsibility rests in the first instance on the presumption of causality, we cannot go further and find any clear relation between the amount of responsibility and the degree of causality. The realm of values has its own, albeit ever varying, principles. The study of causation must proceed on altogether different lines. This conclusion we shall bring out more fully when we examine certain theories of legal responsibility that refuse to admit it. But first we must clear the way by exposing the plausible errors that are associated, by way both of affirmation and of denial, with the doctrine of the " freedom of the will."

---

[6] In a multi-group society, such as characterizes our urban civilizations, the forms of responsibility become, of course, further differentiated. But the obligations imposed under the various forms of responsibility are coincident over a wide range of behavior.

II

THE FREE WILL CONTROVERSY

The age-long barren controversy over the " freedom of the will " belongs to a series of philosophical and theological disputations the very existence of which depends on confusion of thought. In the first place " the will," taken in abstraction from the person, suggests some bodiless independent principle of decision, detached from need and circumstance, detached from thoughts and feelings, detached from flesh and blood, operative in the intellectual void. What genuine issue underlies this ancient logomachy? What is it the freedom of which is vindicated or denied? " The will " is the agent as willing. Nobody doubts that the agent wills. If he wills then he is free to will in the sense that when he wills he is exercising a capacity to will. If, then, the capacity for willing is postulated, what is meant when the question is raised whether the act of willing is " free " or not? To ask if the will is free to will is a perfectly idle question. When we ask about the freedom of the will we must be asking about the freedom of the person who wills. And then the question surely answers itself.

An agent is either free or constrained. He is constrained in so far as some power outside himself prevents him from doing what he wants to do. When a man wills something he acts on the assumption that his objective is attainable. If some one forbids him to pursue this objective or compels him to do something he does not want to do, then he is constrained, he is in this respect no longer free. But he still retains some freedom to act and to will. Even the slave has some freedom, has some alternatives between which to choose. Even if he decides to die rather than to live, or to suffer punishment rather than to obey, he is choosing between available alternatives and is to that extent free. His freedom is grossly limited but is not utterly abolished. The amount of freedom a man has is always a matter of degree. An emperor and a slave have different degrees of freedom. The one can perform many voluntary acts, the other only a few. Freedom exists so long as restraint is not total.

Now those who argue about the freedom of the will must mean something else by " freedom," for they do not deny these common-sense facts. They do not deny that acts are voluntary or willed. They want to get behind this datum of consciousness. The question they are asking is whether voluntary acts are *determined* or *indeterminate*. They reason somewhat as follows: If the decision that characterizes voluntary actions is itself determined, so that given the whole situation it could not be otherwise, then the choice between alternatives is illusory. A man acts as he must act, chooses as he must choose, decides as he must decide. Many who uphold the " freedom of the will " reject determinism, generally on grounds derived from considerations of morality or religion. Those who deny the " freedom of the will " vindicate determinism, generally on the ground that the doctrine of free will is anti-scientific, since it postulates a break in the realm of law, an exception to the universality of the principle of causation.

Confusion befogs the issue on both sides. The possibility of choice between alternatives does not depend on a mysterious principle of indeterminism. Neither is it negated by the acceptance of the principle of causation. " Free " and " unfree " have no meaning outside of conscious life. The laws that all things " obey " are not imposed on them, do not make them less " free," do not " restrain " their nature but merely express it. The controversy over " free will " rests on the logically false antithesis of restraint and freedom. Human actions are not deprived of freedom because they are causally determined. They would not be free if they escaped from the causal nexus. Instead they would be incomprehensible, chaotic, void.

Those who oppose determinism to "free will" are apt to forget that human beings, as individuals and as groups, are themselves dynamic participants within the causal order. They often speak of human behavior in the plausible but misleading language of stimulus-response. This conception implicitly attributes the dynamics of behavior to the environmental factor that is named the stimulus. It is a modern form of the old conception that the mind is a *tabula rasa*, a clean slate, until the "impressions" of the outer world are recorded on it. The response is the result of the stimulus, the stimulus the cause of the response. The environment calls the tune and the organism plays it. Such language does not concede to the conscious agent any initiative, any efficacy. It misapprehends the interactivity of the factors within the causal complex. Moreover, in this interactivity the role of the conscious agent is a distinctive one, to express which the term "response" is wholly inadequate. As we have seen he envisages a total situation, relates it to his own ends, seems to make it, in whatever measure he can, instrumental, so as to turn its intrinsic dynamism into his own means. He adapts the comprehended situation to his desires, in the measure of his comprehension and of his control. Always his comprehension is imperfect, always his control is limited. He is not master nor is he wholly slave, and all his actions are the expression of this fact. His action changes the situation, and the nature of the change depends on what he is and on what the situation is. He, being what he is, modifies the situation accordingly in so far as he is potent to control it. The onus of responsibility lies here, in that it is his particular being that thus meshes with the total external situation. Being what he is, he acts as he does, and so becomes an agent of change within a larger system of change.

Again we have stated only the obvious, but the free will controversy skirts the obvious to seek elsewhere irrelevant ground. Those, for example, who deny " free will " point out that the human agent is the product of heredity conditioned by environment, that his nature is itself not of his own making but the inevitable outcome of his parentage, nurture, and circumstances. There is nothing the matter with the claim, except the conclusions they draw. It is indeed salutary to insist, against certain moralistic and theological prepossessions, that human beings are not abstract wills choosing between right and wrong, that they are not detached from the universal nexus of causation, that the good and the evil we attribute to them can be explained by what they have become in the formative processes that have made them what they are. But again all this has nothing to do with the genuine problem of freedom. The opponents of " free will " say in effect that a man is not responsible for his actions. They start on the trail of an infinite regress in which both freedom and responsibility disappear in the mists. When we speak intelligibly of responsibility we mean the responsibility of the man for his actions. A man is not deemed responsible unless he acts of his own volition within the range of alternatives externally open. If we punish him for his actions we are adding a new factor to the situation and thereby weighting one or more of the alternatives between which he chooses. The method we adopt may be wise or foolish, but in any event we are implying that action is both free and determined. Free—or else punishment could not influence a man's *choice* of alternatives; determined—or else punishment could not become a *determinant* of his choice. There is no logical inconsistency in this position. In virtue of what he is, a man chooses as he does. If he were different he would choose differently. Therein lies his responsibility — and his freedom. If the circumstances were different, he would choose differently. Thus the causal nexus remains unbroken in the realm of will.

The free will controversy would pass into oblivion if the opposing parties admitted that action can be both free and determined. The admission would, as we have shown, be easy if freedom were given its proper antithesis of constraint, and determination were properly construed as the opposite of indetermination. But neither side will make the admission. The one side rejects causal determination in order to vindicate man's freedom, the other side denies freedom on determinist premises. Let us, then, pursue them to their last retreats.

The proponents of free will assert that an agent *could* have chosen differently if he *ought* to have chosen differently; that otherwise the act of choice, the presumption on which morality and responsibility rest, is illusory. To save morality, as they grossly interpret it, they are willing to stand by an assertion to which neither they nor anyone else can give any meaning. For what does it mean to say that precisely the same person in precisely the same circumstances can act, or could have acted, in either of two different ways? Or rather — for otherwise he is in part determined — in any of all conceivable different ways? These doctrinaires would turn the world into a nightmare of eternally capricious contingencies. The " free will " they vindicate is an enigma independent of the character or personality of the agent. The morality they uphold is the legacy of an obscurantist theology. The only evidence they adduce is negative; all the positive evidence is on the other side. They draw support from the fact that we cannot predict with certitude how men will act, no matter how well we know them and their circumstances. Since our knowledge of others is always partial and external, since character is complex and many-sided, since circumstances are intricately divergent, the limitations of prediction are not surprising. But we can predict with some measure of success, and the more we know the person and the situation, the better we can predict. We can tell what considerations are likely to weigh most strongly, what influences are likely to bring a particular response. The routine of common life testifies to this, and no less does the disruption of routine when new forces are brought to bear. All our dealings with our fellow-men are based on some kind of prediction of their actions. And the formidable modern development of one of the most ancient of the arts, the art of propagandism, is wholly due to the skill with which the experts of that art can predict the responses of their fellow-men. We can go further and say that all knowledge is, in so far, predictive, since we know things and persons not as momentary apparitions but through time.

We turn to the last stand of the other side, of those who in the name of determinism deny the existence of freedom, who claim that the choice of alternatives is an illusion of the agent, and that the imputation of responsibility is, in an age of science, an outmoded myth.[7] The argument may be stated briefly as follows: Since behavior, like everything else, is subject to the principle of sufficient cause, we have no choice but to act as we do. We think we are choosing between alternatives but that is only the subjective aspect

---

[7] So, for example, P. C. Knapp, " Criminal Responsibility," *Journal of Criminal Law and Criminology* (1915), Vol. 4, pp. 571–585. See also W. W. Waller, " A Deterministic View of Criminal Responsibility," ibid. (1929), Vol. 20, pp. 80–101, in reply to C. O. Weber, " Pseudo-Science and the Problem of Criminal Responsibility," ibid. (1930), Vol. 19, Part 2.

of the process which eventuates in a predetermined action. We could not choose otherwise if we would. Our action is no more free when it is seemingly spontaneous than when it is externally coerced. It is merely determined in a different way. Once more we observe that the argument cannot be stated without the identification of " determined " with " unfree." The different way is the way of freedom, in the only intelligible sense of that word.[8] The difference is precisely the issue, and the false antithesis arises only because the difference is disregarded or dismissed as insignificant. The original fallacy dogs the argument wherever it is set up. Freedom is a way of being determined that is different from the way of coercion. When an act is voluntary, or free, we are determined, within the limits of the situation, by our own objectives and motives. We may claim that these mental factors lie outside the deterministic system, are merely " epiphenomenal," play no role in the " real " determination of behavior. But this dogmatic assertion, unsupported by and indeed conflicting with empirical evidence, can carry no conviction. It is equivalent to saying that a whole realm of existence lies outside the web of existence. We may distinguish this kind of determination from the determination that characterizes a purely physical system, but we do not thereby dismiss it from actuality.

This kind of determination culminates in an act of choice. Certain alternatives are passed in review by the agent, those that have some weight with him. They are alternatives because it is he who decides which shall be

---

[8] See my article, " The Meaning of Liberty and Its Perversions," in *Freedom: Its Meaning* (New York, 1940), edited by Ruth Nanda Anshen, pp. 278–287. Incidentally, I can draw no distinction between " liberty " and " freedom " where both are used as generic terms, though the opposite claim is made by H. W. Schneider in another article, " The Liberties of Man," in the volume here referred to.

chosen. They are not alternatives in the sense that he is indifferent or equipoised towards them. He may deliberate over them or he may choose without hesitation. The choice means that he has related them to his wants or desires by some kind of preview of their respective consequences. His personality operates in the choice, *determines* the choice. That is his freedom. That is what freedom means. That is all it can intelligibly mean.

In discussing the free will controversy let us observe that the question at issue has been whether the agent is free with respect to his particular acts. It was narrowed to the decision between alternatives, since to that decision the onus of responsibility belongs. But another issue of larger import lurks behind the controversy. The intrusion of this other issue often beclouds the argument and prevents us from seeing the relatively simple nature of the problem. Every particular conscious act involves a decision between alternatives, and every decision is free, in the sense already indicated. What is free, however, is the choice between alternatives, *not the choice of what the alternatives shall be.* The agent assesses the conditions of decision, he does not make them. On every side he is bounded by necessity. External nature sets limits, his organic nature sets limits, his society sets limits. Because the conditions of choice are not his own, he is powerless to attain many things he wants to attain. He is balked in this direction and in that. Because he knows freedom he knows also constraint. He forms his habits in accordance with the limits placed upon his choice. His character becomes canalized along these lines. But because he is not wholly canalized he often seeks to transcend them. In many respects the bounds of choice are widened by the social applications of science, but the struggle is unending. No man, unless his vital energies are low, thinks of himself as being what he would have chosen to be. Here too there is little ground for controversy, but the sense of constraint engendered in this struggle against the bounds of choice has sustained the barren controversy over the question whether choice itself is " free."

The writers on the subject are generally agreed that legal responsibility requires authorship, in the sense already defined, as its ground. Only in so far as a person is the cause of an act can he be, or at least should he be, held legally responsible for it. We may indeed have to stretch our notion of authorship to include all degrees of contributory action and of failure to act, and we must always remember that legal definitions of prohibited behavior are pragmatic and depend on external and readily accessible criteria. But this qualification does not affect the issue that law attaches responsibility to persons on the ground of their having acted or behaved in specified ways. Law does not attach responsibility to all acts, nor even to all " harmful " acts, but only to such acts as presume fault or blame in terms of the prevailing legal scheme of values. " No case or principle can be found, or if found, can be maintained, subjecting an individual to liability for an act done without fault on his part." [9] This statement is relevant to civil as well as to criminal law. It is true that civil liability is addressed to reparation, damages, the redistribution of loss as between individuals. But the law does not, for example, undertake to indemnify a man for loss due to the invasion of his business by a competitor. The loss must be

---

[9] Chief Justice Nelson, in *Harvey v. Dunlop*, Hill and Denio (Lalor), 193, quoted by O. W. Holmes, *The Common Law* (Boston, 1881), p. 94.

attributable to some fault or at least default towards the injured party. To some acts the law attaches a penalty other than that of reparation. Such acts fall under the criminal code. The reason they fall under the criminal code is not necessarily that they are regarded as more heinous or blameworthy, but that for reasons of public policy, or because of the emotions excited in the public by the acts themselves, a different sanction is attached to them. Fault or blame, in the eyes of the law, attaches to civil and criminal offence alike. This fault is not at all equivalent to moral " guilt." It is the fault of doing things that, on whatever ground, the law prohibits. The law is not the conscience of the community, even where it is in accord with the mores. It has a more determinate province. On this point an outstanding legal authority writes: " So far from its being true, as is often assumed, that the condition of a man's heart or conscience ought to be more considered in determining criminal than civil liability, it might almost be said that it is the very opposite of truth." [10]

We again conclude: (1) that legal responsibility implies authorship, (2) that the responsibility attaches to the author by virtue of fault or blameworthiness as determined by the prevailing scheme of legal values. Some writers who accept this conclusion want to go further, still pursuing the attempt to identify responsibility and causation. Since there are many types and degrees of legal responsibility they seek to correlate these with types and degrees of causality. They go down to particular acts, particular obligations, particular offences, and seek to discover some precise proportion between the sanctions attached to them by law and the repercussions of the acts themselves on the system of value. We have seen that responsibility is an imputation of causality — and something more. They

---

[10] O. W. Holmes, op. cit. pp. 49–50.

claim that the something more is the degree in which the act and its consequences — actual or intended — impair the established order of values. They reason as though there were some nicely calculated — or at the least calculable — adjustment between the specific consequences of the specific act, the specific damage or hurt it inflicts on the value system, and the specific treatment it receives at law. They reason as though the legislator or judge somehow determines, by examining the various situations, an equivalence of punishment and crime, based on an equivalence of causality and " guilt." This position is taken, for example, by the German school of von Buri.[11] According to the tenets of this school responsibility is relative to the actual accomplishment, the actual consequences of an intended act. Others modify the formula, while remaining within the orbit of the same general assumption. Some claim that the degree of responsibility is measured, not by the actual achievement, but by the consequences that the agent, as a rational being, could foresee or ought to have foreseen as being " objectively possible."

We need not pursue the endless disputations and ratiocinations concerning the precise relation of causal efficacy and criminal responsibility.[12] For we must deny the assumption on which they alike rest. Responsibility cannot be regarded as a kind or degree of causality, and therefore cannot be proportioned to the amount of doing or of suffering, of intending or of accomplishing. The amount of damage or of achievement that can be objectively measured is a quite different thing from the consequent subjective appraisal of the doer, and that in turn is a different thing from the measure of punishment, or of reward, meted out

---

[11] M. von Buri, *Die Causalität und ihre strafrechtlichen Beziehungen*, Stuttgart, 1885.

[12] The volumes of *Der Gerichtssaal*, through the last quarter of the nineteenth century, contain numerous articles on the subject.

to him. If the author of an act, in the eyes of those em-
powered to judge him, offends against their value-system
he is deemed legally responsible on that account. But
various considerations, also emanating from the value
scheme, deflect the treatment accorded him from the strict
reckoning of the impairment of value. He is a member of
a community. How he is treated will affect his relation to
other members, his service to the community, his own
future behavior, the future behavior of others. The range
of value considerations cannot be confined within the
limits of the doer and the deed. Historically, the treatment
of crime has moved along a strange diagonal of conflicting
considerations, one set of which was addressed to the recom-
pense proper to the deed, while the other contemplated
the value effects, not of the deed, but of the treatment to
be administered to the doer. Thus causality is one thing,
responsibility another, and the penalization of the responsible party yet a third.

In fact, the attempt to make punishment proportionate
to the evil or hurt committed presumes a mechanical and
superstitious equivalence that confounds the very concept
of responsibility. It substitutes the concept of retaliation,
a sort of negative reparation, equating evil done with evil
suffered, with little regard for the consequences to the total
scheme of values. There is some plausibility in the contention that, with respect to torts and breaches of contract,
the object of the law is to give the injured party a reparation equivalent to the loss he has suffered. But we have
seen that the law redistributes loss between individuals
only on the ground that one or other party is at fault or
blameworthy, so that even in cases of contract it frequently
admits other considerations than those proper to actuarial
science. When, on the other hand, the formulas of account-
ing are applied to crime, as in certain stages of primitive

criminal procedure, the meaning of responsibility is ignored. The *lex talionis*, eye for eye and tooth for tooth, cannot distinguish between accident and intent. The Anglo-Saxon *wergild*, which evaluated on the basis of injury done and set a price on each offence, was possible only because considerations of legal ends were omitted. As Saleilles put it, " The system of the *wergild* may be described as one that takes no account of responsibility."[13] In various other systems the concept of requital, of reparation proportioned to the injury committed, held a prominent place. The notions of retribution, of revenge, of expiation, of vengeance, human or divine, controlled — and still in some measure control — the theory and the practice of punishment. But while they express the spontaneous reactions of men towards those who offend them they obscure the notion of responsibility. When punishment is a " repaying " of the crime, at most the deed, not the doer, is viewed in the light of social or legal valuations. It is still in effect the public settlement of a private affair, the only public concern being that it should be duly settled. But the law and the judge are the guardians of public policy. Punishment no less than crime must then be envisaged from this point of view, and neither can be adjudicated by looking merely at the objective results of the criminal act.

In the history of criminal law the recognition of the subjective character of responsibility, and therefore of criminality, gradually emerged, and the principle of objective equivalence between crime and punishment correspondingly ceased to dominate the code.[14] At length various schools of criminology, notably the Italian, began

---

[13] Raymond Saleilles, *The Individualization of Punishment* (Boston, 1911), translated by R. S. Jastrow, p. 31.

[14] See, for example, Saleilles, op. cit. Chap. II: A. Levi, *La Société et l'Ordre juridique* (Paris, 1911), Chap. I.

to focus attention not on the crime but on the personality of the criminal. At a much earlier stage theological and philosophical doctrines of free will were invoked to explain the nature of criminality and to justify punishment. What was punishable was the moral guilt of the wrong-doer. This principle was expressed in the concept of the *mens rea*, the guilty state of mind, the law-violating attitude, the presence of which makes a hurtful act also a crime.[15] This concept served a useful purpose in so far as it promoted the admission of distinctions of criminality for the same objective act and encouraged some degree of individualization in the treatment of the offender. But no clear and specific meaning was conveyed by the term. The idea of the equation of punishment and authorship, though now limited to that of the *mens rea*, still held its vogue. Men argued, for instance, that the accessory is equally responsible, or not equally responsible, with the principal author; that he is subject to the same penalty, or not thus subject — *on the ground* that he is equally, or not equally, the cause of the act. They treated mere intention as a lesser degree of accomplishment, in order to justify a lesser amount of punishment. They tried to solve by considerations relating to causality a thousand problems that cannot logically be solved in that way. They ran into numerous contradictions and confusions. The only way to avoid these, as we have been suggesting, is to take the position: (1) that authorship (which can include acts of omission as well as acts of commission) is the primary condition rendering a person subject to legal responsibility; (2) that the consequent legal responsibility is assessed in accordance with a complex legal scheme of values and cannot be made porportionate to the objective consequences of the act; (3) that the conse-

---

[15] F. B. Sayre, " Mens Rea," *Harvard Law Review* (April, 1932), Vol. 45, pp. 974–1026; D. A. Stroud, *Mens Rea*, London, 1914.

quent legal punishment need not be, and because of various value considerations cannot strictly be, proportionate to the degree of responsibility attaching to the offender.

Let us take one or two simple cases. There is a " Stop " sign at the intersection of a local road with a main highway. A driver fails to stop, is summoned by a traffic policeman, and pays a small fine in court. Another driver fails to stop and a collision occurs, involving loss of life. The punishment of the second driver is much more severe, and on the whole public opinion supports the judicial discrimination, even though both drivers committed the same offence and though the first may have exercised no more vigilance than the second. Again, a man who attempts murder and fails is not punished as severely as a man who succeeds in the attempt, though no distinction can be drawn with respect to culpability. The obligation may be the same in two cases, but the penalty is different. At first blush it might seem as though the differentiation were simply relative to the degree of accomplishment. But the legal scheme of values must include other considerations, such as the effect of severity of punishment on the ability to secure convictions, the attitude of the public towards the offence, the amount of punishment necessary in different cases to be deterrent or to secure the protection of the public, the previous history of the offender, and so forth. In the light of these considerations it cannot assess an offence solely in terms of accomplishment nor yet solely in terms of the legal responsibility of the offender. Still less can it make the *moral* gravity of the offence the measure of the penalty. A moral code may proclaim that it is equally wrong to commit adultery and to commit adultery " in the heart." But law, with its external standards, must distinguish between intention and performance. The value scheme of law is not identical with the value scheme of morals.

Indeed it may be claimed that a pretension to identify the two has been a particular weakness of the American legal system. Many moral issues cannot, and many others should not, be taken cognisance of by law.[16] Many legal issues are properly weighted by other considerations than that of the moral enormity attaching to the offence. The ends of law are more precise and circumscribed than those of any moral code. The distinctions it makes are or should be relevant to these ends.[17]

We conclude that considerations of causality are directly pertinent only at one stage of the criminal process, the preliminary stage of imputation, at which the agent is rendered liable to penal sanction. From that point on, considerations of causality have no specific merit. Enquiry into the complications of the causal nexus of criminal behavior follows one road; the legal assessment of the sanction of crime and of the treatment of the offender follows a different road that does not run parallel to the first. If we follow the first road, we seek to discover the causes of specific criminal behavior as a scientist seeks to discover the causes of a *specific* disease.[18] In doing so we investigate the mental and organic characteristics of individuals who commit these crimes, of the groups in which they are prevalent, relating these characteristics to environmental factors and to the cultural milieu. We do not stop with the fact of responsibility — we are no longer particularly concerned with it, any more than a physician is concerned with the " responsibility " of a patient for a disease. There is a scientific criminology that follows this road, and it tends to

---

[16] See the writer's book, *The Modern State* (Oxford, 1926), Chap. V.

[17] For an examination of the grounds of one important set of legal distinctions see Herbert Wechsler and Jerome Michael, " A Rationale of the Law of Homicide," *Columbia Law Review* (May, December, 1937), Vol. 37, pp. 701–716, 1261–1325.

[18] Cf. Fauconnet, *La Responsabilité*, pp. 278–281.

dismiss altogether the questions of guilt and punishment, as outside the realm of science.[19] The result of such investigations may be of value in suggesting methods for the prevention of crime, not so much by any immediate treatment of the offender as by measures that are applicable to the social environment, measures of economic reform, of therapeusis, of education. But the judge, in his reaction to the offender now before him for sentence, is concerned not directly with the complicated processes of criminal causation but with the preservation of a challenged value-system. It has been pointed out, for example, that the courts are apt to look askance at psychiatrists because "from the psychiatrist's point of view the question is not one of abolishing responsibility but of ignoring it, and of planning treatment to fit the offender rather than his offence." [20] The value scheme envelops the law and the court. These may indeed receive enlightenment from scientific criminology, but even if that science were vastly more advanced than it is, its conclusions would not solve the problems that the legislator and the judge must somehow face. The science of the criminologist may save them from bad errors of judgment — for example, from wrong conceptions as to the effect of the sentences they impose — but it can never be a substitute for the precarious art that the guardians of responsibility must continue to practise.

---

[19] This approach is found, for example, in the Italian school of Lombroso, Ferri, and Sighele.

[20] Cited by Wechsler and Michael, loc. cit. p. 757, from Dr. H. Douglas Singer, in *Illinois Crime Survey* (1929), p. 743.

CHAPTER NINE

FORMULA OF CAUSAL INVESTIGATION

I

THE UNIVERSAL FORMULA

FROM a variety of angles we have seen that the task of causal investigation can be defined as follows: Having first made our why specific, we identify the situation or type of situation in which the phenomenon occurs, as against a comparable situation or type of situation from which it is absent, and engage ourselves to discover how the phenomenon is related to the differential organization of the situation containing it. If x is the specific difference and it is found within the situation or conjuncture C we proceed to the consideration of C_1, the comparable situation or conjuncture lacking x. Sometimes we arrive at two closely comparable situations of this type. If, for example, we find that when the " islands of Langerhans " are intact in the liver, the disease diabetes x is absent but when they are impaired or atrophied the disease is present we have advanced a long way towards the etiology of x. Often, however, and particularly with respect to social phenomena, we cannot establish such clean-cut comparisons. But in all cases alike our question becomes: What is the causal series associated with x in the conjuncture C, such as does not obtain in the conjuncture C_1, where x is absent? When we enquire into effect instead of cause our question takes the alternative form: What causal series emerge or are initiated in the conjuncture C_1 when the conjuncture C is changed to C_1 with the introduction of the phenomenon x? In passing we may note that in the simpler enquiry into effect our comparable situations are usually two successive stages of the same system or order, the latter stage being distinguished by the manifest presence of a new phenomenon not revealed in the former. In all causal investigation we posit a larger or inclusive order, a single frame of reference, including both C and C_1. Every problem of causation is a challenge concerning the specific orderly way of things — concerning the routes they follow in their various associations with one another, the modes in which events or phenomena contingent to a system react upon it, the processes the system itself undergoes by virtue of the changing inter-relationships of its elements, the differences occurring in a system through the introduction of a " precipitant," and so forth.

The preliminary investigation into causes is addressed to the establishment of a specific difference x and thence to the more precise determination of the most closely comparable C and C_1 that we are able to discover. Where it is possible to proceed experimentally, our final C_n and C_{n+1} may represent a stage of scientific refinement far advanced beyond our initial C and C_1. Where experiment is precluded or where situations are highly complex, variant, and non-repetitive, we may have to rest content with the original C and C_1, our effort being directed the more to the clearest possible delimitation of the difference x. The latter type of investigation, characteristic of the social sciences, we have illustrated in Chapter Six. The former type is more easily illustrated from the procedure of the physical and the biological sciences. Whichever type concerns us, the main problem is the discovery of the particular causal series, within the larger conjuncture in which it occurs, to which our x belongs.

Let us take an illustration from the science of medicine. Until recently deep-sea divers nearly always fell victims to a very painful and dangerous disease known as " the bends." The general problem was: Why do deep-sea divers suffer from a disease that would not have affected them had they pursued other occupations? But in so stating the question we have not yet defined our comparable situations so that the difference between them is specifically relevant to the specific effect. Men who go down to similar depths in mines are not subject to the disease. On the other hand men who work in compressed air at or near the earth's surface, for example in the caissons employed in the construction of tunnels under rivers, are also affected. So our problem becomes: Why do men who work in compressed air get " the bends," whereas those who do not work in compressed air are not susceptible to the disease? But we have not yet fully defined our x-containing C.

It appears that divers and caisson-workers do not experience the malady while they are working in compressed air but only after they return to normal pressures. So our problem becomes: What is the causal series relating " the bends " to the process of emerging from compressed air after being subjected to it for some time? Various experiments showed that the onset of " the bends " followed an abrupt transition to normal atmospheric conditions. At last we have our definitive C and C_1, and we can proceed to the investigation of the causal series associated with x. The difference we have been in quest of is the peculiar physical condition of men who have breathed compressed air for some time and thereafter have quickly returned to normal air pressure. When we have gone thus far it is relatively easy to determine the processes and stages of decompression requisite under various conditions to prevent the occurrence of the disease. These experiments were carried out by a succession of scientific investigators.[1] The discovery of preventive measures was not in itself a solution of the causal problem but only a step towards it. On the other hand the discovery of these measures was itself, as not infrequently happens, accelerated by an hypothesis of causation. Investigation and hypothesis thus co-operated to confirm the finally established theory that the specific causal series associated with " the bends " was the absorption by the body of air under high pressure, the release of the oxygen and the retention of the nitrogen under quick decompression, and the consequent formation of nitrogen bubbles in the blood stream, inducing the physiological processes manifested as " the bends."

What, then, does it mean when we impute " the bends " to nitrogen bubbles in the blood stream? It is not the complete solution of the question why. The complete solution of the simplest why would involve the complete understanding of the universe. But the answer is sufficient for all practical purposes and for some scientific ones. It satisfies the biological investigator because now the phenomena of the disease have been brought within a causal scheme already familiar to him. That bubbles of gas in the blood will cause this particular type of organic disturbance is in accord with what he already knows.

We may observe that instead of attributing the effect to the totality of the situation in which it occurs, as certain philosophers prescribe, we must, on the contrary, make our main objective the discovery of that causal series within the total conjuncture which is most immediately associated with the effect. Within the total interdependence of every conjuncture, at whatever level of inclusiveness we take it, there are more specific and limited interdependences, mul-

---

[1] See J. S. Haldane and J. G. Priestley, *Respiration* (Oxford, 1935), pp. 333 ff.

titudinous linkages of elements in virtue of their distinctive attributes or properties. There are various ways in which every item is involved in the smaller and larger systems that contain it. We seek among these ways according to the particular scientific interest that controls our investigation. For example, we find that in the complex of rural poverty characteristic of some southern portions of the United States there is present the disease called pellagra. It scarcely affects the well-to-do or the urban dwellers, though it is occasionally found in the cities. In other countries where pellagra occurs it is also a characteristically rural disease associated with poverty. Scientific investigation is made, inspired by the desire to control the disease. Experiments show that within the rural poverty complex there is a more direct nexus of pellagra and dietary deficiency. Improvement of the diet by the addition of fresh meat and milk proves to be a preventive of the disease. But we have not reached our final C and C_1, differentiating the pellagra-manifesting situation from that in which pellagra is absent. For although meat and milk are proteins, the addition of pure protein to the diet does not curb the disease. The discovery leads on to the isolation of a specific vitamin, the deficiency of which is the crucial factor in the causation of pellagra.[2] Now we have reached a causal series to which our x, the disease in question, immediately belongs. It does not follow that we reject any relation between pellagra and the embracing complex, rural poverty. But now our problem is to discover why within that complex the mode of living and other conditions should be associated with a comparative lack of the amount of the vitamin B factor needed under these conditions to prevent pellagra. The requisite amount no doubt varies with the conditions. Earlier investigations had shown that the

---

[2] Seale Harris, *Clinical Pellagra* (St. Louis, 1941), pp. 126 ff.

incidence of pellagra is subject to seasonal variations, that it occurs particularly in the productive stage of life, that females are more subject to it than males, and so forth.[3] These evidences point again to the fact that the answer to any why poses another why, and beyond that endlessly another. The specific discovery of Goldberger and his associates becomes the established ground from which investigators set out to attack further problems of causal connection within that area of knowledge.

II

THE SPECIAL CASE OF THE SOCIAL SCIENCES

The examples we have offered thus far have been of causal series that repeat themselves in many separable instances, that are on this and other counts relatively isolable within the larger configurations containing them, and that therefore are amenable to experimental controls. The primary function of experiment is to vary the x-manifesting C, by the removal, modification, or addition of factors, until the particular nexus relating x to its immediate causal context has been located. Obviously this can be done only where the x-determining series recurs over and over again, and where the later instances are essentially indifferent to the time interval between them and the earlier instances. These conditions are available in many areas of physico-chemical and biological investigation; they are much less available to the social investigator. For one thing, the phenomena in which the social scientist is interested are presented in a particular historical setting, whether of the past or of the present. The method of experiment cannot be freely applied where we are dealing with the events and processes that constitute the unreturning stream of history. Historical events are unique configurations that do not

---

[3] Op. cit. Chap. X.

recur as such; historical processes are endlessly variant, even though we may trace certain broad resemblances between them. The resemblances provide no more than analogy, an unsafe ground for causal inference. One revolution follows another, one nation after another rises to power and declines. But we cannot with scientific assurance eliminate the differences between pre-revolutionary situations so as to establish one specific causal series culminating in revolution. Nor is revolution itself a phenomenon as clearly defined as, say, an eclipse or a disease. Empires rise and fall, but the empire of Genghis Khan is so different from the empire of ancient Rome, and the empire of Rome so different from the empire of Britain, that the search for a single explanation is greatly embarrassed or altogether baffled.[4] If, consequently, we are driven to seek a special explanation of *each* historical event or process, concerning both its causes and its consequences, the method of experiment is precluded. Whatever comparable situations we may find, we cannot control them. Each situation passes, merges in a new one. It does not abide for our renewed questioning. The empire of the Caesars does not return, so that we may examine in its presence the conditions of its rise and fall. This difficulty is not confined to the social sciences. The pleistocene period does not recur any more than does the empire of Rome. In the evolutionary record

" The Moving Finger writes; and, having writ,
  Moves on."

---

[4] Sometimes the attempt is made. Thus F. J. Teggart attempts to prove that throughout the period 588 B.C. to 107 A.D. every barbarian uprising in Europe followed the outbreak of war either on the eastern frontiers of the Roman Empire or in the "Western Regions" of the Chinese, and he concludes that during the whole period " the correspondence of wars in the East and invasions in the West was due to *interruptions of trade*" (*Rome and China: A Study of Correlations in Historical Events*, Berkeley, California, 1939). The causal inference, even if we accept the adequacy of the evidences cited by Teggart, remains open to question.

The peculiar embarrassment of the social sciences does not lie here, but in the further difficulty that its present and immediately observable data are also so repugnant to scientific control. For the most part we cannot experimentally add factors to the social conjuncture or remove them at will. At best, with few exceptions, such additions or subtractions as we can make are directed to the total changing situation, not to some distinctive causal series within it. A law is passed or repealed. We change some of the regulations of an organization, some of the features of an institution. The change has its repercussions over the whole situation, merging with the forces of change within it. Nowhere are we presented with the clearly demarcated C, containing the causal series associated with x, over against an equally demarcated C_1, from which that series is absent.

Where we cannot experiment we still follow the same process of analysis, but now one of our alternative situations, C and C_1, usually remains hypothetical, a mental construct. We ask: What *would* have happened if the Persians had won the battle of Marathon? The alternative situation is not presented, cannot be reproduced, in the world of reality. We ask: How *would* the situation have developed if this law had not been passed? Or we ask: What did happen because x intervened which but for its intervention *would not* have happened? Sometimes the answer, or at least a partial answer, is relatively easy, when the intruding event disturbs a familiar and well-established routine. At other times it must be contingent and precarious. But in all such cases, in fact in the great majority of investigations into social causation, we must use what evidence we can muster, with whatever skill or comprehension we possess, to construct imaginatively an alternative situation that is never objectively given.[5] Experiment is a way of avoiding the resort to imaginative reconstruction: that way is often blocked in social investigation.

This difficulty is closely associated with another. Our general formula requires for its full application the availability of two comparable situations in one of which the phenomenon under investigation x is present while it is absent from the other. But in the study of social trends and processes we are rarely, if ever, presented with so clean-cut a distinction between situations. What we typically find is that certain attitudes, opinions, or beliefs become more dominant or more recessive, or that certain institutional forms develop and are elaborated while others play a more limited role than before or even become atrophied, or that there is a recombination of structures and a redistribution of functions so as to constitute a relatively new social situation, or that there is a greater or less volume or frequency of certain activities as registered in our statistical facts. Such phenomena are of course not peculiar to the social sciences — we find them notably in the biological sphere. But wherever we find them — and it can be said at least that they form the major subjects of causal enquiry in the social sciences — they compel a different procedure in the application of the universal formula. The difference or change we are investigating is generally one of degree. Sometimes we have a simple quantitative difference. We find, for example, that more of the well-to-do than of the poor vote for the conservative candidate. Or we find that more country-dwellers than city-dwellers vote republican. Or we find that more unmarried men than married men are convicted of crimes. But because some married men are

---

[5] On this point compare Max Weber's schema of causal imputation. See Talcott Parsons, *Theory of Social Action*, pp. 628 ff.

convicted of crimes, because some poor men are conservative, because some city-dwellers vote republican, we cannot seek the causal nexus simply in the difference constituted by the marital condition or by the possession of
wealth or by residence in an urban environment.

We still apply the universal formula, but since the difference is relative we cannot assume that the answer to our
why is to be found inside one of our comparable situations
and outside of the other. The answer may not lie at all in
the dynamic character of, or the dynamic response to, the
factors immediately associated with our x (say more conservatism, or more republicanism, or a greater ratio of
crime). For example, it may not be the direct impact of
rural life that explains the tendency to vote republican. A
generation ago we might have been tempted to conclude
that the lower birth-rate of the well-to-do was a function
of economic status — unless we took warning from the fact
that the differential birth-rate had itself arisen in rather
recent times. To-day, in some places, the birth-rate of the
class of skilled workers is as low as, or even lower than, that
of the well-to-do. Clearly, then, we must look for the solution in another direction. Our specific why becomes: Why
did the well-to-do exhibit the tendency to a lower birth-
rate at an earlier historical stage than did the skilled
workers? We are dealing with a movement that spreads
from group to group, from social class to social class. Why
were the well-to-do exposed to it earlier — or more fully —
than the classes of manual workers? Now factors such as
wealth take on a new character in the causal quest. Similarly factors such as urban or rural residence may appear
as involving a greater exposure to or a greater shelter from
certain cultural influences that at a particular time arise
within a large area of social life. The issue is complicated
by the double role some of these factors play, as directly

promoting change and as permitting exposure to the influences that make for change. But unless we include the second consideration we may totally misapprehend our problem; we shall not understand the growth and decline of social movements.

Suppose, to take another example, that we are asking the difficult question why some marriages are more " successful " than others, that we have a definite and intelligible criterion of " success," and that we confine our quest to reasonably comparable groups. We may again go wrong if we assume that the factors we find associated, solely or to a greater extent, with the " successful " marriages are the explanation of their " success." For one thing, these factors may themselves be mainly indications or expressions of the fact that the marriages are " successful." For another, they may be, as in the previous illustration, conditions that in different degrees, and in different combinations, shelter the " successful " marriages for a time from the influences that make some other marriages less " successful." Hence, to weight these factors as contributing this much or that much to a total effect called " success " would be, as we have already pointed out, an unjustifiably mechanical procedure. Let us take as a last example the relation between marital status and a low crime ratio. The difference to be explained, x, is a lesser amount of criminality, and the comparable situations are those of two groups within the same social milieu, our C and C_1. Here it might seem that since the presence or absence of marital status is the sole criterion by means of which our two groups are distinguished the explanation of our phenomenon is to be found in a particular change of attitude towards crime that marriage with its attendant conditions and responsibilities induces. But all we are given is that marital status and crime are negatively related. What we have to discover is what distinguishes, in such a way as to be relevant to our phenomenon, the married from the unmarried group. Since marriage is not an accident, we may discover characteristics of temperament, of economic condition, of mental or physical make-up, and so forth, that exist prior to marriage, that prompt to or dissuade from marriage, and that therefore distinguish, no less than the marital status itself, the married generally from the unmarried. Such distinctions must also be explored before we can solve our problem.

From these examples it is sufficiently clear that when we are seeking the causal explanation of a difference of degree, when our phenomenon is the presence of a particular attribute to a greater or to a lesser extent in one situation as compared with another, our investigation is apt to run into special difficulties. We must still follow the universal formula, but the modes of its application must be different and our results are often less final. These difficulties we shall seek to face at a later stage. We shall see that they reinforce our argument for the greater need, in the study of social causation, for the resort to imaginative reconstruction, though this must be disciplined and safeguarded by the rigorous use of the more secure methods of scientific enquiry.

The resort to reconstruction plays a particular role in social investigation. In spite of all its perils it is both peculiarly necessary and peculiarly congenial for the interpretation of the teleological aspects of social phenomena. Here again we touch on the distinctive properties of the subject-matter of the social sciences. There is a school of social scientists which seems reluctant to admit that there are significant differences of subject-matter characteristic of the social sciences. There are some, again, who, while recognizing these differences, reject the conclusion that they involve also significant differences of approach and methodology. Those who hold such opinions regard the fact that the social sciences are so lacking in exact quantitative formulations as due solely to their backwardness, a state of things they believe can be overcome when we have learned to apply the methods and techniques of the physical sciences. But the same difference of subject-matter that makes it hard for us to find here causal relationships universally valid and susceptible of precise formulation offers us some compensation in another kind. As human beings we are immersed in the strivings, purposes, and goals that constitute the peculiar dynamic of this area of reality. On however small a scale, we have transcended the externality of things — elsewhere we have merely discovered it. The chain of physical causation does not need mind except for its discovery. The chain of social causation needs mind for its existence. What importance we attach to this difference depends on our respective philosophies. But the difference remains, whatever these philosophies may be. There is that which characterizes all reality and there is that which is revealed only in some areas of it. There are therefore principles and methods common to all science, including the principle of causal investigation we have just been discussing, and there are principles and methods relevant only to distinctive aspects, simply because they have proved applicable to the investigation of these aspects. There is no point in seeking to apply to social systems the causal formula of classical mechanics, to the effect that if you know the state of a system at any instant you can calculate mathematically, in terms of a system of co-ordinates, the state of that system at any other time. We simply cannot use such a formula. It fits into another frame of reference. On the other hand we have the advantage that some of the factors operative in social causation are *understandable as causes*, are validated as causal by our own experience. This provides us a frame of reference that the physical sciences cannot use. We must therefore cultivate our own garden. We must use the advantages we possess and not merely regret the advantages we lack.

We must, so far as possible, supplement our very limited power of experimentation by the more precarious but nevertheless, as we shall seek to show, highly valuable processes of imaginative reconstruction. In our everyday relations we apply it incessantly in the assessment of the behavior of our fellows. In fact, we could scarcely live any kind of human existence, we certainly could not enter into effective relations with others, unless we reconstructed, from overt but often subtle evidences, the hidden system of thoughts, attitudes, desires, motivations, that lie behind them. Constantly, with friend or foe, with neighbor and with stranger, we strive to envisage a meaningful design that not only never is but by its very nature cannot be presented in the world of the senses. It is an operation as familiar to us as that of construing the linguistic symbols by means of which men partly reveal and partly conceal their thoughts. All communication is indirect or semantic, through the medium of symbols. Our experience, according to its degree or kind, enables us to interpret these symbols. In this process there is always an element of imaginative reconstruction. The situation we envisage is never given as such. The same process is involved in the quest of social causation. Some event, a war, the death of a leader, a new law, a scandal, a big financial failure, a flood or a drought, disturbs the social equilibrium. What changes do we impute to it? We study the changed situation. Which of its changes are men's responses to the precipitant event? How have their responses been changed by it? How *would* the situation have developed had it not been for the event? What differences, say, did the Civil

War make to the social structure of the United States, differences that would not have emerged had the dispute between the Northern and the Southern states been settled without that war? Here is an example of the more difficult and never fully answerable question that meets the student of the social sciences. The best answer we can reach demands not only an interpretation of the responses of different groups, as revealed by various signs, to the event itself but also a reconstruction, derived from the indications of their objectives and motivations, of what their behavior *would* have been had the event not happened. Here our actual C, scarcely less than our hypothetical C_1, is a construction requiring all our resources of insight as well as of knowledge. The full challenge of social causation is now before us.

PART FOUR

INTERPRETATION

CHAPTER TEN

THE REALM OF CONSCIOUS BEING

I

THE DYNAMIC REALMS

THE PHYSICIST investigates the universal realm that is bound in the nexus of invariant law. Here and there within it is manifested organic life, but with that more limited realm he is not concerned. Here and there within it the phenomena of conscious life emerge, but with these also he is not concerned. He can investigate his own phenomena without consideration of these other phenomena — if you grant his primary hypothesis that he as conscious being can know a reality that exists independently of the knowing. Nor is he as physicist concerned with human culture or with social relationships. On the contrary, he seeks to assure himself that no influences emanating from these conditions intrude to distort his impartial perception of the physical realm. All the phenomena he studies belong to one great order of being. When he pursues any x to its specific causal nexus he remains throughout within that order. He finds the same laws revealed in the electron and in the galaxy. His highest aspiration is to embrace all the phenomena of this order within one close-knit theoretical scheme, and in a relatively short time he has achieved a remarkable advance towards that goal.

The social scientist is in all these respects at the farthest remove from the physicist. His proper phenomena are de-

pendent on or partake the nature of all the other orders of
being. They do not exist apart from the physico-chemical
realm. They are bound up with the conditions of organic
life. They are found only as expressions of conscious being.
They are intimately associated with cultural patterns and
with the devices, instruments, and skills that all the sciences
provide. Consequently, when the social scientist pursues
his x to its specific causal nexus, he is embarrassed by the
discovery that his causal factors belong to all the diverse
orders of being. He has vainly sought to liberate himself
from this problem by conferring dominance or priority on
one of the orders, by proclaiming some key cause. If, for
example, an empire falls, he tells us that the decisive cause
was political, say the failure of Rome to provide a form of
unity and allegiance appropriate to an empire instead of
to a city-state; *or* that it was economic, say the exactions
of tax farmers or the struggle of economic classes; *or* that
it was technological, say the cumulative effect of a slave
basis of production; *or* that it was cultural, say the loss of
moral standards or of an ancient religious faith; *or* that it
was biological, say the deterioration of stock produced by
warfare or by the failure of the culture-bearing groups to
reproduce themselves; *or* that it was physical, say the impoverishment of the soil whether due to natural changes
or to the acts of men. But we need not continue the list,
for each factor alleged to be dominant is inextricably
bound up with others, so that our problem remains un-
solved. Always we are confronted with diverse factors that
belong to different dynamic orders and are incompa-
rable and scientifically intractable as such. For how shall
we assess, one with the other, the decline of a religion
and the impoverishment of the soil, the centralization
of political power and the decline of the birth-rate? How
shall we discover a specific causal nexus when so many
utterly disparate factors are attendant on our phenom-

enon x? If we merely list our various factors we are at the mercy of an arbitrary selection and we never attain any systematic interpretation or any assurance of scientific advance.

Our first constructive task would, then, appear to be the classification of these diverse conditions or factors under dynamic realms, that is, under categories representing the various major types of causal nexus. In our opening chapter we gave reasons for distinguishing the physico-chemical nexus, the biological nexus, the psychological nexus, and the social nexus. These provide the basis of our classification of dynamic realms. There is first the universal physical realm, which reigns everywhere, whether life is present or absent. There is next the realm of organic being, characterized by the life principle whether or not it reveals itself in conscious or teleological activity. Beyond these lies the emergent realm, in which the psychological nexus obtains. We distinguished three varieties or aspects of the psychological nexus, exhibiting respectively objective, motivation, and design. These three are alike modes of teleological activity. In this form of activity we introduce for the first time the relation of means and ends, the emergence into the realm of consciousness of the relation of organs and functions. As this form of activity becomes socially articulated, two interdependent systems or orders gradually become distinct, the system of apparatus or means and the system of values or ends. These we designate respectively the technological order and the cultural order. The social order itself is the scheme of relationships between social beings. Within it the cultural and technological orders are developed, though it is in turn dependent on these orders. In the social order the further type of nexus we call specifically the social nexus for the first time appears.

We begin, then, with the three great dynamic realms, distinguished as follows:

THE PHYSICAL REALM

Including the fundamental phenomena of matter and energy, as revealed in light, heat, sound, electricity, magnetism, and physical mechanics; together with the phenomena of the transformations and differentiations of material substances, whether occurring apart from or in association with organic life (inorganic and organic chemistry)

THE REALM OF ORGANIC BEING

Including the phenomena of life in all its forms and aspects, whether as vegetative or as animal life

---

THE REALM OF CONSCIOUS BEING

Including the phenomena we distinguish as psychical or mental

---

The three dynamic realms together constitute, so far as we can observe it, the all-embracing reign of nature. Each has its distinctive coherence, its own dynamic quality. Under certain conditions the realm of organic being manifests itself within the more inclusive physical realm. Under certain conditions the realm of conscious being manifests itself within the more inclusive realm of organic being. There is thus a unilateral dependence of the realm of conscious being on the other two.

Within this last realm we have distinguished three orders, as follows:

THE CULTURAL ORDER

Comprising the patterns, interadjustments, and trends of operative valuations and goals, as revealed in the mores, the folkways, the traditions, the faiths, the fine arts, the philosophies, the play-activities, and generally the modes of living of social groups[1]

THE TECHNOLOGICAL ORDER

Comprising the patterns, interadjustments, and trends of the multiplicity of devices, instruments, and technical skills applied to the achievement of human valuations and goals, as revealed in the industrial arts, the arts of engineering and design, economic systems of production and distribution, military systems of attack and defence, political agencies of control and manipulation, and broadly in the cumulative though ever-changing apparatus of civilization

THE SOCIAL ORDER

Comprising the patterns, interadjustments, and trends of the modes of relationship between social beings, as revealed in their group formations and in the multifarious modes and conditions of association and dissociation[2]

---

[1] A fuller account of the distinction between the cultural order and the technological order will be found in the works of the writer, as follows: *The Modern State* (Oxford, 1926), Chap. X; *Society: A Textbook of Sociology* (New York, 1937), Chaps. XIV, XXIV–XXVI; Harvard Tercentary Publication, *Authority and the Individual* (Cambridge, Massachusetts, 1937), pp. 126–153.

[2] Since the distinction of the social from the other two orders, and particularly from the cultural, is often misapprehended or ignored, a further word may be said by way of justifying it. One reason why this distinction is a source of difficulty is that everything existing under

Our focus of interest is the causation of phenomena characterizing the social order. To this end we must explore the manner in which these phenomena depend on the conjuncture of factors belonging to all the dynamic realms. Our argument will depend on the grouping of these factors according to these realms and orders. It is therefore necessary that we explain why this classification is particularly relevant to the study of social causation. We need not pause over the main distinction of realms, especially as it is in harmony with the universal procedure of science. But the classification of the phenomena of conscious being under our three orders requires further explanation.

---

social conditions, "within society," is apt to be designated social. We do not find any cultural configuration or any system of apparatus outside of society. In other words, men create these values or these means not as detached beings, but only where they have also established social relationships. There is indeed no artifact of man that has been developed outside of social relationships or that has not been influenced by social relationships. If on that account we call every manifestation of humanity a social phenomenon, the term " social " ceases to have any definitive meaning. It becomes practically equivalent to " human." Yet there are certain phenomena that have a peculiar claim to be named " social," such as the modes in which human beings group together or stay apart, the rules they lay down for the intercourse of the members of the group, the attitudes they display towards one another. Men have created an elaborate changeful scheme of these interrelationships — this scheme is society. It is of course closely interwoven with their cultural life. The ways of their belonging together express their valuations. It is also closely interwoven with their pursuit of means. The forms of social organization are to a large extent determined by the use men make of one another, either as relatively free reciprocal beneficiaries or under some system of exploitation. But the fact that cultural values are socially fostered need not blur the distinction of the cultural order, as a value configuration, from the social order, as a web of relationships. And similarly the fact that some aspects of social organization are specifically utilitarian need not prevent us from distinguishing a pattern of social relationships from a system of techniques. Thus two people may form a relationship on economic grounds. It is a social arrangement because it is a relationship of persons; it is also a technological arrangement because it is contrived to provide some utility. To take a broader example, the sociology of religion is a study of the interdependence of religious experience and social organization — it is not a study of the positive content or substance of religion.

II

THE CULTURAL ORDER

In the simpler societies the distinction between the cultural and the technological order is undeveloped. The distinction of means and ends holds there as everywhere else. But there is no relatively detached apparatus or system of utility, maintaining a relative indifference to cultural ends. All the artifacts of the folk are at the same time culturally expressive and determinately functional. The dances, the chants, the rituals, the sacrifices, are in this regard scarcely distinguishable from the devices of hunting or trading or hut building or mat weaving. The writer has elsewhere stated it as follows:

" In primitive life the utilitarian system is utterly undetachable from the cultural life. No device, no lore, no art, is solely utilitarian. The cultural is deeply interfused with the utilitarian, and *vice versa*. Ritual is as important as craftsmanship in the making of a canoe or in the cultivation of the soil. Prayers are as important as arms in the conduct of war. Religion is compounded with magic and cannot be divorced from the business of living. The dance is as much a means of warding off evil spirits or of inducing fertility as it is a mode of social recreation. The success of a fishing expedition is as much endangered by a woman's touching the fishing tackle as by unfavorable weather. Sickness comes from spells and the breaking of taboos. The people are bound in spirit to the soil, the home of their ancestors and their gods. Everything in nature is instinct with social meaning and enshrined in social ceremony. Culture, technique, authority, people, and land are subjectively unified." [3]

---

[3] Harvard Tercentenary Publication, op. cit. p. 143.

The value is socially wedded to the instrument. The instrument is socially wedded to the value. There are cultural aspects and technological aspects of the folkways but there is no cultural order, in our sense, that can be identified in contradistinction to a technological order.

That is why the anthropologists can conveniently use the single term " culture " to signify a totality of artifacts and folkways. A similarly inclusive use of the term is made by those philosophers of history who, like Spengler, regard complex societies as also presenting a close and determinate unity through all their aspects.[4] But, without prejudice to these usages, it is for us a very significant fact that in the process from the simple to the complex society there occurs some demarcation of the cultural order, as above defined, from the technological order. The value-systems, the creeds, the ideologies, the styles and modes of group expression, attain some degree of independence or at least of detachment from the more complex technological apparatus. On the other hand it is a characteristic of advancing technology that its superior efficiency leads to its adoption over the widest areas, even though these exhibit the greatest divergence of cultural attributes. The same methods and instruments of transportation and of communication link the whole earth together. The same apparatus of industrial production is employed with practically no modifications in England and Japan, in the United States and in Russia. Against this new universalism of technology the different value-systems reveal the more closely their distinctiveness. They are systems of varying degrees of cohesion and inter-

---

[4] One may note, for example, that the Nietzschean epithets "Apollonian " and " Dionysian," applied to distinguish one type of primitive society from another by the anthropologist Ruth F. Benedict in *The Patterns of Culture* (New York, 1934), pp. 78 ff., follow the mode of designation applied by Spengler to the advanced " cultures " of complex societies.

adjustment, varying considerably for different groups within the larger social unities. But all groups, large and small, can fairly be said to have characteristic values, characteristic symbols, and characteristic modes of expression, brought to some degree of internal consistency by the endless interplay of life and environment. The group style, the symbolic modes, the cultural order generally, are evidenced, no longer so much by a special technology of the group as by the manner in which the universal technology is directed and applied. Just as artists who use the same pigments and brushes nevertheless fall into very different schools, so groups and peoples, no longer possessing exclusive apparatus or technical equipment, exhibit nevertheless distinctive mores, distinctive cultural styles, distinctive *Weltanschauungen*.

Since this classification of orders will play an important role in our treatment of the central problem of social causation, we shall first consider an objection that has been raised against it. It has been objected that our distinction between the cultural and the technological is in effect a distinction between ends and means, a distinction that is therefore completely relative. What is end in one relation is means in another.[5] So fluid a distinction cannot serve as a sure ground of classification.

In reply we may point out, first, that the distinction of culture and technology is not *identical* with the distinction of ends and means. The fact that cultural styles and valuations depend on appropriate means for their realization does not exhaust or even define their meaning. Being values for us they become also ends. They are ends when viewed as not yet attained or as being maintained. But

---

[5] See R. K. Merton, "Civilization and Culture," *Sociology and Social Research* (1936), Vol. 21, pp. 103–113. See also the writer's statement in Harvard Tercentenary Publication, op. cit. pp. 134–135.

what makes them ends is that in the first place they are values. The term " end " does not suggest their content. By the cultural order we signify the system of primary human interests; by the technological order, the apparatus constructed and utilized for their pursuit. Thus while ends and means, taken in abstraction from content, become purely relative categories the same objection does not apply to the initial distinction of culture and technology.

The objection may still be raised that those ends we have defined as culture fall also within the circle of means, in fact that there are no human values, however primary, that are not employed as means as well. The artist may cultivate a style not because he expresses himself thereby but because — or also because — it pays. The prophet may proclaim his gospel not because — or merely because — he is himself inspired by it but because he thereby can dominate people and win his private aims. How, then, can we draw any line between the realm of utilities and the realm of primary values? We might reply that unless some people got direct satisfaction from the work of the artist, unless some people found inspiration in the words of the prophet, the artist and the prophet would evoke no response. Unless their activity gave direct satisfaction to others or to themselves, their activity would cease. And a similar statement does not hold of the trader or the manufacturer or the banker or the engineer or the armament-maker. The utilities they provide, as means to their own ends, remain also means for those who receive them. But there is a more complete answer to the objection, since our distinctions refer not to the motivation of individual occasions but to the systems or patterns of activity established by groups. In every complex society there is an elaborate system of means, composed of lesser systems, its central framework an economico-political organization, supplemented and diversified by various special embodiments of the current technology. It is this specific and relatively coherent system that we call, in the larger sense, the technological order. It is readily distinguishable from the cultural order. The latter has its own institutional embodiments, typically cultural even though they function also as agencies of control. They are instrumental only because they are something more. Thus from the sociological standpoint the activities of the bank, and in fact all the products of these activities, are purely instrumental. The activities of the factory as well as the objects on which these activities are expended, the machines, the raw materials, the office equipment, and so forth, are also purely instrumental. But no such statement can be made concerning the activities of the church, the theater, the concert hall, the tavern, the debating society, the gossip group, the recreation center, the club. These are foci of " final consumption," and the process of participation in them is itself in large measure their end product. This fact, as the writer has elsewhere shown, determines some very important differences between the characteristic institutions and organizations of the cultural order and those of the technological order.[6]

In fact one of the major problems of a complex society is the interadjustment of these two orders. Forever interactive, forever conjoined in every achievement of individuals or groups, they are yet subject to different modes and tempos of change. The technology advances, and the culture, inevitably changing both in response to the new conditions thus presented and in accord with its own principle of change, moves along an embarrassed and wavering diagonal. The technology provides new military weapons, vastly destructive and far-ranging, and the nations, employing them for their national goals just as

---

[6] *Society: A Textbook of Sociology*, Chaps. XIV, XVII.

they once employed spears and bows, are laid prostrate in mutual ruin. The technology provides new modes of production, and over against their clear efficiency stand the disturbances, the insecurities, the class cleavages, the wastages, frequently the lack of direction, shown in the cultural utilization of them. The technology advances the arts of medicine and of sanitation, thus raising the expectation of life; it provides contraceptives, thus operating to lower the birth-rate. Thereby many problems are created for the prevailing culture, problems that it meets with fumbling steps. The technology enables men to live increasingly in great urban aggregations, but under conditions that balk some of their cultural needs, while evoking and satisfying others that formerly were balked. In a myriad ways the relations of technology and culture require continuous readjustment.[7]

The characteristic situation has sometimes been described as one of " cultural lag." But this phrase assumes too easily that the role of culture is mainly that of adapting itself to the technological conditions, that the culture is essentially the responsive factor while the creative and initiating factor, the precipitant or stimulant, is the technology. There is, however, no genuine meaning in the proposition that the culture, in our sense of the term, must or should " keep pace " with the technology, as though it were the lagging partner to be advanced in accordance with a common standard of efficiency.[8] The efficiency standard is relevant solely to technology, and it is relevant solely because technology is a system of means. The issue

---

[7] Some representative statements of the problem are as follows: Thorstein Veblen, *Imperial Germany and the Industrial Revolution*, New York, 1915; W. F. Ogburn, *Social Change*, New York, 1922; Lewis Mumford, *Technics and Civilization*, New York, 1934; Werner Sombart, " Technik und Kultur," *Archiv für Sozialwissenschaft und Sozialpolitik* (1911), Vol. 33, pp. 305–347.

[8] See the writer's *Society: A Textbook of Sociology*, Chap. XXV.

is the adjustment of specific means to inclusive value-
systems, and the controlling and guiding principle must
always reside somewhere in the cultural order. This great
and many-sided issue lies beyond our present scope. But
simply to refer to it is to suggest the practical no less than
the theoretical necessity for the distinction between the
technological order and the cultural order.

The distinction works. It helps us to state and to understand some of the major problems of social adjustment. We
shall presently find it helping us to state and to understand
the major problem of social causation. It is thus vindicated
against those viewpoints that make cultural phenomena
and the systems they compose merely derivative, merely
reflective of some other order, whether named economic or
technological or " material." We must not, however,
assume that the cultural order over any particular social
range is as completely integrated and articulated as the
technological order. There are conditions under which it is
relatively homogeneous and unified, such as those of many
primitive tribes, feudal communities, Puritan settlements,
and Southern plantations. But under the conditions of a
complex civilization it is most apt to exhibit not only great
diversities but also great conflicts and contradictions.
There are groups and schools and sects of every sort. In
fact, if we conceived culture merely in terms of explicit
creeds, philosophies, and goals, the most we could find
would be some degree of social or political dominance
attained by one value-system over others. But the cultural
order manifests itself not only in the faiths men profess,
the mores they cultivate, but also in the whole *style* of
living, comprising at every level of life the subtle as well
as the obvious ways in which their needs of every kind
find expression and seek fulfilment. Every social group,
every community small or large, develops its characteristic

though ever-changing style or complex of styles, and the style controls the activities of its members, not by the more superficial ordainment of authority, but by the myriad influences that pervade all the associations of men. The cultural order of a complex society may be hard to describe, but its reality is attested by numerous signs, signs that have always challenged the historian to his greatest and most difficult task.[9]

---

[9] It may help to clarify further our distinction of the cultural from the technological if we refer to certain misconceptions of it contained in an attack on it by P. Sorokin in his *Social and Cultural Dynamics*, Vol. IV, pp. 157 ff. He accuses it of being " dichotomic " in the sense that it maintains that " technological, economic, and political activities are always and everywhere utilitarian, while the family, religion, arts, science, philosophy, and so on, are uniformly and perennially devoid of the utilitarian character and usefulness" (p. 175). There is of course no such implication. It is true that for some people " the only justifying reason for religion and church is that they are socially useful " (p. 174). If we take religion to be a cultural activity, involving communion on a supra-social level, our claim is simply that unless there were for some people an attachment to it as a primary value it could not also serve as an instrument of social control. Our distinction does not mean, as Sorokin charges, that culture and technology are separately embodied in human artifacts. I have frequently pointed out that under primitive conditions the two are thoroughly fused and that under all conditions they interpenetrate in various ways. Nor is there any implication that the cultural always " lags " behind the technological (p. 283), a viewpoint I have repeatedly repudiated and criticized. What I claim is that the cultural and the technological are distinctive aspects of human activity and that in a complex society systems develop that are typically or primarily cultural and others that are typically technological. The economic system falls in the latter category, and so does the mechanism of government. Sorokin's objection that the state has been taken by " a host of the greatest writers " as itself the realization of a supreme end does not touch the issue since these writers, such as Plato and Hegel, do not differentiate the state as a system of government from the community as a way of life.

In several places Sorokin himself implicitly accepts the distinction. Thus when denying the position that the " total culture " of a community changes " together, *in toto*, as one system " he highly commends Arnold J. Toynbee because he " shows convincingly that, for instance, the technological change in each of these civilizations has proceeded quite independently from the rest of the civilization " (p. 150 n.).

III

THE TECHNOLOGICAL ORDER

By a technique we mean a specific formula for obtaining a specific result. Usually it involves both a mode of procedure and an instrument, or set of instruments, appropriate to it. The technique may be regarded as the adaptation of a principle or method to a particular objective. The objective may be of any sort. There are techniques for cooking a meal and techniques for ruling an empire. There are techniques for building a bridge and techniques for the worship of God. Techniques permeate all human activities. Many are sporadic and occasional, arising out of individual situations and expressive of individual ingenuity. Others are socialized, constituting an articulated system representative of the established stage of technological advance. The progress of science in general is accompanied (and in turn stimulated) by an interdependent series of practical discoveries and inventions, which find multifarious applications in the industrial and other arts. This system of techniques, particularly as applied to the primary production of goods and services, together with the special lores of the corresponding occupational categories, may be said to constitute the basic technology. It is the ground of the acquired skills which form, as Veblen and others have pointed out, the work-a-day habits of the mass of the population. By the acquired skills we mean the technical abilities of workers and specialists, developed through their training in the lores and practices of the basic technology.

The basic technology is in turn directed and organized by two other systems, the economic system and the political system. The three together compose our inclusive technological order.[10] The basic technology determines broadly the extent to which the material resources of a society are at any given time exploitable as well as the modes in which they are actually exploited. But the processes of the basic technology must be carried out in accordance with some socially established arrangement, and the products of the basic technology must be exchanged and distributed in accordance with some socially established arrangement. In order that a ship may sail from port to port it is not enough to have a seaworthy craft, the lores and instruments of navigation, and men versed in the lores and skilled in the use of the instruments. There must also be captain, officers, and crew, operating according to a predetermined hierarchy of command and a predetermined division of labor. And there must also be a system for the payment of the various ratings and for the financing of the whole enterprise. So for the larger business of a society. The political system is from this point of view an organization of means for the control of means, an authoritative ordainment for the social regulation of the basic technology. The economic system is also an organization of means for the control of means, directing, under conditions and within limits laid down by the state, the production, exchange, and distribution of commodities and services. This function the economic system fulfils not by authoritative regulation but by the interadjustment of diverse and conflicting interests that bargain and compete in terms of their respective command of money and credit. The political and the

---

[10] It is necessary to find some term to cover the three major systems through which men exercise control over the conditions under which they live. We have elsewhere embraced them under the term "civilization," viewed as antithetical to "culture." We have also at times used the term "utilitarian" to designate their generic character. Present usage offers no term that is free from difficulties. Since our interest is here centered in the causal relationship, we regard the inclusive use of the term "technological" as the most serviceable of the alternatives available.

economic systems together form a coordinated "institutional complex," the character of which is always changing according as more or fewer regulative functions are performed by one or the other system.[11]

Our larger technological order embraces all three systems because they are alike in being elaborate mechanisms available for the service of almost any interests or goals. The basic technology can be turned to the production of any desired goods. The economic system is peculiarly devoted to the acquisition and distribution of a sheer means, money and monetary control, that is itself indifferent with respect to the vast range of its potential employments. The political system is a mode of regulation applicable to the establishment and maintenance of any kind of ordered society. It is true that there are in this regard certain significant differences between the three systems. The political system is more directly controlled by cultural valuations. It is not merely an arrangement for the massing and distributing of power in the way that the economic system is an arrangement for the massing and distributing of wealth. It is not merely an exploitative agency or a "spoils system." The ordered life it establishes is qualitative, not merely a condition for the attainment of cultural values that lie beyond it. The state is itself an expression, a partial realization of cultural values. Nevertheless the main instruments of government are at the disposal of any set of interests or any philosophy of life that can gain control over them, whereas the organizations that belong more distinctively to the cultural order, like the church, are committed to the pursuit of particular cultural goals that from the first define their character. A church, for example, could not make science its business instead of theology, or trade instead of religion, without losing its identity as a

---

[11] See the writer's *Society: A Textbook of Sociology*, Chaps. XIV–XVI.

church. It is a church in so far as it stands for a particular way of life that we call religious. But there is no particular way of life that we call political.

The devices of the basic technology are primarily designed to control things, whereas those of the economico-political complex are primarily designed to control the relationships of men with respect to things. The latter are thus more directly responsive to social valuations; they change as these change, without seriously affecting the character of the basic technology. The economico-political complex is an *aspect* of the social order. We nevertheless make the social order a separate category, because economic and political relations, as such, are regulative rather than constitutive of the social order — a fact that traditional doctrines of the state have for the most part ignored. The growth of the science of sociology can be viewed as a sign of the increasing recognition that the social order exists in its own right, as comprising the fundamental scheme of human relationships. Apart from this recognition our doctrines of the state are likely to be unrealistic and misleading, with practical consequences of no small moment.[12]

Since political and economic systems are so directly affected by social valuations, they can vary very widely within the range of the same basic technology. We find, for example, the most diverse types of social control among primitive peoples that nevertheless exhibit the same technological stage. The contrast is no less obvious within modern civilization, where the same machine technology supports, with remarkable impartiality, the fascist, communist, and liberal-capitalist regimes, the relative social freedom of democracy and the enveloping authority of totalitarianism. The problem of the control or exploita-

---

[12] See the writer's *Modern State* (Oxford, 1926), Chap. V.

tion of nature, the main objective of the basic technology, is similar for peoples differing widely in their dominant philosophies of life. The problem of the control of men varies with the cultural conditions and social attitudes of different peoples. The economico-political institutional scheme is subject to tides of change and revolutionary surges that do not at all resemble the tempo of advance characterizing the basic technology.

By contrast the basic technology is peculiarly detached from cultural imperatives. This statement does not imply that the basic technology may not profoundly influence our valuations but only that, whatever our valuations, it is completely, and without any transformation of its own character, at their disposal. In a complex society the basic technology is highly articulated and coherent. A dominant type prevails at any time and, though subject to rapid change, tends to have an increasingly wider range. This is because standards of efficiency are easy to apply and give demonstrable results. The play of competition and the urge to acquisition and to power render the less efficient instruments and techniques speedily obsolete. Hence the basic technology is not particularly subject to the demands of *style*. In other words, it is, as a system, relatively independent of cultural norms. In its essential operations the instruments define the techniques and the techniques control the instruments, and both together determine the product.[13] The more efficient instrument and the more efficient technique supersede the less efficient. Thus a powerful process of progressive standardization is always at work.

---

[13] The combination of specific products into a finished " consumer's good " may of course be highly stylized, as in the case of fashions. Here cultural controls, relatively independent of the basic technology, take charge of the specific products of machines and techniques.

Modern civilization has thus developed an antithesis between the basic technology and the cultural order. We can distinguish, in a way that is not possible under simpler conditions, between technical activity and cultural activity. The operation of the instruments of production is more completely divorced from the processes of cultural realization, creating thereby a large part of the problem of the modern industrial worker. Whether he works a ten-hour day or a six-hour day, his working time becomes for the most part purely instrumental and devoid of intrinsic satisfactions. It is true that all cultural activity has also its appropriate techniques, but there are important differences. In cultural activity the distinction between *style* and *technique* is paramount. In music, for example, we distinguish between technical efficiency and creative ability, whether of the performer or of the composer. But we do not similarly distinguish in industry between technical efficiency and productive ability. In the cultural arts the techniques and the instruments do not *specifically* determine the product. The product changes as the style changes, without involving any necessary change of the instruments, while such changes of technique as may be involved are adaptations of skill not to the requirements of the instruments but to the demands of the style. The difference between jazz music and swing music or between classical music and modernistic music does not depend on the introduction of new instruments, although new instruments may be added to heighten the particular effect. There is not the same close gearing between techniques, instruments, and products that characterizes industrial production. This freer relationship is still more obvious in the literary arts. The novel, for example, passes through many phases and exhibits also many contemporaneous diversities of style, together with endless variations of quality, in almost complete independence of the changes in the technical arts of book-making. Such considerations alone would justify us in distinguishing the heterogeneous and freely variant patterns of culture from the highly integrated and standardized scheme of the basic technology.

The classification of orders and systems with which we have been concerned in this chapter can be applied in various ways to the discovery and comprehension of the tides of change in human affairs. Here we are interested in it solely from one point of view. Throughout this work we have insisted that the first advance towards the interpretation of social causation must be the organization under appropriate categories of the vast multiplicity and endless diversity of the " factors," " conditions," or " forces " that constitute the ever-changing conjunctures of events and processes within human society. Our classification is directed to this end. We shall find that in the larger perspective of historical movements and trends each of these orders and systems exhibits a significant causal coherence in relation to the others. It is seen, for example, in the impact of a new technology on the prior system of social relationships, or in the resistance of the cultural order to the introduction of a new technology, or in the rise of new cultural values that direct to new objectives the established technology, or in a political revolution that seeks to maintain itself by the inculcation of favorable cultural attitudes, and so forth. It is seen no less in the specific event or in the shaping of the specific situation, where a differentiated configuration of individual and group values enters into dynamic relations with the particular techniques available under conditions physically and biologically defined. In short, we have now at hand a principle for the organization of our multifarious data into relevant causal categories. But before we can apply it we have a further step to take. We must consider how, in the realm of conscious being, we pass beyond the heterogeneity of causes, as physical and biological and psychological. We must apprehend the synthetic function of conscious being, the function of bringing all these dynamic factors together into one causal focus.

Our classification of systems, orders, and realms implies a ground of unity that still remains to be explored. For us here the problem is how the factors of the various categories are selectively unified in the processes of individual and group behavior. To classify these factors is to reveal the problem, not to answer it. Together, in every conscious act, they enter into dynamic conjunction. The problem would exist even if we could ignore the external factors altogether. For every person and group, at every moment of conscious action, there is a multiplicity of concordant and conflicting values; and there is a multiplicity of means and conditions. How is this multiplicity resolved in the dynamic moment? To answer the question we turn to the process we name the dynamic assessment.

CHAPTER ELEVEN

THE DYNAMIC ASSESSMENT

I

THE INDIVIDUAL FOCUS

1. A BUSINESS man sits in his office. He has concluded an important deal. The tension under which he had been working is relaxed. He is back to the everyday routine and it has less savor than before. He is conscious of a vague restlessness. He wants a change of some sort. His days have been too slavishly devoted to the demands of business, he has been missing other things. He has been making money — why shouldn't he spend some, indulge himself a little? Why not take time off and go on a voyage? The business can get along without him for a few weeks. A steamship company's advertisement of a " luxury cruise," which he had read some days before, comes to his mind. " It is just the thing I need," he says to himself, " a complete change of scene." His wife has been warning him against overworking. His family will appreciate him more when he comes back after an absence. The air and sunshine will do him good. He will make new acquaintances. It will be pleasant to visit Rio and Buenos Aires and other places he has merely read about. The more he thinks of the idea the better he likes it. Before the day is over he " makes up his mind " and telephones the steamship company for a reservation.

What has our business man been doing? He has been assessing a situation and arriving at a decision. He has had alternatives before him and has chosen between them. He is going to travel, for recreation or health or adventure. That is the way he puts it to others — or to himself. His statement of objective is necessarily incomplete and is probably a simplification. Anyhow he has reached a decision, probably without any meticulous calculation. He cannot really tell you how he arrived at it. *It is his dynamic assessment of a situation.* Let us take it at that for the present. In the process of making a decision, some desire, some valuation, simple or complex, has become dominant for the time being, as a determinant of action within the individual's scheme of values.

▼

2. Having made his decision, our business man reorganizes his activities in order to attain his objective. He gives instructions for the conduct of his affairs during his absence. He makes arrangements for family needs. He foresees certain contingencies and provides against them. He cancels some engagements. He buys some travelling equipment. He turns resources hitherto neutral and undirected, such as the money he pays for his transportation, into specific means, the means for his new objective.

In all conscious behavior there is thus a twofold process of selective organization. On the one hand the value-system of the individual, his active cultural complex, his personality, is focussed in a particular direction, towards a particular objective. (Sometimes, as we previously pointed out, the incentive to the reorganization of activity may be a dominating motive that is not attached to a specific objective.) On the other hand certain aspects of external reality are selectively related to the controlling valuation, are distinguished from the rest of the external world, are in a sense withdrawn from it, since they now become themselves value factors, the means, obstacles, or conditions relevant to the value quest. The inner, or subjective, system is focussed by a dynamic valuation; and the outer, or external, system is " spotlighted " in that focus, the part within the spotlight being *transformed from mere externality into something also belonging to a world of values*, as vehicle, accessory, hindrance, and cost of the value attainment.

▼

3. The traveller sets out on his voyage. He enters into a new system of social relations. He is subjected to new influences. He may be deflected thereby from his original objective, he may find new additional objectives, or he may pursue exclusively the first one. Even in the last event he may fail to attain his goal. The experience of adventure may fall flat, he may not improve his health, he may not achieve whatever other end he sought. His assessment of the situation may have been faulty. He may have miscalculated the chances of success. He may have left out of the reckoning some important considerations. Or it may be that developments of an unforeseen character intervene and make his voyage nugatory.

In all conscious behavior we relate means to ends, but the process of establishing this relationship is contingent and involves an attribution of causality that may or may not be confirmed by experience. Before embarking on his ship our traveller had somehow assessed the situation. This assessment, whether superficial or thorough, involved a reckoning of alternatives. It contained, as do all decisions to act, a speculative element. A dynamic assessment weighs alternatives not yet actualized, sets what would be the consequences if this course were taken over against what would be the consequences if that course were taken. It is in this regard a causal judgment. We pointed out in a previous chapter that the attribution of social causation always contains a speculative factor of this sort.[1] But the dynamic assessment, that is, the judgment that carries a decision to act, differs from the *post mortem* judgment of history or social science in that it is doubly contingent. In the historical attribution we imaginatively construct what would have happened if the historically presented event or act had not occurred, or at the least we postulate that certain happenings would not have occurred but for the event or act in question. One of the alternatives that must be weighed in the process of causal attribution is always imaginatively constructed. But in the practical judgment that unleashes action *both* of the final alternatives are constructs, for both refer to the future. The voyager chose what he thought likely to happen if he travelled in preference to what he thought likely to happen if he stayed at home.

▾

4. Our traveller set out on his voyage without reckoning all the contingencies. No one does or could calculate all the possible combinations of circumstance that may conspire against — or in favor of — his enterprise. When a man decides to act he generally has two or three alternatives before him and he assesses these alternatives in the light of a few expectancies. These alone come within the focus of decision. But " there's many a slip 'twixt the cup and the lip." We can perhaps distinguish three types of contingency that may frustrate the attainment of an objective once decided upon. Two of these we have already suggested. The traveller may " change his mind " while he travels and be diverted to another quest. Or he may carry through his project and at the end find that he had miscalculated the means-end nexus — if he travels for

---

[1] Chapter Nine, § 2.

health the voyage may not restore him. The first contingency occurs in the structure of the inner or subjective system; the second in the relationship of the inner and the outer — the relation of means to ends was conceived to be such and such and it turned out to be different. But there is a third type of contingency which has reference to the dynamics of the external order alone. Our traveller probably did not consider the chance that his ship might strike a rock or founder in a storm. He certainly did not consider the chance that he might fall on a slippery deck and break his leg. He thought of the ship as an instrument of his ends and since most ships make the port they sail for he gave no consideration to the fact that the ship, as physical reality, is subjected to forces that are oblivious of its instrumental quality. It enters, like all instruments, into two causal systems, the means-end system of the conscious realm and the neutral system of physical nature. The adjustment of the dependent causality of the first system to the independent causality of the second is imperfect, and thus a new set of contingencies arises. Our traveller did not concern himself with these contingencies. He was content to assess a certain routine of experience that he expected would continue if he stayed at home and a certain alternative to that routine that he expected would occur if he took the voyage. He foresaw, under the impulse of the emotions congenial to his temperament, a preferable train of consequences as likely to occur if he decided to travel — and decided accordingly.

In all conscious behavior the situation we assess, as preliminary to action, is in no sense the total objective situation. In the first place it is obviously not the situation as it might appear to some omniscient and disinterested eye, viewing all its complex interdependences and all its endless contingencies. In the second place it is not the situation as inclusive of all the conditions and aspects observable, or even observed, by the participant himself. Many things of which he is aware he excludes from the focus of interest or attention. Many contingencies he ignores. The situation he assesses is one that he has selectively defined, in terms of his experience, his habit of response, his intellectual grasp, and his emotional engrossment. The dynamic assessment limits the situation by excluding all the numerous aspects that are not apprehended as relevant to the choice between alternatives. At the same time it includes in the situation various aspects that are not objectively given, that would not be listed in any merely physical inventory. For in the first place it envisages the situation as impregnated with values and susceptible of new potential values; and in the second place the envisagement is dependent on the ever-changing value-system of the individual, charged with memory of past experience, moulded by the impact of previous indoctrination, responsive to the processes of change within his whole psycho-organic being. Thus no two individuals envisage and define a situation in exactly the same way, even when they make a seemingly identical decision and even although social influences are always powerfully at work to merge individual assessments into a collective assessment.

Our simple instance of the traveller has brought out a number of points, which we recapitulate as follows:

▼

1. A preliminary to conscious activity is a decision between alternatives — to do this or to do that, to do or not to do. In the process of decision-making the individual assesses a situation in the light of these alternatives. A choice between values congenial to the larger value-system of the individual is somehow reached.

2. The decision once taken, the other purposes or valuations of the individual are accommodated to it. Preparatory actions follow. In this orientation certain external factors are selectively reorganized and given subjective significance. They are construed as means, obstacles, conditions, and limitations, with reference to the attainment of the dominant desire or value. The dynamic assessment brings the external world selectively into the subjective realm, conferring on it subjective significance for the ends of action.

▼

3. The dynamic assessment involves a type of causal judgment that differs from the *post factum* attribution of causality characteristic of the social sciences, in that it is doubly speculative. It rests always on a predictive judgment of the form: if this is done, this consequence will (is likely to) follow *and* if this is not done or if this other thing is done, this other consequence will (is likely to) follow. We may observe in passing that even the most simple-seeming choice may conceal a subtle and unfathomed subjective process.

▼

4. The selectivity of the dynamic assessment, as it reviews the situation prior to decision and as it formulates the alternatives of action, makes it subject to several kinds of contingency and practical hazard. First, the dominant objective registered in the decision to act may not persist throughout the process leading to its attainment. Second, the means-ends nexus envisaged in the decision to act may be misapprehended. Third, the physical order assumed to be under control as the means and conditions of action may "erupt" into the situation in unanticipated ways. All conscious behaving is an implicit reckoning of probabilities, which may or may not be justified by the event.

Before we take leave of our simple case we may point out that the analysis of it contains already the clue to our main problem. What has particularly troubled us is that the various factors we causally relate to any socio-psychological phenomenon belong to different orders of reality. Yet they must somehow get together, they must somehow become comparable and co-ordinate, since they must operate with or against one another in the determination of the phenomenon. But how does, say, a moral conviction " co-operate " with an empty stomach in determining whether or not a man will steal? How does the prevalence of a particular religion combine with rural conditions in determining a high birth-rate? How does the decline of religious authority combine with urban congestion and the improvement of contraceptives in the lowering of the birth-rate? The suggested answer is that *in the dynamic assessment all the factors determining conscious behavior are brought into a single order*. The external factors enter not as such, but as considerations affecting or relative to the pursuit of ends. A change of religious attitudes and the expense of bringing up children both affect the value systems of the individuals concerned. At every moment of deliberation or decision the individual is faced with alternatives. He has not one desire but many, and they are not independent but interdependent. He seeks attainment not of one value but of a system of values, for that is what it means to have, or be, a personality. What choice he will make, what end he will here and now pursue, depends on the urgency of particular desires, the intensity or depth of particular valuations, relative to the variant conditions of attainment. The intensity and depth of particular valuations will in turn register a recognition of the different possibilities of attainment. The change in religious attitudes is not wholly independent of the conditions of urban living. In any event, it introduces a change in the individual's scheme of values. But so, indirectly, does the fact of urban congestion. It makes some values easier of attainment, and some harder. Values are values only as calling for attainment or for maintenance — there would be no values in a static world; conditions and means are such only as they make for or against the attaining or the maintaining of values.

As we proceed we shall follow this clue. With its aid we shall endeavor to explore the particular patterns of social causation. Its justification will be the use we can make of it. We shall therefore not spend time on the purely metaphysical objection of those who reject the language of " motives and goals " and require a common frame of reference for physical and social causation — which in effect means that they would restate the problems of social causation in the language of physics. Thus one writer seems to object to our drawing a distinction between the type of causality involved when a paper flies before the wind and that revealed when a man flies from a pursuing crowd.[2] When we mention the surely obvious fact that " the paper knows no fear and the wind no hate, but without fear and hate the man would not fly nor the crowd pursue," this writer takes it as an illustration of " the tendency to regard familiar words as essential components of situations." [3] He informs us that " the principle of parsimony requires that we seek to bring into the same framework the explanation of all flying objects." He suggests that because we can describe the amoeba's approach to its food without reference to fear and hate we should learn to abandon such references when applied to human

---

[2] G. Lundberg, *Foundations of Sociology*, Chap. I, pp. 11–14. The distinction is made in our *Society: A Textbook of Sociology*, Chap. XXVI, pp. 476–477.

[3] The identification of subjective aspects with *words* is a characteristic confusion of this school. Of course not the words, but the experiences we call " fearing " and " hating," are aspects of the situation.

beings! And he expresses an almost mystical hope that by resort to " operationally defined terms " science may attain this goal. Presumably in this new synthesis science will still have goals, but not human beings. But until that brave new world is disclosed we must continue to regard the physico-chemical nexus as one manifestation of the nature of things and the psychological nexus as another, as a different manifestation. No operational defining can charm away a difference that nature itself reveals.

II

THE GROUP CONVERGENCE

The social sciences are not concerned with the particular behavings of individuals but with the inter-related activities that constitute or reveal group behavior. In the study of social causation we are not confronted with the endless task of explaining how or why different individuals act differently in different situations. It is not a question of how you or I behave, but of how *we* behave. And the " we " is not to be construed distributively, as though one were asking about the ways in which like animals react to like stimuli or independently satisfy like needs. It is the " we " of associated beings, whose ways of behaving, whether like, complementary, unlike, or opposed, are inter-related and in some measure interdependent. The social sciences are concerned with the modes of behavior characteristic of social beings who belong within the same culture, who possess the same institutions, who together face the same problems, who pursue common causes, who, when they act in like ways, are still subject to influences that pass from one to another and envelop them all. Hence in the study of social causation our interest centers in the like or converging dynamic assessments that under-lie group activities, institutional arrangements, folkways, in general the phenomena of social behavior. These like or converging assessments we shall speak of as group assessments.

That the group to some extent and for some purposes acts as a unity in the assessment of situations is evidenced in many ways. Anthropological and sociological studies make it very clear that whenever a people or tribe takes over any doctrine, creed, myth, or philosophy from another people or tribe it endows the borrowed cultural form with its own imprint. The creed, for example, is selectively different for every distinctive group, no matter what uniformity of ritual or acceptance of a single authority may prevail. The characteristic difference holds whether the creed in question be the Christianity of modern civilization or the belief in the " guardian spirit " found among American Indian tribes. (We have already seen, by way of contrast, that essentially instrumental or technological devices are borrowed without significant change.)[4] The group is thus in some sense a focus of assessment, imposing its own pattern on policies and events as well as on the opinions and faiths of its members. Wherever it is allowed to express itself, there is a style of the group as well as of the individual, a manner of living, a manner of thinking, a manner of acting. This style the group is always seeking to perpetuate, by establishing conventions and standards, by institutionalizing in an at least semi-compulsive form the main lines of its system of assessment, though individual variations and deviations forever play upon them. The thought-forms, the valuational constructs, thus perpetuated among the members of a group, serve as the group focus of dynamic assessment.

We may now distinguish three types of social phenomena according to the manner in which these socially conditioned

---

[4] Chapter Ten, § 2.

thought-forms are related to them. Our first type includes changes in mores, styles, usages, in the modes of living, in the tides of opinion, and in such statistical facts as the birth-rate, the crime rate, the suicide rate, the frequency of marriage, and so forth. These phenomena do not express the concerted or collective activity of the group to which they refer. The crime rate is not the objective — nor any part or aspect of the objective — of the persons who commit crimes, as a revolution or a celebration is the objective of those who participate in it. The crime rate is, in effect, a way of saying how many people in a given population have acted alike in violation of a criminal code — or rather have been convicted of acting alike in this respect. Similarly, when the opinions or attitudes of a number of people change at the same time in the same direction the registered volume of change expresses a consensus only, not a collective action but the aggregate of many individual actions. The rate or the volume of change is nevertheless a social phenomenon inasmuch as it is responsive to group or community conditions and is moreover in some measure dependent on suggestion, imitation, intercommunication, leadership, and other social interactions. Through such interactions the varieties of individual assessment become congruent and tend to fall into conformity. Thus also the way is prepared for phenomena of the second type.

Our second type includes statutes, regulations, administrative policies, organized social movements, political revolutions and demonstrations, social agreements of every sort. The distinctive feature of this type is that individuals who are more or less in accord in their assessment of a situation take *concerted* action, either directly or through agents, to bring about a single or common objective, some change in the social structure or in the conditions to which they are together subject. Here congruent individual assessments are the basis of a collective determination. A particular objective is formulated and "blue-printed." It is of the kind that admits actualization through a specific agency in fulfilment of a preconceived design.

Our third type embraces the vast array of phenomena we have already denominated as social resultants, the products of social conjuncture. It includes the greater structures of the social order, the extent of the division of labor, the modes of politico-economic control we call capitalism, socialism, and so forth, the changing equilibrium of economic organization, the business cycle, the volume of unemployment, the various patterns and exhibits of social disorganization. Under this type we should perhaps distinguish two sub-types. There are social phenomena that partly correspond to some preconceived design but in the process of actualization many uncalculated changes have occurred, so that the final result is in important respects different from the "blue-print," and often much more complicated. Again, it frequently happens that around the formally established institution there is woven a subtle network of unplanned usages that in time become an integral part of the operative system. For example, around the law court and the law there develops a scheme of customary practices — what one writer calls the "law-ways."[5] On the other hand there are social resultants that in no measure depend on any preconceived design. Take, for example, the fluctuations of business activity commonly referred to as the business cycle. No one plans a business cycle, no group engineers it; the most men hope for is to control or limit it. Under all conditions the multifarious activities of economic life,

---

[5] K. N. Llewellyn, "The Normative, the Legal, and the Law-jobs," *Yale Law Review* (June, 1940), Vol. 49, pp. 1355–1400.

complicated also by social processes and political regulations, produce unplanned effects. Whether these effects
constitute an orderly scheme of things, a precarious moving
equilibrium, or a realm of confusion; whether they lead
men to bless the " invisible hand " or to demand a social
revolution, they belong equally to our third type. So do
the various rhythms, patterns, waves that are forever
manifesting themselves within a complex society. Certain
statistical facts also find place here, instead of under type
two. Contrast, for example, the unemployment rate with
the crime rate. The former does not presume any kind of
like behavior, like objective, like dynamic assessment, on the
part of those who fall within the category. The volume of
unemployment is a social phenomenon not because it expresses the purposes of social beings but because it is an unpurposed aspect and product of a social system, of complexly
interdependent activities falling under our first two types.

In sum, we have distinguished three causal types of
social phenomena, as follows:

TYPE ONE. DISTRIBUTIVE PHENOMENA

Directly expressive of the like or converging assessments of a number of people, as they issue in separate
activities of a like nature, together constituting an
aggregate or ratio of the same order, such as a crime
rate or an opinion trend

TYPE TWO. COLLECTIVE PHENOMENA

Directly expressive of the like or converging assessments of a number of people, as they issue in concerted and unified action, such as a legal enactment or
an organizational policy

TYPE THREE.   CONJUNCTURAL PHENOMENA

Arising from the variant assessments and activities of
interdependent individuals and groups, as they issue
in unpurposed resultants, such as the business cycle
under a capitalistic system

In all complex social processes phenomena of all three
types are combined. Obviously, phenomena of type one
are implicated in the phenomena of type two. Obviously,
many phenomena of type two are responses to the problems
created by the phenomena of type three. Political systems
are usually classified according to the manner in which
phenomena of type two are organized and controlled,
under such names as democracy, dictatorship, oligarchy,
and so forth. Another line of distinction takes primary
account of the range of phenomena that fall respectively
under type one and under type two. On this basis we
distinguish socialist from capitalist systems, co-operative
societies from other economic corporations, and so forth.
The causal relationships that exist between phenomena of
type two and those of type three have been a main issue
of politico-economic controversy. Some economic doctrines, including laissez-faire, marginal utility, and equilibrium economics of all sorts, announce a socially advan-
tageous harmony; others deny it or assert its inadequacy.

Our immediate concern is with the fact that back of all
these phenomena lie the socially interdependent assessments made by individuals as members of a group, whether
they act collectively or distributively. The dynamic assessment is for us the preparatory stage of the particular nexus
we call social causation. It is that which differentiates it
from every other form of causation. It is also that which
enables us to attack the peculiar problem of the relation of

factors in social causation. These statements we shall endeavor progressively to justify.

The causal role of dynamic assessment is to bring into a single order of coherent relationships the objectively diverse factors involved in social behavior. We begin with the dynamic assessment, while recognizing that back of it lie causal factors of another order. Our problem is not how the evaluating and synthesizing function of conscious being, in its manifold embodiments, is derived and constituted as a psycho-physical system in the realm of universal nature. Our problem is how it operates in the realm of social behavior. We are not asking what determines the focus but what the focus determines. We can see that it is forever being modified and conditioned by the organic processes, by the state of the nerves, the blood stream, the digestion, by the biological effects of emotional experience, by the rise and fall of the atmospheric pressure, and so forth. Nevertheless for the study of social causation we can take it as a datum, since; however determined, it inaugurates another kind of causal nexus, that on which our interest happens to be centered.

The assessing process, whether it takes effect as an individual or as a collective activity, is a function of the personality of the social being, as it apprehends alternatives of behaving, as it discerns their relation to the value-system it incorporates. This personality is constantly changing, is perhaps never fully engaged in any conscious action, is evoked in different degrees and in different aspects by the particular challenges and demands of the occasion. It has nevertheless some coherence and unity through time. A split personality, in the strict sense, is a relatively rare phenomenon. The character type and the character idiosyncrasy are on the whole quite persistent. Otherwise we could not have the complex ordered relations of men.

Sometimes there is bewilderment, lack of orientation, cleavage, whether associated with nervous disturbances and other organic impairments or more directly with tense conflict situations. But sometimes the contradictions attributed to personality are such only because different behavings are compared too abstractly. For example, the envisaged alternatives may be of a momentary nature or of superficial content. Shall I go to this party or stay at home? Shall I read this novel or that one? Such assessments involve only a narrow range of the personality. The action taken with respect to them may be no criterion of the principle of action when larger alternatives are under review. Shall I choose this career or that? Shall I marry this girl? Shall I offend my conscience to please my friends or offend my friends to satisfy my conscience? The presented alternatives vary with every situation. But the mode in which the alternatives are selected and presented, delimited and assessed, is revelatory of the personality structure. The value-system is incorporated in personality, finding partial, variant, and aspectual expression in the flux of behavior.

When we turn to consider the group convergence, under our first two types, we are no longer concerned with the elusiveness and complexity of the individual personality. We now enter an area in which the signs are somewhat easier to discern, in which we can neglect the more subtle variations of the value schemes of different individuals, in which the data are equally open to many observers. What is there in this area that corresponds to the individual personality as a focus of behavior? We might speak of a group personality except that the concept is so liable to misconstruction. But as back of the individual assessment there is a relatively coherent personality, so back of the like and converging assessments of many individuals there is a relatively coherent culture complex. It is a common-place of observation that every group tends to have and to hold its distinctive culture, even though it may be only a variation of a circumambient culture. Anthropologists have dwelt on the " patterns " of this complex, historians have described its manifestations over groups of every scale and through greater or shorter spans of time, sociologists have found a " trend to consistency " in its various aspects or have sought to portray its coherence through the conception of an " ideal type." [6]

Let us look more closely at the manner in which the group assessment operates. We shall take an instance falling under type one. The past seventy years have witnessed a notable and nearly continuous decline of the birth-rate in the countries of Western civilization. We need not here offer the reasons for regarding this decline as a phenomenon primarily attributable to conscious restriction of parenthood and not to purely biological factors. The restriction has been a separate determination on the part of myriads of family circles. But it was not that these myriads of families simultaneously happened to diverge from the ways of earlier generations. Nor was it merely that these myriads of families were alike faced with a new situation to which they alike independently responded by exhibiting a new pattern of behavior. True, the situation, in the sense of the objective conditions under which people lived, had undergone change. The proportion of the population living in towns and cities was increasing; the proportion engaged in industrial and white-collar occupations, as distinct from agricultural occupations, was increasing; the proportion of women in " gainful occupations," especially of young

---

[6] As examples, R. Benedict, *Patterns of Culture*, Boston, 1935; V. L. Parrington, *Main Currents of American Thought* (3 vols.), New York, 1930; W. G. Sumner, *Folkways* (Boston, 1940), Chap. I; Max Weber, *Wirtschaft und Gesellschaft* (Tübingen, 1925), Chap. I.

women, was increasing; the proportion of families that remained settled in one more or less permanent location was diminishing; the economic costs of bringing up a family were, for large numbers, becoming relatively greater. Thus the means-ends schema, with respect to the values attaching to the larger family, was being modified in a direction congenial to the preference for a smaller family. Individual assessments were changing under these conditions but that was not enough to explain the emergent phenomenon.

For individual assessments are not independent, self-contained operations, especially where issues of moment to the whole group are involved. They are responsive, alike in stability and change, to the group-sustained mores. It is not without significance that for each of the chief countries concerned the beginning of the continuous downward trend can be dated rather accurately. The afore-mentioned changes in economic and social conditions were cumulative; certainly they had been proceeding for a considerable length of time before the birth-rate turned definitely downward. The myriads of families followed their traditional way, in spite of greater uncertainties and new problems, until new influences broke through the traditional controls and created a new tide of opinion. The effective assessments of family situations made by most of those concerned remained unchanged until the group-sustained mores became congenial to or at least tolerant of the change. For every revaluation affects and must be related to the larger system of values. Until that system has been adapted to the specific revaluation, only aberrant, pioneering, or disorientated individuals are likely to adopt it. Thus the groups which first exhibited the trend of the smaller family were not those which faced the most severe problems in raising a family, but those whose value-schemes were furthest removed from the patriarchal type of mores and from certain traditional patterns of religious indoctrination. Where, on the other hand, the dominant value-scheme became less congenial to the specific preference for the smaller family, as in Germany after the establishment of the Nazi regime, the trend was for a time reversed.

It is not necessary to dwell on the more obvious facts of fad and fashion to show that the cultural complex of the group lies back of the like behavings of individuals. Even those phenomena that seem peculiarly referable to the conscience or private judgment of the individual, such as religious conversions, can be shown, by the course they follow, to be at the same time expressions of group-sustained attitudes or values. Any attempt, therefore, to derive what we have called statistical facts, such as the suicide rate of a group, from the specific conditions to which the categorized individuals were severally exposed — say, to attribute the prevalence of suicide to individual misfortune, individual isolation, individual neurosis, and so forth — is likely to leave out an important aspect of the problem. The individual assessment cannot be separated from the group assessment. Each has nevertheless its own coherence. There is the individual personality on the one hand, there are the group-sustained mores on the other. The evaluational scheme is imperfectly coherent on both levels, deviates on both levels from the professed norms, and is forever subject to change. But these interdependent schemes of valuation together constitute the assessing system by means of which the diverse factors are brought within the single order of social causation.

Let us return briefly to our previous example to illustrate how the system operates. In the statistical fact of the declining birth-rate we have before us a number of specific whys ready for causal investigation. Why, for Western civilization as a whole, and why in different degrees for different economic, occupational, and class groups, has there been an increasing restriction of the size of the family? It is not difficult to discover the main aspects of the culture complex that went with the earlier relatively unrestricted family. The woman's place was the home; there was no career for her but marriage, no continuing function but the raising of a family: the command was, " Be fruitful and multiply," and with whatever other blessings its fulfilment was associated there was also the sheer necessity of survival, for the expectation of life was so low that even the fruitful did not multiply. Thus an ample progeny was the first of social values, and this value was fortified by the whole constitutional order of church and state. The culture complex was strongly opposed to the restriction of the family, once marriage had been entered upon. The myriads of married pairs, steeped in the patriarchal tradition, fulfilled accordingly their " duty to God and man." The value-scheme of the parents was on the whole congenial to that of the church and the state. Another addition to the family could hardly lower their standard of living while it gave additional assurance of support for their later years. The education of the family was a minor problem, since in the pre-industrial age the children learned their unspecialized jobs on the family land — or on the land to which the family was tied. Under these conditions it is easy to understand also why, although relatively efficient prescriptions for contraception were known even in ancient Egypt and in Greece, contraceptive practices in the modern sense did not spread to the common people and were utterly alien to the mores.[7]

In time all the premises of this scheme of values were undermined by technological and economic changes. The

---

[7] Norman Himes, *Medical History of Contraception*, Baltimore, 1936.

social value attached to a high birth-rate was ultimately contingent on the coexistence of a high death-rate. The death-rate fell as sanitation and medical science advanced. At length the infant death-rate fell remarkably.[8] With these changes went various other changes affecting the value formerly attached by the individual family to a high birth-rate — the general transference of family functions to other organizations; the specialization of work and the increasing cost of raising a family, especially for urban dwellers; the opening up of non-domestic occupations and careers to women; the competitive and unstable maintenance of group standards of living; and so forth. The value-schemes of the units directly concerned, the husbands and the wives of the myriads of families, were undergoing change — not infrequently in the transition the valuations of the two partners went out of accord.[9] But outside of France, which had passed through a tremendous revolution, the momentum of the established culture complex persisted until late in the nineteenth century. The group assessment dominated, in its characteristic way, the individual assessment, but disharmony was growing between them. The disharmony prepared the way for readjustment until, rather suddenly for many groups, the mores became accommodated to the new valuation. There came a definite date, for country after country around the civilized world, at which

---

[8] For the facts and figures see L. I. Dublin and A. T. Lotka, *The Length of Life*, New York, 1936.

[9] That the changing value-scheme is the primary explanation of familial and other social transformations has been explicitly or implicitly recognized by the most penetrating investigators in particular areas of social research. Thus, for example, Thomas and Znaniecki give it first place in their study of the disorganization of the Polish family in the United States: "The real cause of all phenomena of family disorganization is to be sought in the influence of certain new values — new for the subject — such as: new sources of hedonistic satisfaction, new vanity values, new (individualistic) types of economic organization, new forms of sexual appeal." *The Polish Peasant* (New York, 1927), Vol. II, Part II, Chap. II, p. 1167.

the new trend appeared.[10] The historical evidences associated with these definite turning points make it sufficiently clear that somehow there was reached an implicit social acceptance, for larger groups at least, of the restricted family.[11] For these groups birth control and the use of contraceptives ceased to be taboo. The taboo ended before the official guardians of the mores admitted the fact, long before there was any institutional recognition of the fact. But the effective group assessment had changed, and the change permeated even into those groups which accepted a religious authority definitely opposed to it.

Our example has suggested the way in which the culture complex of the group lies back of the dynamic assessment of the individual. We have seen how in this process the various factors of social causation, however disparate in other respects, are brought into a single system. We are now ready to consider more particularly the way in which the different factors are combined, how each has its role and place and weight in causal determination. But before doing so we shall examine our third type of social phenomenon, the phenomenon of social conjuncture, for this depends not on like and converging assessments but on unlike, conflicting, and diversely related assessments of every kind.

III

THE SOCIAL CONJUNCTURE

Everywhere the combination and opposition of dynamic elements produce structures of remarkable complexity as well as events of a spectacular nature. Thus biologists

---

[10] See, for example, W. S. Thompson, *Population Problems*, New York, 1935.

[11] See J. A. Field, *Essays on Population* (Chicago, 1931), Chap. VII.

since the days of Darwin have been pointing out the intricate functional adaptations involved in the fertilization of various plants, in parasitism, symbiosis, and so forth. Our concern here is with another form of dynamic combination and opposition, that revealed in the interplay of the behavior of individuals and groups. The purposive actions of men, expressive of a diversity of dynamic assessments, bring unpurposed results that are no less remarkable than, say, the hexagons of the hive of the honey bee. It is scarcely an exaggeration to claim that the larger framework of every society, its institutional complex, is a resultant of this type. It may be compared with the physical layout of a city every single edifice in which has been built according to some one's plan, whereas the total structure, whether it serves well or ill the purposes of those who inhabit it, has not come within the compass of any controlling design. So men build their social cells, form and re-form their associations, enter into changeful relations of one kind or another; and through this multitude of activities there comes into being a larger pattern to which also their traditions and habits became attached. Now and again a revolutionary spirit may be bred that seeks to control and to remake the entire fabric. However far it succeeds, along whatever new channels the multitudinous activities of men proceed, patterns other than those designed and superintended again emerge.

Various social philosophies have been founded on a perception of the role of social conjuncture, thus understood. We have already referred to the tendency to interpret social change in terms of rhythmic recurrence or symmetrical variation regarded as inherent in the nature of society. Aside from this, certain schools of thought have dwelt on the manner in which human activities fulfil social functions entirely beyond the cognisance of those who engage in them. This doctrine underlay the ancient notion that strife was the father of things, but it gained its greatest impetus in the nineteenth century when the Malthusian form of the doctrine passed through the Darwinian lens and issued in the sociologies of Gumplowicz, Lapouge, Spencer, Karl Pearson, and many others. To some the great constructive force was war, especially as the struggle for supremacy between peoples or races. To others it was the struggle of individuals in the free arena of " natural selection," assuring the progressive fitness of those who survive. To others it was the qualified economic struggle, the competitive process that maintains the level of human endeavor and begets the wealth of nations.

But it is not alone the clash and grapple of opposing purposes that is to be credited with unpurposed achievement. The main difficulty presented by the doctrines just mentioned is the difficulty that has dogged social theory from the beginning of reflection, the intemperate attribution of total results to a single agency or cause. Not alone the clash of purposive activities but also their multitudinous interactions have brought into being the changeful fabric of society. In a famous passage Adam Smith declared that the whole scheme of the division of labor is due to " a certain propensity in human nature which has in view no such extensive utility; the propensity to truck, barter, and exchange one thing for another." [12] Again a simplification, since the division of labor is responsive to the many diversities of human aptitude, opportunity, condition, and interest; to the ease of communication and transportation; to the state of the industrial arts; and so forth. The division of labor is in fact an excellent example of a social resultant, arising without design from the interplay of many factors, involving the co-operative and complementary as well as

---

[12] *Wealth of Nations*, Book I, Chap. II.

the conflicting purposes of men. The real problem is the way in which the various factors are related in the processes of social change. All too rarely is it examined. All too frequently the "wealth of nations," or whatever other resultant is under consideration, is attributed to "liberty of competition" or to the division of labor or to the advance of technology or to geographical opportunity or to the policies of government or to the productive power of labor — without much consideration of the place of the chosen factor in the complex interdependence of things.

We shall see the nature of the problem better if we begin by setting out some typical social resultants corresponding to different modes of social relationship. Let us take first the different forms of conflict or opposition. In war or unmitigated hostility each side endeavors to maim or destroy the other. The total destruction thereby produced is an unpurposed resultant of the purposed unilateral activities of destruction, and thus a large part of the immediate consequences of war, with all the sequelae they entail, falls into our category. So much is this the case that the issues at stake at the outset of a war are very frequently changed or altogether lost to view as the war proceeds. The predicaments created by the means employed transform the ends to which the means are addressed.

In the competitive conflict another kind of social resultant is more apparent. If two persons enter into economic competition there is always the third party, the party for whose custom or favor the competitors contend. Each competitor offers the "third party" his product or his service on more favorable terms than he would have been likely to make were it not for the contending offers of his fellow competitors. There is thus, as an immediate consequence, the total lesser advantage of the competitors themselves — an unpurposed resultant of the kind inherent in all conflict, though this immediate consequence is an entirely different matter from the net final resultant of the whole competitive process. The latter is an exceedingly complex product, varying greatly according to the conditions under which competition takes place. But the most distinctive feature of competition is the immediate (not always by any means the final) advantage of the " third party," in the degree in which the " third party " is not engaged in reciprocal competition. A special type of third party advantage occurs when there are two strong contestants for an office or honor, neither of whom can be chosen without giving serious offence to the powerful or influential supporters of the other, so that both sides fall back on a third and less conspicuous candidate. This is the typical situation of the " rejoicing third," the *tertius gaudens*.[13]

There are various other forms of conflict which possess some of the aspects of competition but which for the sake of clarity ought to be distinguished by other names. If we mean by competition the bidding for the custom or patronage of a third party by the alternative offer of similar or substitute services, there are certainly many types of rivalry and struggle, often loosely called competitive, that do not fall under this definition.[14] When two teams struggle for victory they do not make alternative offers to the spectators. In many contests there is no third party — in friendly games, for example, or in certain more serious conflicts in which one party tries to keep the other down or to get ahead of him. Here we must look for resultants of another kind. The social phenomena arising from the interplay of conflicting desires for dominance, distinction, and relative

[13] An admirable account of the sociology of the *tertius gaudens* is given in Georg Simmel, *Soziologie* (Third Edition, Munich, 1923), pp. 82–89.

[14] It would be useful if we could employ another term, say, " concurrence," for these types.

position are numerous and complex, but we may perhaps single out the class system as a characteristic resultant.

We turn next to a mitigated form of conflict closely associated with competition but really quite different in its mode of operation. In bargaining the two contenders offer their services to one another, not to a third party. In the immediate transaction both gain something and both give up something, but in the assessment of both parties the gain exceeds the loss, or the transaction would not take place. Bargaining is a process of exchange, arriving at a kind of compromise. It is thus an important aspect of the far-flung system of exchange relationships that is central to the economic order. The exchange rate is itself obviously a social resultant, since it is not the objective of any of the parties concerned but arises from the meeting, opposition, and relative accommodation of their respective desires. The combination of competing and bargaining, as these processes are pursued through multitudes of particular transactions, makes possible the various functional balances characteristic of any complex economic order, the temporary ever-disturbed " equilibrium " of debts and credits, of saving and investment, of prices and costs, of production and consumption, and so forth. Even more obviously the economic phenomena of disequilibrium, such as those associated with the " business cycle," fall into our category of social resultants, responsive to the interaction of divergent and opposing economic interests.

These relations between conflict situations and typical phenomena of social conjuncture may be presented as on the following page. It is of course to be understood that in many conflict situations more than one form of conflict is in process, and also that in all forms of conflict except warfare the conflict is on a level that permits

TABLE II

Social Conjunctures Associated with Conflict Situations

CONFLICT	PROCESS	CONJUNCTURE
1. War	Reciprocal destruction	*Immediate* Inclusive destruction and impoverishment within and beyond the belligerent area *Other* Enormous repercussions on national life, involving also the transformation of original objectives on both sides
2. Competition	Alternative offering of goods or services to a third party	*Immediate* Inclusive loss of advantage by the groups most subject to competitive stress. The *tertius gaudens* *Other* Stimulation of functional efficiency, tendencies to monopoly, etc.
3. Concurrence	Non-violent struggle for domination, prestige, and so forth, not necessarily involving a third party	*Immediate* Social tension and disturbance of the *status quo* *Other* Formation of hierarchies and class systems. Succession of elites and so forth
4. Bargaining	Reciprocal offering of goods or services between two parties, each seeking its respective advantage	*Immediate* Compromise and accommodation *Other* Stimulation of the division of labor

or even requires the coexistence of co-operative activity on another level.

Social conjunctures are so numerous, variant, and complex that we must here be content merely to indicate a few familiar types. Wherever men get together for any purpose, unintended and unforeseen processes are set in motion. The most universal of all social phenomena — the effect on one social being of the presence of another, the effect of the congregation on each member of it — is a social resultant in this sense. Here we can include a vast range of phenomena stretching from the heightened animation of lovers to the accelerated tempo of urban life. Another type of social resultant that has been the object of frequent comment arises from the manner in which the means men have designed become converted into ends, while the ends they have struggled for undergo a process of degeneration into means.[15] Men build organizations, and they find that the frame of organization somehow holds them in its grasp. They develop institutions to serve their particular purposes, and they sometimes end by worshipping them. Seeking to preserve institutions from change men turn them into the sanctuaries of bureaucrats. Or they overthrow the established order, and something else comes into being than the shining goals they sought. Again, we may cite as a well-recognized type of social resultant the unpurposed consequences of technological advance. Men invent aeroplanes, and thereby revolutionize the art of war. They devise the assembly line for automobiles, and the consequences reach

---

[15] See, for example, R. K. Merton, "The Unanticipated Consequences of Purposive Social Action," *American Sociological Review* (December, 1936), Vol. 1, pp. 894–904, and the same writer's "Bureaucratic Structure and Personality," *Social Forces* (May, 1940), Vol. 18, pp. 1–9; E. C. Hughes, "Institutional Office and the Person," *American Journal of Sociology* (1937), Vol. 43, pp. 404–413; E. T. Hiller, "Social Structure in Relation to the Person," *Social Forces* (October, 1937), Vol. 16, pp. 34–44.

into home and school and church. They develop the electron tube, and the remotest hamlet responds to the newest voices of the city.

Since the causal sequence is continuous without end we could logically extend the range of the social conjuncture to include all social phenomena whatever. For they are all the unpurposed consequences, near or remote, of prior behavior in prior situations. A war of a thousand years ago is a determinant, co-operative with countless other things, of the composition of the population today. An advance in sanitation changes incalculably the relation of city and country — and everything else besides. Every birth has consequences of which the parents could not dream. In this sense every being and every event is the product of an inconceivably complex conjuncture. We must merely recognize this truth and pass it by. Such conjunctures, bred in the " dark backward and abysm of time," are beyond investigation. We can at best deal only with dynamic moments of the endless process. For practical reasons we limit ourselves to the conjunctures that are the near unpurposed sequels of purposive actions. Man schemes and contrives under conditions that change and divert his actions into new conditions for new scheming and contriving. But through it all he contributes the causal factor that distinguishes the area of social causation from all others, the factor of dynamic assessment.

OPERATION OF THE DYNAMIC ASSESSMENT

I

HOW THE DYNAMIC MOMENT IS PREPARED

THE DYNAMIC assessment does more than bring diverse elements within one causal system. It is an organizing principle of greater range. The coherence, consistency, or degree of integration attained by each of the three orders of the conscious realm is itself the work of the continuous and successive dynamic assessments of individuals and groups. Everywhere we find the patterning of culture and within it the particular styles of schools and groups, the particular direction and impetus of movements old and new. Everywhere we find characteristic schemes of social relationships, institutional complexes the various aspects and parts of which are somehow congenial to one another. The social scheme in turn is closely bound up with the dominant cultural pattern. Everywhere we find also not a mere aggregation of utilitarian devices or techniques but a close-knit functional unity of interdependent means. And this unity is in turn expressive of the dominant cultural pattern. Hence it is almost universally assumed that the inclusive scheme of things, which, because of our lack of distinctive terms we call the " society " or the " culture " or the " civilization," is also a coherent whole. On this assumption the historian deals with countries and periods and whole civilizations and whole epochs. Perhaps we are too apt to assume that things that are found together on that account belong together. Certainly there are various kinds of unity and various degrees of cohesion which ought to be distinguished and analyzed. The unities we discover are imperfect; they are in process of formation and disruption; they contain incompatible or even alien elements. There is needed here a much more profound social analysis than the subject has yet received.[1] The tendency to integration of some sort is, however, universally acknowledged. Just as there is a selective and integrative process behind the successive acts of a single personality, so there is a selective and integrative process, subject though it is to various rifts and disturbances, behind the successive movements of group convergence.

We shall consider briefly, in so far as it is necessary for our purpose, the characteristic form of cohesion belonging respectively to each of our three orders of the conscious realm, the cultural order, the technological order, and the social order. Our purpose is to bring out the manner in which the various phenomena of the three orders combine in the dynamic complex. We shall therefore not be concerned with the question of how far and in what sense the culture, say, of a whole people forms a unity. Our concern is with the dynamic moment, with the culture scheme in so far as it is exhibited in group convergence towards action. Our concern is to explain an activity

---

[1] The easy habit of conceiving all unities in organic terms has been peculiarly besetting in the social sciences. Obviously the functional (not mechanical) unity of a technological system is different from the valuational or meaningful unity of a culture style. The unity of the dynamic complex in which values and means are conjoined is again different. A suggestive analysis of different types of integration is contained in P. A. Sorokin, "Forms and Problems of Culture Integration," *Rural Sociology* (1936), Vol. 1, pp. 121–141, 344–374. See the same author's *Social and Cultural Dynamics*, Vol. I, Chap. I, and Vol. IV, Chap. I.

that, in so far as it lies within the conscious realm, begins with a *change* in assessment.

Let us look again at the phenomenon of the declining birth-rate. For causal investigation we must take that phenomenon as it appears within one recognizable culture complex. We measure change only against continuity. The birth-rate has declined within the continuity of Western society. If it has declined also among the Central Australians or in some South Sea islands, that is another phenomenon, and the explanation may be either similar or utterly different. The statistical fact is not a decrease of births or an increase of marriages or an increase of divorces or an increase of crimes, but an increase or decrease within an order of things — and it is not a rate, but only a meaningless arithmetical manipulation, if we combine in one statistical expression the figures representing the birth-rate of the United States with the figures representing the birth-rate of Tahiti. Even the rates we more properly construct are subject to qualification in this regard, as including figures for areas that are islanded from the prevailing order of things. There are culture areas that cling to traditions elsewhere outmoded. There are economic areas that are scarcely subject to the impact of technological change. The birth-rate of certain mountainous sections, for example, may express conditions that are not characteristic of the country as a whole; and when we include, say, the figures for the Kentucky mountains in our rate for the United States or the figures for the Piedmontese Alps in our rate for Italy, there is introduced into our rates some degree of artificiality. In fact all rates have in this sense an element of "impurity." The continuum or system to which they by assumption refer is imperfect, but it is only because there is nevertheless a dominant or characteristic system that they are at all meaningful.

Now if we rule out as inadequate a biological explanation in terms of increasing sterility, the change in the birth-rate is a revelation of purposive behavior and thus of a change within a valuational order. In myriads of families the dynamic assessment, the choice of alternatives, has undergone change. The balance of valuation with respect to alternatives of action has shifted. The nature of the valuational change is indicated by the differential birth-rates of different categories. A fuller knowledge of it is obtainable from case studies, from the study of cultural trends that accompany the decline of the birth-rate, and from various other sources of evidence. Conditions and considerations that at an earlier period were not operative have now developed so as to favor a limitation of the size of the family.

But to see this fact aright we must view it as a change in a larger scheme of valuation. A whole set of values cluster about the family life. A whole set of values (for the parents and other near relatives) depend on the existence of offspring — there are other values for the greater unity, the nation or the " race," but these need not at present detain us. There is the sense of perpetuity, of the enduring name, of the home, of the stake in the community; there are the more intimate satisfactions and fulfilments that outreckon the troubles and costs of rearing a family. In the period when the size of the family was relatively unrestricted there could indeed have been little reckoning of alternatives. There were no easy and accessible means for diverting the sexual act from its end in reproduction, but this condition was in accord with the whole situation, cultural and economic, of the patriarchal family, and with the mores of the larger community. The lack of careers for women, the lack of a controlling standard of living so far as the majority of the people were concerned, and the early entrance of the young into the service of the agricultural economy were again facts that harmonized with religious doctrines and social traditions. But changes of various kinds came to disturb this valuational scheme. It would take too long to discuss these in detail, though it would be quite possible to show how the cultural complex of family life responded to them at different stages and under different conditions. Every cultural complex at every stage strives to maintain itself in action. Incessantly it readjusts changing means under changing conditions to somewhat changing ends. Every cultural complex has to be conceived as a unity, *sharpened to a specific objective at the spear-point of action.* In this way we must apprehend the effective desire for a smaller family that is registered in the decline of the birth-rate.

Next let us consider the technological aspect. It was no historical accident, no fortuitous invention, that brought the development and wide-spread application of contraceptive methods in the later nineteenth and in the twentieth century. Devices for limiting the number of offspring, such as mutilation, abortion, the imposition of prerequisites for marriage, and even crude contraceptive practices, are very ancient. Under some conditions, in China and elsewhere, the size of the family was restricted also by infanticide. But these practices were for the most part sporadic and occasional. For the most part some kind of balance of births and deaths was maintained by what Malthus called the positive checks — disease, famine, misery, and war. The advance of hygiene, sanitation, and preventive medicine in general, accompanying the improved standards of living made possible by the increased " command " over nature, found its greatest triumphs in the reduction of child mortality and above all of infant mortality. Whereas at one time an average of five or more births per family was requisite to maintain the population level, in the second decade of the twentieth century an average of a little over three sufficed for many countries of Western civilization, in spite of a less favorable composition of population. It was while this most significant change was in process that modern contraceptive methods evolved. It was then that cultural attitudes became widely receptive to contraceptive practices. It was then, too, that medical art devised more effective methods. These methods were in fact special applications of a wide-ranging advance of medical knowledge, which in turn was closely bound up with the broader advance of science. We can safely say that the same technological principles that made possible the reduction of child mortality also made possible the improvement of contraceptive devices. In short, at every stage the technology is applied in the various directions that are congenial to the demands of the culture. The inclusive and coherent technology is specialized and elaborated into the various instruments and agencies of the culture. Just as the cultural complex becomes focussed in particular objectives, so does the technological system become effective as corresponding selective means. In the dynamic assessment the two meet. It is there and then that they become respectively objective and means.

We need not spend much time to show that a congruent process of adaptation occurs in our third order, that of the social relationships themselves. Under the impact of many other changes and in conformity to them the scheme of family relations had been undergoing change. The conditions of modern urban life were favorable to the detached unitary family, dissolving the relationship cluster of the patriarchal household and promoting a mobile family unbound to any location and at the same time less immersed in the tradition of the successive generations.[2] The various

---

[2] It is significant that modern writers on the family bestow less attention on the continuing genealogical family than did earlier writers,

specializations of work and interest characteristic of an industrial civilization reduced the functions of the family proper, so that it became less and less the center around which the activities of its members revolved. Of particular importance was the fact that the women members of the family, especially the younger women, were engaging in non-domestic occupations. As the family became less engrossing or less demanding in other respects, its primary function, that of reproduction, was becoming accommodated to the new conditions. The new scheme of relationships, responsive to both cultural and technological change, required, at least in the highly urbanized and the highly industrialized areas, a restriction in the size of the family. For our present purpose it suffices merely to indicate that this special aspect of the social order is congruent alike with a special aspect of the cultural complex and with a special application of the technological system. Continuously the dynamic assessment maintains and reselects the relevant aspects of the inner as well as of the outer environment.

II

HOW THE DYNAMIC PROCESS IS ORGANIZED

We have now seen that the simplest conscious act presupposes a preparatory stage in which relevant aspects of the three orders of the conscious realm are selectively marshalled and directed towards the point of action. The ever-changing scheme of values, responsive to change throughout the whole realm of being, becomes focussed at each moment in this objective or in that. Likewise, from the available system of apparatus particular devices and instruments are selected and adapted as means appropriate to the objective. The social organization in its turn presents

---

and that present-day American books on the subject, somewhat in contrast with European books, almost completely ignore it.

a particular conformation congenial both to the objective and to the means. Countless prior actions have created the larger correspondence between the cultural complex, the technological system, and the social framework. This correspondence, especially in the more advanced societies, is always incomplete and subject to various disturbances.[3] It is always in process of readjustment and reintegration. And every act, while itself deriving from a pre-established correspondence, may also be regarded as reasserting or readjusting the relationship of the orders within its own range and perspective.

We should, of course, bear in mind that the interadjustment of the three orders is dependent on and responsive to the biophysical conditions. Thus, to return to our recent example, the limitation of the size of the family postulates not only the biological requirements for reproduction, but also the particular biological factors that are manifested in the lower death-rate preceding and accompanying the fall of the birth-rate. It postulates also the physical and biological conditions that lie back of those technological applications that enhance economic productivity and make higher standards of living possible. The " fitness " of the environment is a primary requisite for the interadjustment, as well as for the prior existence, of our three orders. We have then, in any conscious action, a new dynamic relationship set up between particularized aspects of various systems that through long time have been undergoing continuous readjustment one to another. From this point of view we envisage:

1. A set of objectives (including conscious drives of any kind), arising within a particular cultural complex and

---

[3] On this subject see the writer's statement, " The Historical Pattern of Social Change," in *Authority and the Individual*, Harvard Tercentenary Publications, 1937.

finding particular expression in the process of dynamic assessment.

2. A set of techniques or controls, derived from the apparatus of a particular civilization, and applied to the specific objectives.

3. A set of social relations, falling within a larger social system, organized conformably to the particular objectives and at the same time constituting an aspect of either or both of 2 and 3, as agency if not as goal of action.

4. A set of biophysical conditions, as relevant to and prerequisite for the particular action. (For our immediate purpose we need not separate the physical and the biological realms.)

Now no one of these factor groups, in whole or in part, has independent efficacy in the causation of the act. A set of objectives or even the most imperative of urges can as such effect nothing. " If wishes were horses, beggars would ride." Motives are impotent apart from means. Goals are idle dreams if no road leads to them. Without goals or motives there are no *social* phenomena. Without some knowledge of goals and motives there is no understanding of social phenomena. But they become dynamic only in the conjuncture that joins them to the particular situation. This last statement can equally be made with reference to techniques or to social relations or to biophysical conditions. A thing becomes a means, instrument, agency, or control only in relation to an objective or motive. Apart from that it effects nothing. Its being as means is its role in the attainment of ends. Even the biophysical conditions do nothing by themselves to create the social phenomenon. Biological changes in the balance of births and deaths do not as such cause a limitation of the size of the family or a movement against " race suicide "; what they do is to

present new alternatives to the social beings who in the face
of these alternatives, as part of the situations they envisage
and define, act thus — or otherwise.

These considerations show once more how unavailing
is the simply quantitative approach that seeks to attach
particular weights to the several " factors," attributing to
each so much push or pull in a total push or pull. We have
just seen that the factors are dynamic only within the conjuncture, and therein they are dynamic, not as such, not
as separate items of reality, not in their intrinsic properties,
but only as they are subjectively apprehended and assessed. Only in the dynamic assessment is there anything
that can be called the weighting of factors. And this weighting employs no objective scales. It varies with every mood
as well as with every situation. In so far as there is weighting it is relative to a value scheme. And we do not weight
ends and means and conditions as coordinate items. Means
are also costs in the value reckoning. They limit as well as
facilitate desires, and even in facilitating they usually
involve a reduction of the immediate net satisfaction we
should gain had our desires a magic potency. Utilities from
this point of view are also relative disutilities. Since in
varying degrees they constitute the minuses of net attainable satisfactions they are forever changing the equilibrium of our effective desires. How much they do so is endlessly contingent and can be learned only, and then within
limits, by the most careful analysis of the particular behavior of men and groups, in which we judge how far their
objectives and motives are evoked by the various facilities
and opportunities at their command.[4] The total appre-

---

[4] This analysis, no matter how elaborately behavioristic, must still
resort to imaginative reconstruction, since it cannot dispense with the
subjective evidences, the direct and indirect communication through
which those whose behavior is being investigated express their experience, their problems, their desires and feelings. Even in the explana-

hended situation, including conditions as well as specific means, controls the value assessment and the direction of the value quest.

Since none of the primary components of the dynamic conjuncture have as such any independent efficacy we must assign that efficacy to the conjunction itself, to the consummation of the dynamic assessment. There are unfathomed psycho-organic processes involved in the formulation of the dynamic alternatives, in the choice between them, and in the passage of decision into action. These are not here our concern. Our concern is with the process wherein changing assessments, changing means, and changing conditions are interrelated so as to bring out *social* action, as revealed in an institutional reform, a group movement, a statistical fact, and so forth. If a like change of attitude or of overt behavior is at the same time manifested by many individuals we can for our present purpose ignore the psychological complexities of their variant assessments. We can look for some significant difference between the conditions to which they alike respond, the means they alike possess, the cultural complex they alike reveal, and the comparable conditions, means, and cultural complexes of those who do not manifest the change of attitude or of overt behavior. We can thus bring the social phenomena within the universal

---

tion of such a *relatively* simple decision as that which determines how a rat will behave at a choice point in a maze the psychologists are impelled to introduce such factors as " demand," " appetite," " learning capacity," and " skill," and to construct elaborate hypothetical formulas indicative of the relationship of these factors. (See, for example, Edward Chace Tolman, " The Determiners of Behavior at a Choice Point," *Psychological Review* (January, 1938), Vol. 45, pp. 1–41.) The decision of a rat to turn right or left in the quest for food at a maze intersection of routes is already a complex act of discrimination and yet incomparably less complex than the problem of decision of the social being, culturally conditioned and technologically equipped, apprehending a total situation in the light of his past experiences and under the impulsion of a variety of not wholly integrated desires.

formula of causal investigation. Since the difference is so often one of degree — increase or decrease of crime, competition, division of labor, radicalism, and so forth — we can endeavor to trace the spread or development of the phenomenon, as one traces a rising or receding tide. We may discover why it rises here and recedes there — *and our explanation will be no longer the listing of a congeries of factors but the exposition of a coherent pervading cause that is not any of the factors nor all of them together nor even any combination of them.* We must seek the dynamics of a spreading change beyond the factors of the individual instances that reveal it. Each single manifestation of the phenomenon of change may be attributed to the changed relationship of the factors in that situation, but now we are concerned with the spread of the phenomenon, from person to person, from group to group, from area to area. What determines the ebb and flow of the tide? What is it that moves, that takes hold, that spreads, that controls the ebbing and the flowing tide?

Now we approach the answer to a question raised much earlier. We were not satisfied with the various attempts to explain such phenomena as an increase of crime by reference to this or that concomitant or group of concomitants. The attribution seemed always precarious, not grounded in any adequate methodology. In Chapter Nine we suggested a different approach. There we pointed out that factors highly correlated with a social trend at one stage of its progression may lose that correlation altogether at a later stage. Economic status, for example, was so closely associated with family limitation in the late nineteenth and early twentieth century that there can be no doubt the correlation was significant. But gradually the association dwindled and in some areas disappeared. It is thus apparent that a high income level was not in any proper sense a cause of the *movement* we designate as the decline of the birth-rate. And so for the other factors. We may regard certain conditions as facilitating the trend. We may regard the antithetical conditions (such as poverty, lack of education, orthodoxy in religion, rural domicile) as resisting the trend, just as rocks remain unsubmerged by the advancing tide that first fills the hollows. But neither the rocks nor the hollows are the causes of the tide. Something that itself moves must be the explanation of a movement. There is the moving moon beyond the moving tides.

III

SOME APPLICATIONS

Let us consider more at length the significance of this approach. It suggests that if we limit our attention to the specific properties or components of individual instances, looking for the causal explanation in some particular linkage between them and the phenomena of change, we may miss the distinctive unity of the causal process. We may fail to perceive or at least may not realize the import of the cultural transmission that is the lifeblood of a trend or movement. We may attach a misleading role to the conditions that favor the spread of the movement, regarding them as its sufficient causes. To bring out this point we shall examine in turn one form or subtype falling under each of the three main types of social phenomenon we distinguished in the previous chapter.

1. Suppose we are investigating the increase of the divorce rate in the United States. While an increase in the number of divorces has characterized modern civilization generally, it has been to an eminent degree characteristic of the United States in the past fifty years. This fact prompts two closely allied whys. Why has the di-

vorce rate increased in the United States? Why is the divorce rate of the United States higher than the rates of other
countries of Western civilization? Each of these

The   questions presumably concerns a difference be-
Statistical   tween comparable situations, the first defined as
Fact   a time difference and the second defined as a
                 place difference. Since in both cases the difference
is a moving one, the investigation of either involves a range
of subsidiary questions concerning time differences and
place differences. Let us limit ourselves to the former of
the two questions. We find that the divorce rate has increased much more in some areas of the United States than
in others. We find that although the East is more industrialized than the West the rate generally increases as we
go from east to west. We find that some of the less urbanized Western states, such as Oregon and Texas, exhibit
markedly higher rates than more urbanized Eastern states,
such as Massachusetts and New York. We find at the same
time that the Southern Atlantic states have comparatively
very low divorce rates. *Within* the different areas referred
to, but not *between* them, the rate is higher for more urbanized than for less urbanized sections.[5] It is much higher
for childless than for fertile marriages. It is higher also
for Protestant than for Roman Catholic groups. It is
higher also for states that admit a number of grounds for
divorce as contrasted with states that strictly limit these
grounds. Now we might regard childlessness, urban environment, religious affiliations that do not prohibit divorce, and accommodating laws as our " factors " and
make them the causal explanation of the increase of divorce. But such an attribution would not explain the
trend. It would not explain the marked differences between
the larger areas, or again between countries. Oregon is

---

[5] For the figures see A. Cahan, *Statistical Analysis of American Divorce*,
New York, 1932.

less urbanized than New York State. California is not as urbanized as Pennsylvania. Catholic Austria has shown higher divorce rates than Protestant England. Laws are reflective of social attitudes rather than explanatory of them. Childlessness exists in similar proportions in states with very different rates. And so for the various other factors that are advanced. Thus some countries, such as England, have a large percentage of women engaged in non-domestic employments and yet show a low divorce rate. In short, for a satisfactory explanation of the increase of divorce we must go beyond the factors. We must no less go beyond the " grounds " of divorce. We cannot conclude that there is more divorce because there is more adultery or more " mental cruelty." Divorce is the legal dissolution of the family. Why do more people resort to it now than formerly? Why are they more ready to take advantage of the " grounds " offered by the law?

Many evidences point to the conclusion that various groups no longer attach as high a valuation as formerly to family cohesion. In the assessment of alternative ends it is weighted less heavily than under earlier conditions. The continuity of the family name, abode, and heritage through the generations plays a smaller part in the thoughts and the activities of large numbers. The family has become more detached, more limited to the immediate circle of parents and young children. Why this should be so is not difficult to discern. The specialization of work, the increase of mobility, the greater economic independence of women, the demands of urban residence, the stripping from the home of many of its former functions, the obsolescence for large groups of former religious sanctions, the earlier initiation of youth into associational activities outside the home — these and other considerations are relevant. How they affect the dynamic assessment that in the face of certain issues chooses divorce instead of the preservation of the family is a matter requiring the careful analysis of many different situations. We might pursue it along the lines already suggested for the investigation of a related phenomenon, the limitation of the size of the family. Here we shall be content with the evidence that there has been a change in valuation affecting the status of the family. The general indication is that *divorce is more prevalent in those areas where the continuity of the family through several generations has less significance in the scheme of cultural values than formerly or than elsewhere.*

We do not put forward this conclusion as though it were a complete explanation of modern divorce, but rather as a heuristic hypothesis to be refined, supplemented, and tested by fuller investigation. What we claim is that any satisfactory explanation must be somewhat of this type. What justifies it is that it throws light on the whole *trend* of the divorce rate. It helps to explain why this trend diverges at various points from the trend of urbanization or of industrialization, why here it follows the decline of authoritative religion and there it does not, why in one environment it is associated with the increase in the " gainful employment " of women and in another environment it is not — and so forth. It explains the very constant association between divorce and social mobility. It accords with the concept of the family characteristic of countries and areas where divorce is prevalent, as shown by literary records of various kinds.[6] In short, we can in the light of

---

[6] We might even include the characterizations of the family offered by sociologists of different countries. Perhaps the approach most current in the United States is that of E. W. Burgess, who treats the family as a " unity of interacting personalities " — see his article on this subject in *The Family* (March, 1926), Vol. 7, pp. 3–9 — an approach adopted by W. W. Waller in his book, *The Family*, New York, 1938. European writers give less prominence to this *aspect* of the family. This observa-

this hypothesis give an intelligible account of the great variations in the frequency of divorce as well as of its general increase under the conditions of modern civilization.

▼

2. Let us take as a second example the rise of a social movement. By a social movement we mean here the concerted advocacy of a program of action or of any doctrine that inspires a program of action. Modern society offers a multitude of instances. Some are politico-economic, such as Marxism, fascism, communism, socialism, the single-tax movement, pacifism, the movement led by men like Coughlin, Townsend, and numerous others who build up a following in the name of some political principle. Some are socio-economic, like co-operative movements and consumers' leagues. Others are philanthropic, educational, moral, recreational, in an endless variety of modes and combinations. We think of a movement as the organized promotion of a cause. If the cause becomes fully established or institutionalized within the social order, this later embodiment is more appropriately given some other name. Thus we think of fascism as a social movement while it is still proclaimed by insurgent groups seeking to control the state, but not when and where it has become the established system of government. This, incidentally, is in accord with the usage of fascist writers, who speak of fascism as being a movement up to the time when the Fascist Party was formed.[7]

The Social Movement

The causal investigation of the rise and growth of a movement requires us, as in the preceding case, to go

tion is similar to that we made in an earlier note where we were discussing the birth-rate. One great advantage of the method we propose, which seeks for a causal formula beyond the factors, is that it reveals the close cultural interdependence of many social phenomena, and particularly of the various trends or movements that occur in the same social milieu.

[7] H. A. Steiner, *Government in Fascist Italy* (New York, 1938), p. 12.

beyond the factors that facilitate or impede its advance. Such factors vary with the milieu and the stage of the movement. By themselves they do not afford us any unified or adequate explanation. The why of a movement introduces, however, certain complexities not presented by the why of a statistical fact. The movement expresses the convergent assessment of many persons directed towards a common objective, in contrast with the parallel assessments manifested in the instances of a particular act, such as a crime or a suit for divorce. A considerable variety of interests and attitudes may converge on an objective of this kind. Hence again the objective may be conceived in different and even conflicting ways by those who nevertheless unite in the common cause. It may also change its character in significant respects as it gains more adherents and advances towards realization.

Let us briefly take fascism as an example. Because of the complexities just mentioned we can do no more, within these limits, than indicate a procedure. In the first place it is necessary to interpret various evidences in order to comprehend the nature of the movement. What is the fascism that gained strength in Italy in 1919 and the succeeding years? There is some scheme of values, some objective, some view of life or at least some proposed way of meeting certain of its problems. What makes it a movement is that it seeks expansion. Its dynamism works outwards. It would convert, influence, control. Let us suppose we have sufficiently identified its initial character — its demand for national, or nationalistic, unity, its activism, its turbulence, its resort to violence, its denunciation of left-wing organizations, its irritation against democratic institutions, its imperial gestures, its invocation of power at the top and discipline below, its exaltation of the leader, its ruthless opportunism. We want to learn why this movement arose and spread; why in the first place it emerged as a distinctive historically dated program, why it gained momentum, and why in doing so it changed its character in particular respects. What we are really seeking is to discover why the assertion of a certain characteristic value complex was effective among particular groups of a particular people at a particular historical moment. The more we know of the pre-existing conditions and the attitudes that accompanied them the closer we can come to our mark. But we must first understand as fully as possible the distinctive character of the value complex called fascism. Then we can hope to relate the various factors of the different situations under which people in different degrees accepted and promoted fascism. Then we can hope to give a unified explanation of why some groups were more responsive than others; why it made headway among war veterans, and industrialists, and youth groups, and anti-communist labor elements, and politicians, and military leaders; why others, such as the feudal nobility, made ready concessions to it; why others again, and particularly the church authorities, made uneasy compromise with it; why yet others, such as the freemasons, supported it at first and then were cast aside. We have here the picture of a myriad dynamic assessments, at a particular conjuncture of events, converging towards a like response.

As we pursue this method the form as well as the dynamics of a social movement becomes clearer — not of one movement only but of the generic phenomenon. It seems to follow, though with endless variations, a fundamental pattern. First a favoring conjuncture arises, frequently in some time of crisis, when prior routines or a pre-established equilibrium is shaken. The time is ripe for a restatement of values. This may be on any level, from the proclamation of a new world gospel to the most opportunistic call for the redistribution of spoils. Men grope about for some kind of salvation. A germinal idea emerges, precipitated by challenging experiences. A leader seizes hold of the idea. A small circle gathers around him. It is the parent cell of the movement. As it grows it devises symbols, elaborates an ideology, builds a fighting organization seeking establishment, incorporation in the social system. It meets opposition, reaffirms its values with new emphasis, often changing and compromising in the process. If it succeeds in the quest for establishment it ceases to be a movement in the old sense. It becomes a part of the institutional order, of a new equilibrium that in its turn is shaken or disturbed by new forces of change, from which again new movements arise. For the heart of every movement is some restatement or re-emphasis of values, about which men rally in an expansive organization. And when we study what happens to the movement, we are studying, above all, the ways in which men respond to a particular value claim, according to their needs, their situations, and their prior indoctrinations.

▼

3. Our third example brings further complexities, a still more intricate interplay of causal relations. We consider now the process of change in an institutional-

The Institutional Pattern ized mode of behavior already incorporated in the social order. Take the economico-political scheme of things we call capitalism. It is forever changing and we distinguish, if somewhat loosely, various phases and aspects such as early capitalism, eighteenth century capitalism, modern capitalism, industrial capitalism, laissez-faire capitalism, state capitalism, and so forth. But here our difficulties begin. Capitalism is not a demarcated system, like a machine. Where it is operative it is inwrought into the total social order. How much of that social order shall we distinguish as capitalism?

Shall we call the law of property a condition or an aspect of capitalism? Is the association between free enterprise and democracy accidental or essential? These and similar questions men answer different ways. We may have some simple criterion of capitalism, say the predominantly private ownership of the means of production. But no such criterion will enable us to mark its boundaries. There will still be significant differences of definition and interpretation. Furthermore, the going system we call capitalistic will contain elements of antithetical systems. It will include collectivistic controls. Private ownership and the profit-seeking economy will be limited at important points. A purely capitalistic system will be as rare as a purely communistic one. The concept of capitalism, however formulated, will not be fully applicable to reality.

We can avoid some of these difficulties if we confine our causal investigation to the processes of change in a single instance of what we call capitalism. But then what we are explaining will not be the transitions of capitalism as such but of a unique economico-political system containing capitalistic features. We may trace the changes occurring in these capitalistic features within the larger changes of the total economy. If we discover similar changes in other instances containing somewhat similar capitalistic features we can regard these changes as the history of a phase or type of capitalism. But we can no longer impute the changes to forces inherent in capitalism itself. What changes is not capitalism but an institutional complex manifesting certain capitalistic attributes. The dynamics of change, as we have already pointed out, are not resident in the institutions that change. Institutions are the social routes men follow; if they change it is because men follow different routes. The co-operating and conflicting desires of men, never fully stabilized under any set of institutions, are forever impelling institutional change. But men change their institutions because they are seeking to change other things, because they are striving to attain values in situations imperfectly equilibrated by institutions. We have to deal not only with a convergent group assessment, as in the social movement, but with the numerous variant and conflicting assessments of the individuals and groups that are embraced within the institutional complex. Hence the causal relations involved in the change of an institutional system are exceedingly complicated.

We must therefore content ourselves with a schematic presentation, since a specific historical illustration would overweight this chapter. Diagram III offers a simplified presentation of the manner in which the changes of capitalism (however defined) are related to the changes of the inclusive structural order exhibiting capitalistic features. The system undergoing change is not capitalism as such. Capitalistic features are bound up with others and together with them constitute the changing system. Some of the changes in the system may be brought about by movements that directly attack or defend the capitalistic principle. But the actual system is not the sheer embodiment of a principle. When we speak of capitalism we put a selective emphasis on certain strands in the web of social relations. But the changes occur in the web itself. This fact is graphically shown in Diagram III on the following page.

A few comments may be added to explain the diagram. Because our interest was focussed on capitalism we singled out the capitalistic features of the inclusive system. If our interest had been different we would have selected some other features. We might have viewed the inclusive system as a class system, a power system, an ethical system, and so forth, giving another meaning to our symbol k. No attempt is made in the diagram to suggest the elaborate

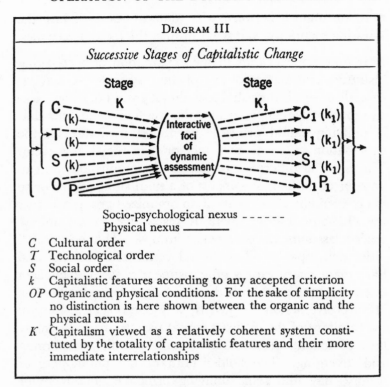

DIAGRAM III

Successive Stages of Capitalistic Change

Socio-psychological nexus - - - - - -
Physical nexus ————

C   Cultural order
T   Technological order
S   Social order
k   Capitalistic features according to any accepted criterion
OP Organic and physical conditions. For the sake of simplicity
      no distinction is here shown between the organic and the
      physical nexus.
K   Capitalism viewed as a relatively coherent system consti-
      tuted by the totality of capitalistic features and their more
      immediate interrelationships

causal interactions of the dynamic assessments, convergent
and conflicting, of individuals and groups. Nor is any
attempt made to distinguish the social resultant from the
intended consequences of group and individual activities.
It will be observed that we show both types of causal nexus,
the socio-psychological and the physical, as relating the
organic and physical conditions to the foci of dynamic
assessment. The point is that biological processes, the
changing state of the organism itself and of its adjustment
to the physical environment, affect the assessing focus and
therefore the nature of its assessment; while on the other
hand physico-organic factors are subject to dynamic assessment and thus undergo changes other than those that come
about in the direct line from OP to O_1P_1. Once again we

must distinguish between what determines the focus, the assessing mentality, and what in turn the focus determines.

It now appears that in the explanation of a changing institutional order, or of any of the " systems " — such as capitalism — distinguishable within it by aid of some selective concept, we cannot assume the presence of the same kind of unifying causal principle we found available for the explanation of a statistical fact or of a social movement. The essential difference is that the latter phenomena can be referred to like assessments of a number of people or to the convergent assessments of an organized group, whereas the changing establishment is responsive to the many-angled assessments of diverse groups. The established order encompasses all sorts and conditions of men, who have made every variety of adjustment to it. The changes occurring in the established order do not represent the line of purposive action dictated by any one objective but are the resultant of the intricate causal pattern made by many lines of action, crossing and running parallel, converging and diverging. The bolder faith of the philosopher of history may find some unifying principle, immanent or transcendent. But the scientific investigator of causal process cannot have recourse to any embracing formula.

At this point we may raise a final question. Since to trace all these complexities of interaction is a baffling task and one that can never be fully accomplished, must we be content merely to follow the broader avenues of change and to record the historically given transitions? In a word, can we distinguish here between historical description and causal analysis? The methodology we have been developing throughout this study furnishes an answer. It can be applied in various ways so as to throw more and more light on processes of change the full revelation of which we may never wholly attain. If we suggest some of these ways it will serve also to recall the route over which we have travelled up to this point.

First let us repeat that all causal investigation is directed to a difference between comparable situations. In the transition from one phase of capitalism to another various specific differences in the capitalistic features of this or that part of the social structure emerge and can be made objects of causal investigation. There are changes in the relations of ownership to control or management, in the relations of employers to wage-earners, in the relations of the financial organization to the producing organization, in the processes of distribution, in the role played by government, in the form and extent and degree of concentration of the various economic associations, and so forth. These offer numerous specific problems of causation. As we attack one we are indirectly attacking others. As we advance towards the solution of one, uncovering its closer relations with certain others in the process of transition, we are gradually disclosing, part by part, the intricate larger pattern of the whole changing system. We are learning, among other things, the modes in which the capitalistic features are bound to other features within particular social structures. In fact, it is only on the basis of many such investigations that we can with any hope of success attack the larger issues of social change. The causal challenge cannot be stated in the vague general question: Why did capitalism change from the stage K to the stage K_1? It must rather take the shape: Why did a system exhibiting a certain characteristic pattern change to one exhibiting this other characteristic pattern? The difference between the two patterns must be clearly designated if there is to be a genuine basis for scientific investigation.

Given this preparation, the search for a synthesizing principle may be legitimately, if still somewhat speculatively, extended to the greater processes of social change, to the transformations and revolutions that befall social systems or even whole civilizations. In particular we may look for some precipitant that here or there disturbs or disrupts the established order. As we have shown, the concept of the precipitant is serviceable only where there is some kind of self-maintaining equilibrium, some well-adjusted and relatively closed system the continuance of which we can reasonably predict on the assumption that no invading or erupting factor breaks or thwarts the prevailing routine.[8] The system operates for a time according to some definite pattern: change is no doubt incessant, but for a time it appears only as the variant modes of an established type. The going system absorbs or integrates the change. Then comes a time when the system, as we have understood it, is challenged. It may be a seemingly sudden revolution or it may be a more gradual process; but if the latter we recognize it, at least in retrospect, as the passing of one order of things into another. Something, we feel, has loosened the bonds of the old order. We search for that something, and often, rightly or wrongly, discover our precipitant.

As an example we may take Max Weber's explanation of the decline and fall of the classical culture of the Roman Empire.[9] The characteristic art, poetry, historiography, jurisprudence, and other manifestations of the Roman

---

[8] All prediction of the recurrence of events or of the continuance of processes is based on the assumption of a relatively closed system. The validity of the prediction depends on the basis for the belief that the system will remain relatively closed during the time interval covered by the prediction. It is this type of prediction — not the prediction of sheer novelty — that belongs within the realm of science.

[9] " Die sozialen Gründe des Untergangs der antiken Kultur," in *Gesammelte Aufsätze zur Sozial- und Wirtschaftsgeschichte* (Tübingen, 1924), pp. 289–311.

spirit, even the genius of the language, were in full decay by the third century after Christ. The manifestations were not merely changing, they lost the essential qualities they had hitherto possessed. The whole pattern of the pre-existing culture was disrupted or destroyed. How did this come about? It is Weber's contention that the determinant factor was not the irruption of alien power or influence nor the break-up of the political system — the latter endured for centuries after the distinctive culture had passed away. The system that first manifested decisive change was what we have called the basic technology. Classical culture was urban culture. The city was the locus of art and literature no less than of political power. It was supported by the free exchange of the products of urban industry with those of rural agriculture. As the city grew, this exchange of goods took on an international character. But gradually slave labor became dominant in the Roman economy, extruding free labor and turning the freemen into owners, overseers, and idle beneficiaries of slave industry. The slave lived characteristically in compounds or barracks, a propertyless and even familyless population. This process transferred the center of social life from the city to the semi-rural slave establishment. It militated against the free exchange of goods. It removed the technological support of an urban civilization, and thus the technological conditions of the cultural pattern of ancient Rome. The servile land, not the free city, set the cultural style, introducing the feudal age.

We are not concerned here with the evidence marshalled by Weber to show the cumulative effects of the development of a slave economy under the Roman Empire. Nor is it our task to evaluate his interpretation. Our point is that Weber's approach shows a true appreciation of the nature of the causal problem. He has asked the crucial question. He starts from the position implicitly accepted by every historian, that in the earlier period of the Roman Empire there was a distinctive dominant Graeco-Roman culture, relatively well integrated, and that in the later period of the Empire this culture was disintegrated or at least profoundly transformed. Where, then, he asks, do we find the progressive intrusion of an alien element into the characteristic pattern of Roman life? Which of the component systems was most directly exposed to the cumulative impact of such an element? Can we show that the operation of this intruding element was such as to bring about the kind of transformation exhibited by the culture of Rome? Obviously the answers to such questions are not final. Obviously the questions themselves are based on certain assumptions. But it is only by asking and attempting to answer such questions that we can expect some fuller clarification of the problem of far-flung historical change. As we shall see in the final chapter, our conclusions regarding these major changes — and many others as well — will at best be proximate and subject to constant restatement.

CHAPTER THIRTEEN

ATTRIBUTION OF EFFECTS

I

EXAMINATION OF INSTANCES

THE LOGICAL NEXUS, unlike the causal, has no time direction. Inference can travel indifferently from effect to cause or from cause to effect. Practical and theoretical considerations alike may lead us to postulate some cause, to take it as datum, and ask concerning its effects. So far we have given relatively little attention to this form of enquiry, where we ask not *why* something happened but *what also* happened because something else did. Such a question comes easily to us on certain occasions, especially when faced by some portentous event. We hear the crash, the earth-shaking repercussions, and we ask: What has it done? So when a war has occurred, or a revolution, or an economic collapse, or any cataclysmic event, we recognize certain manifest consequences but want to know what further consequences, less obvious but possibly even more momentous, it has entailed. In the same fashion we enquire concerning the effects of a discovery or invention, of something new that has emerged or been projected into a situation, of anything we conceive of as a precipitant, disturbing the established routines. Or again, when an occurrence marks a turning point, as it seems, in the life-history of individual or group, when it signalizes the reversal of a trend, or a change of direction, we tend to regard it as setting in motion a train of consequences and seek to explore the manner of its causal operation. What difference has a man's marriage made to the tenor of his life, or the fact that he has fallen heir to a fortune, or the fact that he has lost his job? When we pursue questions of this sort we move downstream, as it were, following the causal sequence along the time order: whereas when we ask concerning the causes of things we move upstream, working back from the datum as effect.

The quest for effects might seem at first sight to be free from some of the problems associated with the quest for causes. The sequence is before us. We have presented to us the situation before the event, the event itself, and the situation after the event. If the event marks a drastic and abrupt change in the course of affairs it is a simple enough inference to make it the cause of the difference. A shot is fired and a man is killed. The causal relationship is plain. A depression occurs, and the marriage rate falls. The nexus is understandable, and we are ready to attribute the decrease in marriages to the depression. But the causal relationship is not so obvious — it has still to be proved. A change of government takes place, and trade revives. But before we can assert any cause-effect relationship we must make a careful analysis of the economic situation, and even when we have done so some doubts may still remain. Of the three examples we have just given the last two involve the operation of the dynamic assessment. They belong within our sphere of social causation, and they suggest that within this sphere the quest for effects has to surmount difficulties similar to those we encounter in the quest for causes.

Sometimes, it is true, the inference from cause to effect is easy. There are situations into which some factor, such as a declaration of war, is suddenly injected and which immediately thereafter exhibit a series of drastic changes. If the injected factor is relatively contingent, so that we could have presumed the continuance of the prior situation apart from the injection of the factor, then the causal inference is reasonably clear, particularly if we can show that the sequence has occurred not once but many times. But usually the problem of inference is more complex. Let us look, for example, at the accompanying charts (Diagram IV). The last three charts, presenting respectively indices of industrial production, factory payrolls, and factory employment, exhibit sharp drops and subsequent sharp upswings on two occasions during the period from 1920 to 1936, the major disturbance beginning in the year 1929. The three phenomena thus charted are of course closely interdependent. For all three both the fall and the rise occur almost simultaneously. The three are in fact aspects of one inclusive process, the process of business activity. The simultaneous fall of all three means that business activity has been suddenly checked. The main problem here is not how a change in one may affect the others, but what combination of conditions has caused the check to business activity that is registered in these three different ways. But turn to the first three charts. The social phenomena to which they refer belong to another category than that of business activity. And the question is: To what extent and in what ways did the decline in business activity affect the marriage rate, the birth-rate, and the divorce rate? We are positing the depression as a causal factor and asking about its repercussions on certain social relationships.

Accordingly we look for indications of concomitance or sequence such as would suggest a causal nexus between the fluctuations of the rates representing social relationships and the fluctuations of the rates representing the volume of business activity. In this instance we find that the marriage rate, which had been tending somewhat downward

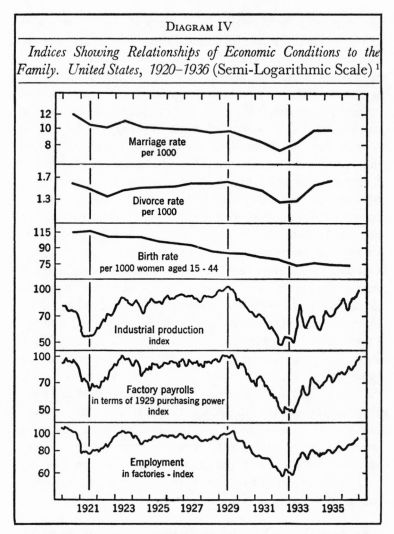

DIAGRAM IV

Indices Showing Relationships of Economic Conditions to the Family. United States, 1920–1936 (Semi-Logarithmic Scale) [1]

previously, exhibits a relatively sharp decline followed by an upturn, with business recovery, to a level slightly higher than before the drop. Here we have a strong presumption

[1] Reproduced with permission of Stouffer and Lazarsfeld, *Research Memorandum on The Family in the Depression*, Social Science Research Council, New York, 1937.

that the depression adversely affected the marriage rate. If we find, as in fact we do, that other depressions have been accompanied by a fall in the number of marriages we have strong grounds for inferring a causal connection, *since there is also an understandable relationship between the prospect of attaining, maintaining, or enhancing an income and the mode of behavior we call " getting married."* Now this understandable relationship or, in other words, the relationship that leads back to the dynamic assessment, varies with social conditions, with the prevailing mores, with status, with age, with income level, with the role of women in the economic system, with the normal expectations associated with different modes of life. Hence, to attain more nearly to the socio-psychological nexus between the decline of business activity and the decline of the marriage rate, it is necessary to have available and to analyze a considerable series of group rates, observing how they fluctuate during and immediately after a depression.[2]

Consider next the divorce rate. The chart indicates that in the United States, for the period in question, it fluctuates in closer correspondence with the volume of business activity than does the marriage rate. It rises definitely with economic prosperity and declines markedly during depression. (This movement, of course, is to be distinguished from the long-time or secular trend of the divorce rate.) That economic conditions exercise a determinant influence on the divorce rate is strongly suggested by the charts, as well as by other evidences, especially since there is an understandable connection to support the inference. Divorce is generally a rather expensive affair, both as a legal process and also because it frequently precedes the setting up of a new matrimonial establishment. The

---

[2] An admirable preliminary analysis of the available data is given in Stouffer and Lazarsfeld, op. cit. Chap. VI.

reasonable expectation that the number of divorces would decrease in hard times is supported by the figures. It is further confirmed by the correlation between the divorce rate and the business index over a much longer period in the United States.[3] Here we may introduce the seemingly contrary evidence that over a considerable period in England no significant correlation is shown.[4] But in England the divorce rate has been extremely low. The prevailing attitude to divorce in England suggests that the evaluation of the continuity of the family is higher than the current evaluation among considerable groups of the American population. Where the higher evaluation prevails the decision to seek divorce might be expected to depend much less on the ups and downs of business activity. We have here again a confirmation of the position that for the causation of a statistical fact we must look beyond the factors associated with it at any particular stage. Incidentally, the decrease in divorce during depressions may serve also to illustrate the limitations of the procedures frequently employed to discover the causes of " happiness " in marriage.[5] There is no reason to assume that family conflicts are lessened during depression — rather is there some evidence making in the opposite direction.[6] Yet the most overt of all the indications of " unhappiness " in marriage, in effect the one indisputably objective sign, the resort to divorce, is present in fewer instances.

Lastly, let us consider the birth-rate. Here the problem of inferring from cause to effect is most fully revealed. The

---

[3] Ogburn and Thomas found a correlation of plus 70 for the period between 1867 and 1896 — see W. F. Ogburn and Dorothy S. Thomas, " The Influence of the Business Cycle on Social Factors," *Journal of the American Statistical Association* (September, 1922), Vol. 18, p. 334.

[4] Dorothy S. Thomas, *Social Aspects of the Business Cycle*, London, 1925.

[5] See Chapter Five, § 4.

[6] See Mirra Komarovsky, *The Unemployed Man and His Family* (New York, 1940), Chap. II.

long continued decline of the birth-rate persisted through the period from 1920 to 1936. There was no marked change in the rate of decline during the more intensive depression, that commencing in 1929, nor was there any marked rise in the number of births during the recovery period. Such minor fluctuations of the general trend as occurred are comparable to fluctuations witnessed at times when there was no depression. Hence it would be very precarious to postulate without further evidence that the depression was the cause of these fluctuations. It is true that just after the low point of the depression, in 1933, the downward trend becomes a little more abrupt and that the direction then turns mildly upward for the next year or two. This deviation may be due to the depression — but in what manner? The marriage rate had been falling since 1929. The decrease in the number of new marriages must surely mean the loss of the contribution they would have made to the number of births. In fact, " the decline in marriages alone would produce a deficit of at least a half million births if those couples who failed to marry had been representative, with respect to fertility, of the normal marrying population." [7] This figure is more than three times the actual loss of births represented by the 1933 deviation from the trend. We might even be tempted to conclude that the influence of the depression was rather to encourage than to discourage child-bearing in already established families! But again we must beware of the *post hoc* argument. It is clear that before we can draw any conclusions we must differentiate types of family, distinguishing our types according to the manner in which they are affected by a depression. There is, for example, the distinction between families receiving relief and families of like economic and cultural status not receiving relief. There are differences again in the impact

---

[7] Stouffer and Lazarsfeld, op. cit. p. 123.

of a depression on families of different income level, different duration of marriage, different religion, different nationality, and so forth. Until studies based on these
distinctions are available we simply cannot tell in what
manner the depression, under the conditions of the period
in question, has affected the birth-rate. In the instance
before us we have not discovered, so far, the specific nexus
between the changes in economic conditions and the
changes in the number of births.

Our example has already shown that inference from
cause to effect is sometimes easy and sometimes hard. The
difficulties to be surmounted are comparable to those that
beset inference from effect to cause. We have seen again
that in the multitudinous interdependence of things the
discovery of correlation, with or without a time lag, does
not of itself justify the postulate that one thing is the cause,
or even the precipitant, of another thing. We cannot
assume that a trend manifested prior to the eruption of
some disturbing factor would have continued to pursue its
previous course had it not been for the disturbance. And
we have seen that the universal formula of causal investigation, the analytic delimitation of comparable situations in
the quest for the specific nexus of the phenomenon in which
we are interested, must be no less rigorously followed when
we postulate the cause and seek its effects than when we
commence with effect and seek to discover cause.

There is, moreover, a further danger when we reverse
the causal quest. We are apt then to isolate some factor
from its context and assign it independent efficacy. Usually
we select as initiating cause some spectacular event, some
eruptive factor, some great moment of change. But the
relation of event to process must always be kept in view.
Most of the one-way determinist theories seize upon the
more external and the more obvious factors within the

complex process of causal interaction. They take, for example, some invention that is widely adopted and exploited, and attribute to its influence a heterogeneous variety of social and cultural changes. Thus W. F. Ogburn lists 150 different "effects" attributable to the radio.[8] We set down a few of these, arranged in three groups as follows:

GROUP ONE

1. An increase in the consumption of electricity.
2. Radio beams, enabling aviators to remain on course.
3. Aid furnished to ships in distress at sea.
4. A new employment for singers, vaudeville artists, etc.

GROUP TWO

5. Aids in correct pronunciation, especially for foreign words.
6. Broadcasting has aided adult education.
7. In government, a new regulatory function necessitated.
8. A new form of advertising has been created.

GROUP THREE

9. Homogeneity of peoples increased because of like stimuli.
10. Distinctions between social classes and economic groups lessened.
11. Cultural diffusion among nations, as of United States into Canada and *vice versa*.
12. Lessens gap schooling may make between parents and children.

---

[8] *Recent Social Trends*, Vol. I, Chap. III. The statement of the several effects, though not the numbering of them, is as in the original.

We shall not ask whether the changes alleged to be effects of the radio have occurred. Our concern is with the grounds of attribution. The effects placed in the first group are either technological changes necessarily involved in the utilization of the radio (1), or adaptations of radio techniques to technological services other than those to which they were first applied (2 and 3), or else such simple socio-economic changes as the sheer operation of the new device demands (4). The nexus in these instances is direct and obvious. Take the last of the four, for example. We might set down as an immediate consequence of the exploitation of the radio the development of a group of radio technicians. But the radio is primarily a new medium of communication, and there must be people who supply the communication as well as people who operate the medium. Hence radio speakers, radio singers and other entertainers, are required if the radio is to serve its function on any considerable scale. In other words, given certain technical advances and certain economic conditions, this new type of employment will also appear. In this sense every new technological change may be said to create new forms of occupational specialization. And we might add that these specializations in turn will engender new habituations—such as the peculiar time servitude imposed on radio speakers. This is the " way of habit " on which Veblen laid so much stress as a primary determinant of social and cultural change.

Our second group introduces some new considerations. There is a difference between the claim that the exploitation of the radio has actually had such and such consequences and the claim that these particular consequences inevitably appear whenever and wherever the radio is exploited within human society. The statements in the second group can be supported by evidence calculated to show that in the United States, and no doubt in some other countries, the radio has actually brought about such changes. But we can at least conceive of conditions under which these changes would not ensue. They depend on the manner in which the radio system is organized and controlled. Even the alleged aid to correct pronunciation (5) would not result if certain far from inconceivable policies were followed with respect to the selection of radio speakers. Again, under certain conditions the regulation of the air waves (7) might fall into the hands of a private monopoly. On the other hand, where the radio is made a public monopoly, as in Great Britain and other countries, it may not provide any new medium for commercial advertising (8).

The moral to be drawn, concerning the inference of effects, will appear more conclusively when we examine our third group. For here the nexus between the radio and the postulated effects is not immediate and practically universal, as exemplified by our first group, nor yet dependent simply on the manner in which the medium is utilized, as exemplified by our second group. It will be observed that the effects now attributed to the radio are specifically changes in social attitudes and in consequent social relationships. They are not obvious effects. They may well be disputed. Even if there were good evidence that since the introduction of the radio social attitudes and social relationships had changed in the indicated direction it would require extremely skilful and difficult analysis of the data to show whether or not the radio had played any important part in bringing them about. Many other conditions must certainly be considered — the whole complex interplay of influences that bear on the attitudes of men towards one another. Even as between the various media of communication how can we distinguish the role of the radio from that of the press, the platform, the moving picture, and so forth? Let us remember also that the radio is an instrument sheerly indifferent to the sentiments it is used to convey, that it can be as readily employed to inculcate, between peoples, feelings of exclusiveness and antipathy as feelings of inclusiveness and sympathy, that therefore it is the policy behind the radio and not the radio itself that determines whether it will be conducive to any " increase of homogeneity " (9). Given a policy so directed, all that can be claimed is that the radio provides a new and extremely pervasive means for the attainment of this end. But how can we discover just what difference this new means makes? The problem seems almost insoluble — and possibly it is not very important. Men use what means are available for their purposes, and the massing of means is a function not only of the stage of civilization but also of the strength and intensity of the purposes.

The insulation of the external instrument as a cause of the type of social change illustrated by our third group appears to rest on unwarranted assumptions, on assumptions of the kind we have found to be back of one-way deterministic theories. In the first place, the indifferent instrument cannot be held responsible for the uses to which it is put. In the second place, since the instrument is indifferent, it can be made to speak with many voices, supplying to different groups the different appeals that are severally congenial to them. Some listen to swing music, some to classical music. Some listen to the orators of one political party, some to the orators of an opposing party. This selectivity on the part of the listener throws doubt on the claim — unless it can be substantiated by some exceedingly expert investigation — that the radio lessens the " gap between parents and children" (12). In the third place, even were there no selectivity in the listening, there may well be selectivity in the response. It does not follow that " like stimuli " (9) will elicit like response. The already like, in that regard, may respond in a like way. Why should not the unlike respond in unlike ways?

These considerations suggest that it is much more profitable to look for effects emerging within the specific process involved in the operation of the neutral instrument or means. Of course we are not denying that the development of a new agency may in fact aid some rather than others of the various purposes to which it can be applied; but we are maintaining that such aid cannot be attributed to the indifferent instrument as such, but is a function of a particular relationship between the instrument and the purposes dominant in those who are able to control and exploit it. On the other hand there is a direct nexus between the operation of the instrument and the skills it calls for, the habits it engenders, the occupational specializations that grow out of its use. The differences thus brought into being can be attributed to the instrument without resort to any precarious assumptions. And these in turn enter into causal conjunction with other phenomena so as to promote further and more far-reaching changes.

II

PROCEDURE IN THE INVESTIGATION OF EFFECTS

We may now draw certain conclusions regarding the procedure to be followed when we postulate some phenomenon as cause and enquire into its effects. We have pointed out that in so doing we usually select some momentous occurrence, some salient or convulsive event, such as a war, a revolution, an economic crisis, and so forth. We usually think of this occurrence as relatively external to the situation in which it occurs, in the sense that it belongs to a different order of things — as when we enquire into the impact of a depression on the marriage rate; or that it invades a process, a trend, a going system, and interrupts the course that otherwise would have been followed — as when we enquire into the impact of unemployment on family relationships. In fact the usual reason why we start from the event and ask about its effects is that it seems to possess this capacity of invasion and interruption. We observe therefore that the postulated cause frequently assumes the character of a precipitant, so that the analysis we have given of this type of attribution in Chapter Six is applicable here. In view of this analysis we can limit the present discussion to certain considerations regarding investigational procedure.

▼

1. Since our starting point is so often a large-scale or momentous event, such as a war, a revolution, or a depression, we ought obviously to delimit the area of investigation. Such events have endless repercussions. It is hard to conceive any aspect of human affairs that is wholly unaffected by them. Even the most munificent and expansive foundation could not undertake a research project big enough to include all the multitudinous effects of a war or a revolution.[9] As we have seen, most of the effects attributed to the great event depend on the manner in which it enters into dynamic conjunction with the various systems and sequences already operative. Hence to compass all the changes that are in some sense dependent on the event would be another way of taking all knowledge for one's province. Even the attempt to deal with the effects of any widely disturbing event on some one category of human behavior may be a vain endeavor.[10] Certainly any inclusive

---

[9] We may note in this context that the Carnegie Endowment for International Peace published 150 studies of the first World War, and that the Social Science Research Council organized a series of thirteen " research memoranda " on the social effects of the depression of 1929.

[10] Thus the *Research Memorandum on Crime in the Depression* (Social Science Research Council Bulletin 27, 1937), prepared by a very capable investigator, Thorsten Sellin, offers practically no con-

enquiry into effects must be lacking in focus, precision, and direction. There is not, to begin with, the same unity of interest in the search for the effects of a particular phenomenon as in the search for its causes. The former search offers no ground for specific attack. It is not addressed to some challenging difference that is manifested in one of two comparable situations — the procedure we have seen to be requisite for the discovery of the causal nexus. Hence we are more likely to attain results when we limit the investigation to well defined issues. This may be done, for example, if our objective is to discover the effects of a phenomenon on those situations where it brings a clean-cut and obviously significant change. Thus unemployment comes abruptly on many families and groups during a depression, sharply dividing the present from the past. We have the comparable situations, we have the challenge of the difference. Here, then, is a field of study where we may expect successful causal investigation, as various researches already have shown.[11] Another type of enquiry into effects that meets our conditions is that wherein we find a somewhat abruptly manifested change in one order of phenomena highly correlated with a specific change in another order, when at the same time it is understandable that the change in the first order would be registered in a dynamic assessment favor-

clusions respecting causation and reports an almost entire lack of agreement among researchers except for the establishment in two areas of a fairly high correlation between depression conditions and offences against property with violence (p. 62). The author of this memorandum points out that an elaborate series of further researches is needed in order to throw light on the causal relationship between economic crises and fluctuations in criminality (Chap. VI).

[11] Such as: E. W. Bakke, *The Unemployed Man*, London, 1933; P. Eisenberg and P. F. Lazarsfeld, "The Psychological Effects of Unemployment," *Psychological Bulletin* (June, 1938), Vol. 35, pp. 358–390; F. S. Chapin and S. A. Queen, *Research Memorandum on Social Work in the Depression*, Social Science Research Council Bulletin 39, 1937; P. F. Lazarsfeld, M. Jahoda. and H. Zeisl, *Die Arbeitlosen von Marienthal*, Leipzig, 1933.

able to the change in the second order. The causal relationship of a depression and a decline of the marriage rate will serve as an instance.

　　　　　　　　　　▼

2. When we begin with a postulated cause there is a peculiar temptation to insulate this causal factor as though it operated independently. Consequently the investigation in this field should be particularly concerned to distinguish types of situation according to the manner in which the postulated cause enters into the dynamic complex. It is not enough, for example, when we are studying the relation of a depression to the crime rate, to distinguish categories of crime and enquire into the effects of the depression on them severally. This procedure may not carry us very far. It is likely that we shall learn more if we prepare the way by enquiring into the mode of impact of the depression on different groups, selected by reference to economic reserves, standards of living, liability to unemployment, social status, marital condition, age, occupational mobility, and other possibly relevant factors. If a depression hits these groups in different degrees and in different ways, their response will obviously be different. A change in the crime rate is one form of response to a changed situation. Unless we know how the situation has changed — unless in the last resort we get close to the comprehension of the changed dynamic assessment — we cannot really cope with the problem of changed behavior, whether it expresses itself in crime or not. Many investigations into effects give little or no attention to the primary problem of social causation, the manner in which a change in the situation is reflected in a change in the evaluation of the situation, and thus leads to a change in behavior. They are concerned, for example, with the correlation of external factors, or specific personality traits, or " test items " of some sort, with some general condition, such as social disorganization or

" happiness in marriage "; but the postulated causes of this general condition appear to be associated with the most contradictory " effects " in different cases. What is lacking is a relevant typology — often there is no typology at all.[12] When we find that a postulated cause is associated with dissimilar changes with respect to some mode of behavior, the problem clearly calls for the discovery of type differences. Thus there is evidence that some workers, when they become unemployed, become more interested in religion, while other unemployed workers become more indifferent to it.[13] Here is a clear challenge to a study of the differences of religious attitude or more broadly to the differences of attitude-complex that undergo dissimilar processes of change under the impact of an economic misfortune. We find again that some unemployed workers turn to radicalism and others to fascism.[14] The discovery of such divergence raises a different but very significant problem of social causation which we cannot attack until we learn to distinguish the cultural situations and the personality types exhibiting these divergent responses.[15]

▼

3. Let us suppose we have already advanced some way in the differentiation of types associated with opposite or at least divergent responses in the presence of a like impact.

---

[12] Thus L. M. Terman, in his *Psychological Factors in Marital Happiness* (New York, 1938), points to the " chaos of opinion on the determiners of marital happiness," but his own work is mainly devoted to a more elaborate and ingenious study of item correlations.

[13] Eisenberg and Lazarsfeld, op. cit. p. 369. For some acute comments on this subject see the analysis offered by these writers, ibid. pp. 371–379.

[14] Ibid. p. 370.

[15] As examples of studies directed to this problem we may cite A. Gabriel and H. D. Lasswell, " Aggressive Behavior of Clients toward Public Relief Administrators," *American Political Science Review* (1934), Vol. 28, pp. 643–655, and Mirra Komarovsky, *The Unemployed Man and His Family*, Chap. IV.

Now we must seek to discover the relation of variant response to differences of personality type or of situation. We have reached a stage where the universal formula of causal investigation is clearly applicable. If, for example, we should find that those workers who have previously been actively devoted to religious enterprises tend to maintain their religious faith when unemployed, while those who have been more passive adherents are more apt to lose their faith altogether, we can at least suggest a socio-psychological explanation. The difference in response becomes understandable. To test the validity of the explanation there are various other evidences that can be examined, as we seek to fathom the socio-psychological process from which the particular response emerges. The study of the process in which attitudes are modified by experience is a difficult but rewarding one. We know, for example, that the attitudes of the unemployed change in a specific direction the longer the duration of unemployment. We know that at the same time there are marked differences in the manner in which different personality types respond at any stage. Some become defiant, some become apathetic, some become bitter.[16] Such differences can be related to other differential conditions, such as economic level, social status, religious experience, sex, state of health, age, and so forth. The life-history of individuals will throw further light on the nature of their response. So we can increasingly run the differences of response down to the particular configurations of personality and situation to which they are respectively congenial.

Even where the differential response of different groups seems susceptible of a simple explanation we should not be satisfied that we have reached the causal nexus unless we

---

[16] See, for example, B. Zawadski and P. F. Lazarsfeld, " The Psychological Consequences of Unemployment," *Journal of Social Psychology* (1935), Vol. 6, 224–251.

have adequate evidence of the psychological process. W. A. Bonger, who has always stressed the dependence of crime on economic conditions, presented evidence that when unemployment relief was established a prior correlation between unemployment and theft no longer held. Some other investigators have come to the same conclusion.[17] It might seem obvious enough that the introduction of relief measures would reduce the temptation to steal. But the statistics of crime do not yield any convincing correlation between the volume of unemployment and the frequency of theft. Studies of particular communities show that minor crimes against property sometimes decrease in number in times of depression, even where there is as yet no system of public relief.[18] It is certain that other factors or complexes of factors besides the urgency of need must be taken into account. If so, it has still to be proved that the reduction of need by the establishment of public relief is the explanation of a decrease in crime. It may be so, given certain conjunctures, but unless we can distinguish the conjunctures and realistically discover the mode of response associated with each of them, we still remain in the realm of unverified hypotheses.

▾

4. A final consideration emerges from the previous three. It now appears that most investigations into effects sooner or later turn into investigations into causes. What they do is to make some particular factor in a situation their starting point. This factor, say a depression, is accompanied or followed by a number of other phenomena. Suppose, for example, a depression is followed by a decline in the birth-rate of certain groups or a decline in religious

---

[17] Thorsten Sellin, op. cit. p. 64.

[18] R. S. and H. M. Lynd, *Middletown in Transition* (New York, 1937), p. 345. These authors warn here against too ready acceptance of the " obvious factor."

observance among certain groups. We are likely to find that other groups are not affected in the same way. Hence our problem becomes: Under a particular set of conditions why does the birth-rate drop from a previous level, or why under a particular set of conditions does religious observance fall off? We have an initial clue to the answer. It has something to do with the intrusion of unemployment or of some other aspect of depression. This factor makes so significant a difference in the total situation that it must certainly be taken into account. It provides us with a number of causal problems — those concerning the causation of changes occurring along with it. But each of these changes still requires explanation. We must enquire how the posited factor enters into and modifies a prior conjuncture. We must comprehend the new conjuncture. The obvious factor does not explain the fall of the birth-rate, where it falls, or the decline of religious observance, where there is a decline. What its intrusion does is to modify, check, facilitate, or redirect certain already operative dynamic processes. What it does is to precipitate or to reinforce certain tendencies. So we have to deal with new causal complexes. But our comparable situations — the necessary basis of causal investigation — are not respectively those in which depression is present and those from which depression is absent. They are those in which a depression and a fall in the birth-rate go together as against those in which a depression and no fall in the birth-rate go together. Clearly we are back on the main road of enquiry into the causes of things.

CHAPTER FOURTEEN

CONCLUSIONS CONCERNING CAUSAL INFERENCE

I

CONSPECTUS

THROUGHOUT this work we have offered grounds for the claim that the phenomena with which the social sciences deal exhibit a special type of causal process differentiated in significant respects from the causality of external nature. We have endeavored to explore and to define this process. In doing so we have suggested an answer to the kindred question: How should we *investigate* the causes of social phenomena? For if we have reason to regard social causation as a distinctive kind or variety of causation then we should adapt our methodology accordingly. Let us review our conclusions under both heads.

▾

1. The primary contrast between social causation and the causation revealed in physical and in biological phenomena is that the former involves the socio-psychological nexus. This mode of causation is not an alternative to or substitute for the physical nexus but it introduces a new or additional process that supervenes within but does not abrogate the universal reign of physical law. The problem of the relation of the physical to the psychological nexus is profoundly difficult and very far from being solved. The fact of the relation is given in all conscious experience. The realm of conscious experience is also the realm of society,

and thus in its actual operation the psychological nexus practically always manifests itself in a socio-psychological form.

Let us once more bring out the contrast. Take, for example, the case of a deserted town, such as a dead mining or lumbering center. The wheels no longer turn, the machinery is rusting and useless. The houses are falling apart, open to the wind and the rain. Vegetation ranges over the forgotten works of man. All his engines have ceased to function; they are no longer related to his purposes. They are reverting to external nature. Now let us look by way of contrast at a busy factory town. All its apparatus is at work, directed by the various consentient purposes of the community. What is the essential difference? There is here a continuous gearing of means to ends, of a kind that is wholly lacking in the deserted town. There is a coherent social system that maintains a multitude of activities and regulates the various relationships of men to the equipment they control. Animating this social system there is a fairly coherent scheme of values, the cultural complex of the community. These systems and these activities depend on the continuous operation of the dynamic assessment, the causal process peculiar to the conscious realm. Responsive to this assessment the wheels turn and multifarious exchanges take place. Every man, every family, every group, as well as the community itself, selectively defines a sphere of action, and thus the busy factory town is kept in being.[1]

The difference here stated is entirely obvious, but in it we have already the clue to the understanding of social

---

[1] Our concept of dynamic assessment is indicated by various other formulations found in sociological analysis, and notably in the works of W. I. Thomas and of Florian Znaniecki. The closest approximation is the manner in which W. I. Thomas uses the expression " the definition of the situation," speaking of the family and the community as " defining agencies." See *The Unadjusted Girl* (Boston, 1923), pp. 43 ff.

causation. Let us look at it more closely. In the busy town there are a thousand routines of action. The wheels keep turning. Children go to school. Men go to their work every morning and return every evening. Types of behavior persist. Modes of relationship are established. But a thousand minor changes are always occurring in the for-- ever new-woven pattern and sometimes a more decisive change occurs. It is these changes, these differences, we seek to explain.

Pursuing them, we are led beyond the overt indications to some change in valuation, to some re-adjustment of ends and means, to some redefinition of a situation. This change in valuation is no mysterious thing; it is no more mysterious than the fact that words have meanings. It is evidenced in various ways. Sometimes the inference is easy, often it is difficult. The flashpoint of a new assessment, turning un-winged desire into winged decision, is the most challenging of the problems of social psychology. It is just as referable to causes as any other phenomenon of nature. Here too there is the relatively constant *ethos* of person and of group; here too there is the intrusive factor, the disturbance of equilibrium, the dynamic motion. Whatever our success in fathoming the psychological process that issues in a change of valuation we can regard that change, the dynamic reas-sessment, as itself the primary organizing principle in a further process that has been our main interest throughout this work, the process of social causation.

We have dwelt at some length on the manner in which this organizing principle operates. A scheme of values, whether conceived in terms of personality or of the culture complex of a group, may be likened to a field of force, highly charged, having a general direction but full of tensions and pressures. There are desires that at every moment remain unwinged, there are aspirations that are held in abeyance, there are felt obligations that do not issue in resolve. Somehow, within this value field, some valuation becomes the immediate dynamic of behavior, investing itself with the appropriate available means and penetrating the total situation so as to bring it into conformity with the value demand. The range of the dynamic valuation may be wide or narrow, its time span short or extended, its linkage with means simple or elaborate, and its relation to the inclusive value configuration superficial or deep-working. In a myriad different ways the dynamic assessment advances from resolution to fulfilment.

For the interpretation of social phenomena we are concerned not with the individual assessment as such but with the modes and processes of interindividual assessment, as they emerge in historical events, statistical facts, social trends and movements of various kinds, institutions and institutional complexes, and the various unpurposed resultants of social behavior. Back of all these lie the converging and conflicting assessments generated within the social situation. In so far as we are able to discover the changes of the evaluative schemes of social groups we can attain, and thus only, a unified explanation of social change. For then we can assign to the various factors of change their respective roles and functional relationships, as they cohere into specific patterns of the interdependent systems and orders that combine, in endlessly variant conjunctures, into the inclusive causal complex.

2. From this standpoint we address ourselves to the methodology of causal investigation. The problem is that of applying to the particular subject matter of the social sciences the universal formula of enquiry into causes. The setting for every such enquiry is a challenging difference between two comparable situations. We must therefore, in the first place, demarcate the difference. It must be so

apprehended as to constitute a well-defined contrast between well-defined situations. In the social sciences this preliminary caution is peculiarly relevant, for several reasons. Too often the attempt is made to investigate the causes of undelimited phenomena, such as criminality, delinquency, suicide, divorce, desertion, and other aspects of " social pathology " — and when the investigator is baffled by the hopeless task of finding specific causes for manifestations that appear in endlessly variant conjunctures he is apt to abjure the quest for causes altogether and even to deny its scientific validity. Again, the social scientist, being concerned with group attitudes and intersubjective adjustments, not infrequently sets out to discover the why of such things as contentment, social harmony, happiness in marriage, and so forth. But these things are the emotionally charged reflections of our responses to some kind of interpersonal equilibrium. They are hard to identify, to demarcate from states of consciousness more fittingly described by other names, to characterize in terms of grade, intensity, or type; and the interpersonal equilibrium on which they depend varies endlessly in accordance with variant temperaments and variant situations. Furthermore, the phenomena with which the social scientist is concerned are largely matters of degree — the more or less of unemployment, business activity, inflation, crime, governmental control, conservatism, radicalism, capitalism, and so forth. The more and the less do not clearly differentiate our comparable situations. It is part of the same problem that the experimental method is less available and gives less conclusive results.

Thus the social scientist, as he pursues the specific linkages between specific phenomena, encounters his own particular problems of classification, research, and analysis. We have dwelt at some length on various aspects of these problems, and so in this review we shall simply re-emphasize the central issue. The process of causal investigation is a process of delimitation, a sifting out of irrelevant elements from the inclusive situation, a more accurate determination of the ways in which phenomena belong together. We pass from one approximation to a closer one and often our final conclusion must be still only an approximation.

Suppose, for example, we are interested in the decline of the yeoman class in England. We provisionally define a yeoman as a working farmer, who owned land and had a certain social status and disposed of a certain yearly revenue, varying with the times. This definition is not entirely explicit, but whatever refinement we adopt there will still remain some question as to the limits of the yeoman class. Moreover, that class, however understood, was itself subject to changes in its character and composition and in its relation to other classes, such as those of the large landowner, the tenant farmer, and the propertyless peasant. Hence it is highly important that, if we set out to study the causes of the decline of this class, we make our category as definite as possible while at the same time we keep it continuous and distinctive for the whole period under consideration. This example brings out the point that in the study of social causation it is sometimes nearly as difficult to define our problem as to solve it. In fact we keep on re-defining it in the process of solving it. We have good evidence that a class of small independent land cultivators which flourished in sixteenth century England no longer characterized English society in the nineteenth century. Was this due mainly to internal readjustments within the class itself, gradually giving it a different economic role and a different social status in the changing economy, or was it due mainly to conditions which prevented the class from maintaining its existence at all? The latter thesis is supported by the weight of the evidence. The yeomen were for the most part forced off their lands by economic pressures. How this happened, to whom, under what conjunctures — these are questions demanding careful research and analysis.[2] In the process we gain a clearer conception of a distinctive socio-economic class of people who occupied a like status, were subject to like chances, and suffered a like fate. So our most acceptable definition of the yeoman class marks the end and not the beginning of our enquiry.[3]

The progressive delimitation of the phenomenon is simply one aspect of the approach to specificity that constitutes the essential procedure of causal investigation. What above all we need to make specific is the *linkage of difference to difference*. We are presented with a phenomenon and a situation within which it occurs. We want to know how this phenomenon, as pertaining to this situation and not to certain comparable situations, is bound up with a distinctive structure or configuration of elements. (Observe in passing that the difference between one social situation and another is never the mere presence or absence of a single factor, never even the more or the less of one particular factor. It is the situation *as assessed* that is dynamic for social change. And the assessment always involves a redisposition of means to ends and ends to conditions, a readjustment of various factors even where a single new factor invades the situation and can be regarded as *precipitating* the change.) We want to discover, as nearly as possible, the precise conjuncture and organization of elements to which the difference to be explained belongs. And

---

[2] For a good study of this subject see W. Hasbach, "Der Untergang des englischen Bauernstandes in neuer Beleuchtung," *Archiv für Sozialwissenschaft und Sozialpolitik* (1907), Vol. 24, pp. 1–29.

[3] We follow the principle of operational definition in the sense that we *refine* our preliminary definition as we operate with it, not in the sense that we define by stating our operations. See note, pp. 157–158.

finally, since in the last resort this difference either is itself or at least depends upon the purposive activity of social beings, we want to identify, as nearly as possible, the evaluational response, the mode and the process of individual and group assessment, the dynamic of the new conjuncture that initiates the behavioristic change.

It should now be apparent why we have characterized causal investigation as a process of delimitation. It is a series of successive discriminations. The phenomenon itself, the situation in which it occurs, the comparable situation lacking the phenomenon, the focal conjuncture relative to the dynamic assessment, the readjustment of the means-ends schema — these must all be brought out in their distinctive relevance for our objective, the discovery of the specific nexus between a difference and a difference-generating system. It is easy therefore to see why causal discovery in the social sciences is often insecure, generally incomplete, and at best approximate.

Let us once more illustrate the problem by reference to a group of studies in a much investigated field that has afforded us several previous illustrations. Among the more significant investigations into the causes of delinquency are those that seek to associate it with a particular set of urban conditions. We take as example the contributions of Clifford R. Shaw. His starting point is certain statistical evidence showing, particularly for the city of Chicago, that delinquency rates are highest in the area just beyond the business center, the area that in the course of city growth is subject to " invasion " by the spread of business and industry, while the delinquency rates tend on the whole to diminish progressively as we pass to the outer zones. How are we to interpret this difference? What features or configuration of features belonging to the difference-revealing or difference-generating area are specially relevant? Our author regards " poor housing, overcrowding, low living standards, low educational standards, and so on " as " only symptoms of more basic processes." What, then, is the basic process? It is, we are told, " the invasion of residential communities by business and industry." The result of this invasion is " a disintegration of the community as a unit of social control." [4] The conclusion is apposite and suggestive, so far as it goes. So far, it is in accord with the evidence adduced. But does it go far enough? Does it have room for all the relevant evidence? Delinquency rates are correlated with other conditions and processes besides " the invasion of residential communities by business and industry." The rates vary considerably for different cities in which a similar " invasion " has taken place, especially if we include cities in other countries. They are markedly different for different economic groups, for different nationality groups, and under different types of civic administration.[5]

So we must ask again why " the invasion of residential communities by business and industry " is given the central role in the explanation of urban delinquency. Above all, how is this " invasion " related to the difference of mores, to the election between available alternatives that exhibits itself not only in the greater amount of delinquency but also in the statistics of desertion, drug addiction, crime, alcoholism, and so forth? We have evidence that urban areas where business and industry are encroaching on residence tend, through the operation of economic forces, to become dilapidated and slummy. But our author tells us that poor housing and overcrowding are only symptoms.

---

[4] *Urban Delinquency Areas* (Chicago, 1929), pp. 204–205.
[5] See the careful analysis of delinquency rates in New York City by S. Robeson, *Can Delinquency Be Measured?* (New York, 1936), Chaps. IX–X. Some good remarks on the subject are made by N. F. Cantor, *Crime and Society* (New York, 1939), pp. 61 ff.

Shall we conclude that the whole economic status of the groups inhabiting these areas is also only symptomatic? Little attention is devoted to economic conditions and relationships within the delinquency areas. On the other hand the point is stressed in a later work that as successive nationality groups moved into and out of these areas their delinquency rates respectively rose and fell.[6] This seems to suggest that the area as such somehow breeds delinquency. At the same time we are told that "more important than the external realities of the area are the traditions, standards, and moral sentiments which characterize the neighborhood life." [7] What, then, is the role of the area itself or of the invasion of business and industry into the area — unless it is assumed that this invasion somehow creates the traditions, standards, and moral sentiments congenial to delinquency? But nothing is presented to support so extreme a position.

So we must question the adequacy and even the consistency of the causal formula employed by Shaw. He has located, for a type of city, the area exhibiting the highest delinquency rate. He has described the process in which this area becomes externally distinguished from other urban areas. These are steps on the road to causal discovery. But we are not shown any explicit relation between these areal characteristics and the "spirit of the community," which latter he acknowledges to be very important for the understanding of delinquency. We need more analysis of the social configuration within the delinquency area as contrasted with that presented in some comparable situation that is relatively free from delinquency. The emphasis on the physical locale as such may be one-sided. Perhaps the

---

[6] *Report on the Causes of Crime*, Vol. II, National Commission on Law Observance and Enforcement (Washington, D. C., 1931), pp. 388–389.

[7] Ibid. p. 108.

author himself is conscious of this danger. In a more recent work he has made extensive use of life-story materials.[8] Such materials are a valuable aid to the discovery of social configurations. They are also particularly useful as suggesting to us the evaluations current among groups that do not conform to the patterns of behavior with which we are ourselves more familiar. The data they liberally provide should help us to improve our frame of reference — but they do not supply us with one. In commenting on the life stories of five " brothers in crime " Shaw dwells more — though still briefly — on the economic factors, the " struggle for a living," the " economic insecurity," and the " extreme poverty " characteristic of the milieu in which the brothers grew up.[9] He also gives some prominence to the aspect of culture clash, the conflict between the mores of the immigrant group to which the delinquents belong and the mores of the larger community.[10] But, again, these features of the delinquency area are not co-ordinated into one integrated and distinctive presentation so as to bring out the effective contrast with areas in which the rate of delinquency is lower. We are still given substantially the same causal explanation as in the earlier works.[11] We are told that the boys grew into criminals as a result of association with criminals, as a result of living in an environment predisposing to crime. This of course merely sets the question back a stage. Why did the neighborhood predispose to crime? What was the particular conjuncture of things that differentiated it *in this respect* from other urban neighborhoods? It was not poverty as such, it was not the proximity of poverty and wealth, it was not the combination of poverty and a particular nationality, and it was certainly not the

---

[8] *Brothers in Crime*, Chicago, 1938.
[9] Ibid. pp. 356–357.
[10] Ibid. pp. 107–108 and elsewhere.
[11] Ibid. pp. 359–360.

fact that business had invaded a residential area. The neighborhood had a certain " spirit," its distinctive cultural complex. How was it generated, and how is it related to a particular system of means, opportunities, obstacles, and conditions so as to find expression in an unusually high rate of delinquency?

This is the form of problem the social scientist is always meeting. It is not solved all at once, but only by the progressive refinement of successive investigations. In all such situations our objective is to discover the distinctive scheme of valuation whose dynamic selectivity is peculiarly linked with a relevant organization of means and external conditions.

II

THE GOAL OF CAUSAL KNOWLEDGE

One conclusion that has emerged in the course of our enquiry is that the discovery of the causes of social phenomena is progressive and always approximate, always incomplete. We seek to trace the routes of specific transitions within the larger flux. What we designate causes are the various conjunctures of things in the process of creating some difference that arrests our attention; effects are then particular properties — or differences — manifested by things in their various conjunctures. We want to relate the difference as closely as possible to the pertinent conjuncture. But our knowledge of the conjuncture, however far we probe, remains imperfect — its unique configuration is not wholly discerned. A simple illustration will serve. We hear some story, say of a quarrel between two of our friends. We are curious, we are also somewhat disturbed — anyhow we want to know the truth of it. We enquire concerning the occasion and the ground of the quarrel. We receive different versions of the story. We approach the parties to the quarrel, and they too give us different accounts. We get all the " facts " we can. We form our own conception of what really happened. We revise it as we learn more about the previous relations of our two friends. We know something of their personalities, of how they respectively react to various situations. So we get nearer to the truth, but some of it eludes us. There remains an element of conjecture, an area of uncertainty, a process of reconstruction, a question of emphasis. Who will dare to claim that he has the whole truth? And if this is so in an affair so close to us, what of the causes of larger conflicts, of labor disputes, of wars, and so forth? Everywhere, behind the changes of human affairs, there is the problem of knowing the unique conjuncture from which the event proceeds.

Some who are hotfoot for absolute and final certainty, for the whole truth wholly demonstrated, reject this conclusion. They refuse to accept partial knowledge. They refuse to employ methods that do not yield verifiable exactitude. Perhaps the very assumption of potential exactitude is mistaken, or at least irrelevant, for some important aspects of knowledge. The causal problem is not one of *how much*, but of *how*, and we should seek to answer accordingly. In any case we should remember that the rejection of partial truth, because it is only partial, is still the rejection of truth — just as much as the rejection of an imperfect light, in preference to none at all, is the choice of darkness instead. This in effect is what the demand for complete objective verification — not merely for objective evidences of subjective data — amounts to. Extreme positivists of this type regard all subjective phenomena as tainted, unfit for scientific consumption. The consequence is that they are quite unable to deal with the issues that mainly concern the social scientist, and least of all do they help us in the quest of causation. We may quote on this head the judicious words with which two of the ablest and best equipped investigators of our day conclude their study of the family in the depression:

" It will be observed that in the foregoing discussions the writers have taken an eclectic point of view with reference to research. . . . It should be obvious . . . that a scrupulous limitation of research to that which will yield immediately an order of verification comparable to what is required in the more developed natural sciences would result in almost no knowledge about the effects of depression on the family. Some of us are extremely interested in helping push sociological research more in the direction of verification. But that cause will not be served by an insistence on an exclusive technique which too often may yield trivial results where valid, and pretentious nonsense where invalid." [12]

In the search for causes we advance to fuller and more precise knowledge, employing whatever methods are available and helpful to this end. We have shown throughout this work that the basic method is a form of the method of comparison, the successive analysis of comparable situations in order to demarcate our phenomenon and to segregate the particular complex of things to which it immediately belongs. This method calls for all the precision and all the ingenuity we can muster. We cannot, for example, be satisfied with an explanation that equally covers other phenomena besides the one we are endeavoring to explain. The causal conjuncture must be seen in its specific relation to the specific phenomenon. Thus if we were to assign the characteristic gang of modern American cities to the complex of poverty, deteriorated urban neighborhood, and so forth, we could no less adduce these factors to account for

---

[12] Stouffer and Lazarsfeld, *The Family in the Depression*, p. 201.

the prevalence of crime in general, drug addiction, desertion, sidewalk peddling, and various other phenomena of slum areas. Our explanation would lack specific relevance. The modern urban gang is a distinctive development, and is the outcome of a distinctive complex of attitudes, opportunities, conditions, and means. To expose this complex, to reveal it in its particular operation, and also in its gestation, this is the kind of problem that in its endless varieties continually challenges the student of social causation.

Causal attribution is therefore the progressive revision of a hypothesis. The process of revision, as already set forth, is also a process of verification. What, we may finally ask, are the tests by means of which, at each stage of the investigation, we can check the adequacy and the validity of the causal hypothesis? In setting up this hypothesis we are claiming that certain things, as coexistent or successive, do not merely coexist, do not merely succeed one another, but are bound together by virtue of their interdependent dynamic properties. Now there are, to begin with, some obvious tests of this claim. Supposing, for example, we put forward the thesis that modern industrial capitalism is a product of democratic conditions, it would be immediately refuted by the fact that this form of capitalism has strongly developed under non-democratic conditions in Germany and in Japan. If, again, we claimed that modern industrial capitalism is the result of technological advance, a reference to the association of technological advance with state-socialism, fascism, and communism would show the lack of precision in the claim. These are gross instances, but in many more refined ways the method of comparison can be employed to show that an alleged nexus does not hold or at least is improperly stated. On the other hand where certain phenomena are found constantly associated over a wide range of situations the claim of a causal nexus between them is strengthened. Thus we found a rather constant association between economic depression and a decrease in the number of marriages. We cannot conclude that under all social conditions economic depression and a decrease in the marriage rate go together. We can, however, claim that, given a certain type of socio-economic organization, the onset of a depression acts as a check on the marriage rate. As we have shown, this claim becomes the starting point of further investigation in which we seek to define the causal nexus more precisely.

We see here the role of the statistical test in the verification of the causal hypothesis. It does not furnish any positive proof, but by giving us exact formulations of the correlations of variables it provides important clues as to where and how we should look for causal connections. There are simple instances in which it leads us immediately to a causal nexus. Thus there is a very high positive correlation between the temperature and the frequency with which the cricket chirps.[13] Below 45 degrees Fahrenheit the cricket does not chirp. Over a considerable upward range of temperature there is a steady increase in the number of chirps for each additional degree of warmth. The conclusion is inescapable — and can, of course, be experimentally confirmed — that the relation is not coincidental but causal. The rise in temperature causes, under the given conditions, the increase in chirping. The correlation of variables belonging to social situations is generally much less conclusive, but it is still very serviceable in a number of ways. In the first place, it enables us to dispose of many false trails to the causal nexus. We conjecture, for example, that the increase of suicides under modern civilization is due to the sharp changes from prosperity to adversity reflected in

---

[13] F. E. Croxton and D. J. Cowden, *Applied General Statistics* (New York, 1939), pp. 651–653.

the movements of the economic barometer. We discover a correlation of, say, $+.4$ between suicides and business failures. So far, we are not discouraged from pursuing the trail. But when we apply the principle of multiple correlation and make the proper adjustment for age differences, the positive correlation between business failures and suicides falls to a quite insignificant figure. " What appeared to be a relationship between business failures and suicides was in fact largely a relationship between average age and suicide rates." [14] So it becomes apparent that there was no such definite nexus as we had supposed. In the second place, the appeal to statistics often helps us to delimit the group or the situation to which a particular phenomenon should be referred. The group has various constituents, and the situation has many aspects. The causal connection may not be predicable of the whole group as such or of the whole situation as a conjuncture. There is, for example, a decline of the marriage rate during a depression. The impact of the depression does not bear equally on all classes of the population, nor does it follow that the decline of the marriage rate for different groups is proportionate to the economic hardship or loss they respectively suffer. Possibly the decline shown for the community as a whole may mask the fact that the marriage rate of certain sub-groups has been unaffected; it is even possible that the rate for some sub-groups may have moved upwards. Further statistical analysis, by relevant categories, will resolve these questions, will enable us to construct a group typology according to the mode in which the contracting of marriage is affected by adverse economic changes — and thus bring us nearer to the central issue, our final why: Why do people in the face of certain new situations act thus and thus?

---

[14] F. E. Croxton and D. J. Cowden, op. cit. p. 769.

It is at this point we must resort to other methods of investigation than that of statistical analysis. We have insisted on the primary experimental fact that back of every social change there is a reassessment of a situation by individuals or groups and a readjustment, in terms of that reassessment, of activities relating means to valuations. This is the unifying process that brings into one dynamic synthesis the inner or subjective order of urges, values, and effective goals and the outer orders of environmental reality. But the unity is achieved on the condition that the outer loses for this synthesis its sheer externality and *becomes the outer of the inner*, operates in this relation no longer as its full biophysical reality but instead as a selectively conceived system of opportunities and obstacles, areas of advance and retreat, things celebrated and things deplored, the soil of memories and expectations and hopes and fears. So conceived, so presented to the dynamic assessment, the social environment bears the multitudinous evidences of social action and of social change. These are objective evidences for the social scientist. He can detach them from the meanings they have to the social agent. He can count and measure them, can subject them to statistical analysis. But when he is through with that, he must reinvest himself, constructively, with his own role as social agent. Otherwise, though he may learn how much a war has cost in men and treasure, he will never learn why men fought the war; what passions and persuasions moved them, what they sought. Otherwise, though he may trace the fluctuations of the marriage rate and of the birth-rate, he will not discover the forces that control and liberate and direct the behavior of human beings.

These forces, as reflected in social or socially conditioned behavior, pertain to the cultural complex. Is this complex, in specific instances, beyond the reach of scientific method, for the discovery of the causal nexus and for the verification of the causal hypothesis? If it were so, the social sciences could never advance towards the goal of causal knowledge. The methods of science as applied to the phenomena of the external world, and particularly as employed in statistical analysis, assure us of the probability that there is a connection between, say, a depression and a decline in the number of marriages. Shall we stop there? Shall we disregard every hypothesis, however obvious and understandable, as to the kind of connection? A change of fortune interposes no physical or biological barrier to marriage. Statistical evidence may show us that under certain social systems a change of fortune interposes no cultural barrier. If it is otherwise in our present Western society we can very properly enquire where, and how, and under what conditions. Thus every method of scientific investigation brings us to the verge of our final problem. It is not the external aspect of a social system, it is the socially accepted scheme of valuation, that deters from marriage during a depression. The inference is here simple and indubitable. That there is a prevailing scheme of valuation is established by the like preferences men exhibit, by the like changes of behavior to which they resort when the conditions of choice are altered by new circumstances.

The dynamic assessment that lies back of overt behavior is thus a fact as validly attested as any other. The scientific difficulty is not the establishment of the mere fact but the determination of the specific scheme of effective valuation dominant in any process of decision. It is never directly revealed to us and though sometimes the discovery of it is a simple enough inference it is often highly precarious. Often we have some inkling of it but the evidence is insufficient to enable us to compass its subtlety and its full scope. Often the objective is clearly indicated while the motivation remains obscure. But there is abundant evidence that every group has its characteristic mores, or standards of valuation, and that the like and common activities of the group express various aspects of a relatively coherent cultural complex. Such a phenomenon as the decline of marriage during a depression is not an isolated manifestation; it is in accord with various other changes of behavior to which at such a time people resort, according to their circumstances, in order to maintain as nearly as possible their prior status or standard of living. We pointed out in another context that the decline of the birth-rate was a particular expression of a general readjustment of values and means that has many other manifestations.

The verification of a hypothesis of social causation is consequently conducted on two levels. We employ statistical analysis and other methods common to all the sciences in order to learn whether and to what extent and in what areas and over what length of time the phenomenon under consideration is associated with certain other phenomena. These methods furnish a test that any hypothesis must first pass before it can be accepted as a legitimate claimant for further investigation. If it meets this requirement we continue the search on another level. We seek to discover whether the association or correlation of phenomena is meaningful, whether it depends on the dynamic response of social beings to changing situations. Again we appeal to evidences, but the interpretation of them follows different lines and requires the application of different methods. These evidences are of various kinds — the other overt activities of those whose behavior in some particular respect is being investigated, the oral, written, and gestural communications of the participants, the expressed opinions of those who are in direct or indirect contact with them, the past behavior of the individuals or groups concerned, the behavior of other individuals or groups in comparable situations, and so forth.

We may distinguish two main types of evidence that lead us beyond the data of correlation to the socio-psychological nexus. One consists of the depositions, avowals, confessions, justifications, and other testimonies offered by agents, participants, or witnesses, professedly or ostensibly giving their own answers, on the ground of their inside or close-up knowledge, to the question of causation. The reliability of such declarations can be examined in various ways familiar to historians, anthropologists, psychologists, psychoanalysts, judges, detective agents, and in fact to all men in so far as they are students of human nature. The other main type of evidence consists of those indications, other than direct testimony, that help us to place the particular behaving in its meaningful context. If a hungry man steals bread it is not necessary to search for the configuration of values that explains his action. If somewhere in our Western civilization a man who has had sudden financial reverses postpones the date of his marriage, the search for an explanation, unless the circumstances are unusual, is not likely to occupy us long. But often the quest is not so easy. We seek for the explanation that is most consistent with the personality and life history of the individual or with the cultural complex of the group, as it bears on the specific situation within which the behavior takes place. But we cannot know the situation fully, as it is presented to or selectively conceived by individual or group, and we cannot fully follow the cultural complex through the subtle processes of readjustment to ever changing conditions. We must here essay the task of projecting ourselves by sympathetic reconstruction into the situation as it is assessed by others, with such aid as we can obtain from the two types of evidence. There must always be, as we have already shown, this process of reconstruction.

What we reconstruct is the relatively coherent scheme of things to which the phenomenon under investigation belongs. Every act is the act of a personality, and every personality is bred within a social system, and every social system exhibits its cultural complex. Everywhere there is some unity embracing the individual life, and beyond that the life of the group, and beyond that the life of the nation, and beyond that there extends the widening area within which men communicate with and influence one another, so that to the synthetic historian continents and epochs have their characteristic being. Every social phenomenon is an expression of *some* meaningful system. We piece the system together from a myriad evidences — not as outsiders but as in some degree ourselves participants. Experience and history provide us, in the measure in which we can learn their lessons, with the background of knowledge into which we seek to fit the specific social phenomenon. The particular methods we have already cited enable us to narrow the margin of error. But complete certitude eludes us. The unity, however coherent, exhibits deviations and conflicts. The systems we construct do not integrate all the manifestations we discover within them. The particular phenomenon may be the offspring of the system, but every birth is difference as well as likeness.

That is why the verification of any significant hypothesis of social causation is never complete, but only approximate. The goal of causal knowledge is never attained, though our endeavors can bring us always nearer. What we cannot fully apprehend is that which is intrinsically dynamic. We measure its manifestations, but it is always revealing new aspects, turning in new directions, entering into new conjunctures, which we did not foresee, perhaps could not have foreseen. In the study of social causation, as no doubt elsewhere, we are in the presence of an intrinsic dynamic in this sense. In this context we may call it simply human nature. We pursue its endlessly changing responses to endlessly changing stiuations; we discover continuity in change and change in continuity; we measure concomitances of factors and regularities of sequence; we infer the pattern of the scheme of values that every group sustains and forever reconstructs, adjusting means to ends and ends to means through all the vicissitudes of its experience. As we follow these trails and indications, not in one instance but in multitudes, we gain a widening and deepening knowledge. From many angles we attack the problem of understanding human nature and its works. And if this human nature possesses any basis of identity through all its changeful manifestations these angles must converge towards a point they never reach, the goal of causal knowledge.

SELECT
BIBLIOGRAPHY
(*Revised, 1964*)

TITLES marked with an asterisk are recommended as supplementary reading for the student. Date and place of publication are given only where the reference has not already been included in a footnote.

CHAPTER ONE

For the agnostic attitude towards causation the *locus classicus* is
DAVID HUME, *Essay on the Human Understanding*, § VII.
The classical answer to Hume was offered by
IMMANUEL KANT, *Critique of Pure Reason*, "Transcendental Logic," Book I and Book II.
In modern philosophy the problem of causality is well presented in
A. N. WHITEHEAD, *The Concept of Nature* (Cambridge, 1926), especially pages 30–41; G. H. MEAD, *The Philosophy of the Act,* Chap. XX; S. P. LAMPRECHT, * "Causality," in *Essays in Honor of John Dewey*, New York, 1929.
A profound appreciation of the problem, particularly as to the relation of causality and power, is to be found in
S. ALEXANDER, *Space, Time, and Deity* (London, 1920), Vol. II, pp. 290 ff.
For the psychological development of the concept of causality see
J. PIAGET, *The Child's Concept of Causality* (translated by M. Gabain, New York, 1930), § IV.

CHAPTER TWO

Modern scepticism is represented by
BERTRAND RUSSELL, *Mysticism and Logic*, Chap. IX; M. R. COHEN, *Reason and Nature*, Book II, Chap. III, and Book III, Chap. I.
More recently the validity of causal attribution has been disputed by the "logical positivists," whose point of view is well represented in

PHILIP FRANK, *Philosophy of Science, New York, 1957.
The claim made by such authors that modern physics has abjured the notion of cause is refuted by statements of modern physicists, such as
MAX PLANCK, *Where Is Science Going? Chaps. IV, V, and Epilogue. See also E. SCHROEDINGER, Science and the Human Temperament, New York, 1935; L. SILBERSTEIN, Causality, London, 1933.
A brilliant attack on the mathematico-philosophical reduction of causality to "pointer readings" and timeless equations is contained in
KURT RIETZLER, Physics and Reality. See also WERNER HEISENBERG, *Physics and Philosophy, New York, 1958 (Harper Torchbooks, 1962). MAX WEBER, The Methodology of the Social Sciences, Glencoe, Ill., 1949; FELIX KAUFMAN, Methodology of the Social Sciences, New York, 1946.
In an issue of the Journal of Philosophy, vol. 39, 1952, Ernest Nagel took sharp issue with the author's conception of causation in a skillfully constructed argument based on a "positivistic" position the author cannot accept. Since the issue does not affect the treatment of the subject in the rest of the volume, the author merely suggests that any sufficiently interested reader might care to compare the opposing viewpoints.

CHAPTERS THREE AND FOUR

While the illustrations of faulty causal analysis given in the text do not refer to any recent studies, the need for more refined methods of inquiry in this field is as great as ever. See, for example:
HENRY A. BLOCK, "The Inadequacy of Research in Delinquency Behavior," National Probation and Parole Journal, July, 1955.
Causal explanation by resort to origins is discussed in
R. M. MACIVER and C. PAGE, Society: An Introductory Analysis, Chap. 27, New York, 1949.
The doctrines of social change as periodicity are summarized in
P. SOROKIN, Contemporary Sociological Theories, Chap. XIII (Harper Torchbook edition, 1964) ; *Social and Cultural Dynamics, Vol. IV, Part II, Chap. IX.

CHAPTER FIVE

There are few studies in the methodology of causal investigation in the social sciences, as set out in Chapters Five to Eight. The requirement of specific definition, as explained in Chapter Five, is met in a number of competent investigations. As examples we may cite

W. A. HEALY and A. BRONNER, *New Light on Delinquency and its Treatment*, New Haven, 1936; GUNNAR MYRDAL, *An American Dilemma*, New York, 1944; W. I. THOMAS, *The Unadjusted Girl*, Boston, 1923; ROBERT K. MERTON, *Mass Persuasion*, New York, 1946; H. WARREN DUNHAM, "The Schizophrene and Criminal Behavior," *American Sociological Review* (June, 1939), Vol. 4, pp. 352–361; KENNETH M. STAMPP, *The Causes of the Civil War*, Englewood Cliffs, N.J. (Prentice Hall), 1959; see also the comments of WILLIAM DRAY, "Causal Accounts of the Civil War," *Daedalus*, 1962.

A caustic but unsystematic examination of some of the more gross failures to clarify the causal problem is made in

V. PARETO, *The Mind and Society*, §§ 254–255 and *passim*.

For the method of operationalism consult, in addition to Bridgman, the following:

R. B. LINDSAY, "A Critique of Operationalism in Physics," *Philosophy of Science* (October, 1937), Vol. 4, pp. 456–470; H. ALPERT, "Operational Definitions in Sociology," *American Sociological Review* (December, 1938), Vol. 3, pp. 856–861; C. S. DODD, "A System of Operationally Defined Concepts for Sociology," *American Sociological Review* (October, 1939), Vol. 4, pp. 619–634.

CHAPTER SIX

The equilibrium-precipitant doctrine is elaborately applied in
V. PARETO, op. cit. Vol. IV, §§ 2060 ff.

The role of the precipitant is suggested in some passages of Max Weber's analysis of the causal problem. See

MAX WEBER, *Gesammelte Aufsätze zur Wissenschaftslehre*, pp. 271 ff., 420 ff.

See also

TALCOTT PARSONS, **The Structure of Social Action*, pp. 610 ff.; A. VON SCHELTING, *Max Webers Wissenschaftslehre*, pp. 255 ff.

On the use of the formula "other things being equal," see
FELIX KAUFMAN, *op. cit.*, pp. 84 ff. and 213 ff.

CHAPTER SEVEN

Numerous works pertaining to psychology, social psychology,
psycho-analysis, sociology, economics, and other fields discuss the role
of "motives," "instincts," "complexes," and so forth, in the causation
of behavior and of social change. They contain, however, little analysis of the problem we have set out, the relation of the subjective
factor to the rest within the causal conjuncture. See, for example,
V. PARETO, *The Mind and Society*, Vol. 11; S. FREUD, *Group Psychology and the Analysis of the Ego*, London, 1922; M. SHERIF,
The Psychology of Social Norms, New York, 1936; M. SHERIF and
H. CANTRIL, **The Psychology of Ego-Involvements*, New York,
1947; K. HORNEY, *Our Inner Conflicts*, New York, 1945.

CHAPTER EIGHT

For the concept of responsibility consult
P. FAUCONNET, **La Responsabilité*; A. LEVI, *La Société et l'Ordre
juridique* (Paris, 1911), Chap. IV; L. LÉVY-BRUHL, *L'Idée de re-
sponsabilité*, Paris, 1884.
On free will and determinism consult
M. TAUBE, *Causation, Freedom, and Determinism: An Attempt to
Solve the Causal Problem through a Study of Its Origins in
Seventeenth Century Philosophy* (London, 1936); Aristotelian
Society, *Symposium on Indeterminism, Formalism, and Value*,
Supplementary Vol. 10, London, 1931; HERBERT MULLER, *Issues
of Freedom*, New York (World Perspectives Series), New York,
1960; R. N. ANSHEN (ed.), *Freedom: Its Meaning*, New York,
1940, esp. Pt. 5.
Much has been written on legal responsibility. An excellent state-
ment is contained in
O. W. HOLMES, **The Common Law*, Chaps. I–IV.

CHAPTER NINE

The formula of causal investigation developed in this chapter has
been indicated by writers on scientific method since the time of

Francis Bacon. It found an elaborate, though defective, expression in Mill's canons of experimental enquiry. See

J. S. MILL, *A System of Logic*, especially Book III, Chaps. VIII–X. For a modern critique of Mills see

M. R. COHEN and ERNEST NAGEL, *An Introduction to Logic and Scientific Method* (New York, 1934), Chap. XIII.

For the distinction between the problem of causation as presented to the natural sciences and the problem of the social scientist see

MAX WEBER, *Wirtschaft und Gesellschaft* (Tübingen, 1925), Chap. I; TALCOTT PARSONS, *Structure of Social Action*, Chap. XVI; A. GOLDENWEISER, * "The Concept of Causality in the Physical and Social Sciences," *American Sociological Review* (October, 1938), Vol. 3, pp. 626 ff.

CHAPTER TEN

The distinction between the cultural, the technological, and the social has been developed broadly, though with relatively little application, by Afred Weber. See

ALFRED WEBER, *Ideen zur Staats- und Kultursoziologie*, Karlsruhe, 1927.

The distinction between the cultural and the technological has been pursued, though with many variations, by a number of writers; for example,

KARL MARX, *Critique of Political Economy*, Chap. I; W. SOMBART, "Technik und Kultur," *Archiv für Sozialwissenschaft und Sozialpolitik* (1911), Vol. 33, pp. 305–347; LOUIS WEBER, *Civilisation: le Mot et l'Idée*, Paris, 1930; O. SPENGLER, *Der Mensch und die Technik*, Munich, 1933; L. MUMFORD, *Technics and Civilization*, New York, 1934.

The writer has dealt with it elsewhere in

R. M. MACIVER and C. PAGE, *Society: An Introductory Analysis*, Chaps. 21, 25, 26, 29; "The Historical Pattern of Social Change," in *Authority and the Individual*, Harvard Tercentenary Publications, 1937; *The Modern State* (Oxford, 1936), Chap. X.

For comments and criticisms see

R. K. MERTON, "Civilization and Culture," *Sociology and Social Research* (November, 1936), Vol. 21, pp. 103–113; J. W. WOODARD, "A New Classification of Culture," *American Sociological*

Review (February, 1936) , Vol. 1, pp. 89–102; P. Sorokin, *Social and Cultural Dynamics*, Vol. IV, Chap. IV.

For the concept of cultural lag see, besides the above, W. F. Ogburn, *Social Change*, Part IV; J. W. Woodard, "Critical Notes on the Cultural Lag Concept," *Social Forces* (March, 1934) , Vol. 12, pp. 388–398; W. D. Wallis, "The Concept of Lag," *Sociology and Social Research* (May, 1935) , Vol. 20, pp. 403–406; M. Choukas, "The Concept of Cultural Lag Re-examined," *American Sociological Review* (October, 1936) , Vol. 1, pp. 752–760; R. M. MacIver and C. Page, *Society: An Introductory Analysis*, Chap. 26.

CHAPTERS ELEVEN AND TWELVE

The concept of the dynamic assessment, though implied in the treatment of social causation by various writers, has been only incidentally the subject of analysis. The nearest approach we know is in the writings of W. I. Thomas. See

W. I. Thomas, * "The Behavior Pattern and the Situation," *Publications*, American Sociological Society, Vol. 22; *The Unadjusted Girl*, pp. 43 ff.

See also

R. M. MacIver and C. Page, *Society: An Introductory Analysis*, Chap. 29.

The subsequent problem of how the dynamic assessment of individuals and groups is modified by various impacts, such as persuasion, propaganda, compulsion, and so forth, is discussed by various writers. See

F. Znaniecki, *Social Actions* (New York, 1936) , *passim; The Laws of Social Psychology*, Chicago, 1935.

Other writers, particularly of the psycho-analytic school, deal with the psychological and organic conditions that determine or modify the dynamic assessment. See footnote references to Chapter Seven.

The choice between alternatives that is basic to the dynamic assessment may involve a preliminary distinction between types of values or of situations or of consequences. In any event, the process of distinguishing types or categories and their subdivisions is a condition of all knowing and of all doing. See, for example

R. F. Winch, "Heuristic and Empirical Typologies," *American Sociological Review*, 1947, pp. 68–75.

The character of the dynamic assessment is of course largely determined by the ingrained habits and modes of response of the individual. On this topic see

GARDNER MURPHY, "The Internalization of Social Controls," in *Freedom and Control in Modern Society* (ed. Burger, Abel, Page), New York, 1954.

In Chapter twelve we take the declining birth rate as a phenomenon exhibiting change in an order of values. With the present great expansion of population the example may not seem so apposite. While in certain areas there has been a modest increase in the birth rate, the major proportion of the rather menacing population increase is attributable to the continuous reduction of the death rate, especially the infant death rate. What has happened here is not a change in purposive behavior but a biological result of improved sanitation, advances in medical science, and various other hygienic developments. A corresponding change in valuations, such as happened in Western Europe and in North America with the increase of the survival rate, may ensue as the knowledge of birth control methods spreads.

CHAPTER THIRTEEN

Of the large number of books dealing with social consequences very few pay much attention to the preliminary causal analysis. Some studies of the consequences of particular situations pay due regard to the problem, as, for example

STOUFFER and LAZARSFELD, *The Family in the Depression*; S. K. WEINBERG, *Society and Personality Disorders*, New York, 1952.
Some aspects of the problem are well recognized in

M. HORKHEIMER (ed.), *Studien über Autorität und Familie*, Paris, 1936.

CHAPTER FOURTEEN

On the problem of sociological inference generally see
F. ZNANIECKI, *The Method of Sociology*, New York, 1934; W. J. GOODE and P. K. HATT, *Methods in Social Research*, New York, 1952.
On the subject of inference in general see

DANIEL LERNER (ed.), *Evidence and Inference,* Glencoe, Ill., 1959. Those who wish to pursue further the question of the relation of correlation to causation will find the following works of service: A. A. TSCHUPROW, *Principles of the Mathematical Theory of Correlation*; CHARLES E. CLARK, *An Introduction to Statistics,* Chap. 9, New York, 1953; L. H. C. TIPPETT, *The Methods of Statistics,* London, 1937.

INDEX